# PLAYING POLITICS WITH TERRORISM

*For Argyró, Georgia and Dionysis*

George Kassimeris

*editor*

# Playing Politics with Terrorism

*A User's Guide*

Columbia University Press
New York

Columbia University Press
*Publishers Since 1893*
New York, Chichester, West Sussex
Copyright © 2008 Columbia University Press
All rights reserved

Library of Congress Cataloging-in-Publication Data

Playing politics with terrorism : a user's guide / George Kassimeris, editor.
   p. cm.
 Includes bibliographical references and index.
 ISBN 978-0-231-70000-9 (cloth : alk. paper)
 ISBN 978-0-231-70001-6 (pbk. : alk. paper)
   1.  Terrorism—Political aspects. 2.  Terrorism—History.  I. Kassimeris, George. II.
Title.

HV6431.P574 2007
363.325—dc22


2007022275

c 10 9 8 7 6 5 4 3 2 1
p 10 9 8 7 6 5 4 3 2 1

References to Internet Web sites (URLs) were accurate at the time of writing. Neither
the author nor Columbia University Press is responsible for URLs that may have expired
or changed since the manuscript was prepared.

# CONTENTS

# CONTENTS

# ACKNOWLEDGEMENTS

Many friends and colleagues helped me in putting this book together, whether they knew it or not, so it is a great pleasure to thank: Tim Knox, Conor Gearty, Crispin Black, Bruce Hoffman, Caroline Soper, Peter R. Neumann, Joanna Bourke, Michael Kenney, Dennis Pluchinsky, Alex Danchev, Moazzam Begg, James Harkin, David A. Charters, Anthony Dworkin, Babis Grammenos, Pedro Teixeira, Jean Gilkison, Jeevan Deol, Stephen Grey, James Cameron, Frank Faulkner, Alun Thorne, Pete Gill, Mark Phythian and Paul Rogers. Special thanks are owed to my publisher in London, Michael Dwyer, for his patience and good humour and to the incomparable Maria Petalidou, production supremo at Hurst. My deepest thanks, however, go to Carolina Salinas, love of my life, and to Carol Millwood my best friend, mentor and editor for her unflagging support and confidence in me over many years.

*May 2007*                                                                    G.K.

# THE CONTRIBUTORS

Jo-Marie Burt is Assistant Professor of Government and Politics at George Mason University, where she also sits on the steering committee of the Center for Global Studies. She is co-editor, with Philip Mauceri, of *Politics in the Andes: Identity, Conflict, Reform* (2004), and has written numerous articles on human rights, social movements and democratisation in Latin America. She is currently a recipient of a Fulbright award to research the struggles over truth, justice and memory in postwar Peru and a visiting researcher at the Catholic University of Peru. Dr. Burt was a research consultant for the Peruvian Truth and Justice Commission in 2002–2003. She is currently completing a manuscript on civil society and political violence in Peru.

Richard Drake received a Ph.D. in history from UCLA in 1975. He then taught at UCLA, UC, Irvine, Wellesley College, and Princeton before moving to the University of Montana in 1982. He teaches courses on European history, specialising in modern Italy and modern European cultural and intellectual history. His books include *The Revolutionary Mystique and Terrorism in Contemporary Italy* (1989), *The Aldo Moro Murder Case* (1995), and *Apostles and Agitators: Italy's Marxist Revolutionary Tradition* (2003).

William L. Eubank is an Associate Professor at the University of Nevada, Reno. A graduate of the University of Oregon, besides terrorism, he has interests in political parties and voting, research methods and law. He teaches courses in American constitutional law; research methods; parties, elections and voting; and the history of political science.

Nicola Horsburgh is a Research Associate of the International Policy Institute, King's College, London. She has worked as a Research Fellow at King's College London on numerous issues, including nuclear weapons proliferation, North East Asian politics and terrorism. She has presented and published several articles on jihadism in Europe and Spain in *Studies in Conflict and Terrorism, International Journal on Intel-*

*ligence and Counterintelligence,* and *Mediterranean Politics.* She studied at the University of Wales, Aberystwyth, the University of Southern California and the London School of Economics and Political Science.

MARK HUBAND is an award winning journalist who has focused on political Islam in the Middle East, Africa and South Asia for the past fifteen years. He was Security Correspondent for the *Financial Times* until June 2005, specialising in terrorism, security and defence issues. He oversaw the *FT*'s coverage of al-Qaeda in the wake of the September 11, terrorist attacks in the United States, reporting from Iraq, Guantanamo Bay, Saudi Arabia, South-East Asia, much of the Middle East, the US and Europe. He is the author of the widely-acclaimed *Warriors of the Prophet* and five other books on Africa and the Arab world. The most recent is *Brutal Truths, Fragile Myths,* which looks at the Middle East in the wake of the invasion of Iraq and US attempts to engineer political change in the region. He is currently an executive with Hakluyt and Co., a London-based investigative consultancy.

RICHARD JACKSON is Senior Lecturer at the Centre for International Politics, University of Manchester, where he lectures on critical terrorism studies, critical security studies and war studies. He is also the convenor of the British International Studies Association (BISA) working group, *Critical Studies on Terrorism.* His research focuses on the discourses of terrorism, the causes of political violence and international conflict resolution, and his most recent book is *Writing the War on Terrorism: Language, Politics and Counterterrorism* (2005).

JAVIER JORDÁN is Lecturer in the Department of Political Science, University of Granada. He was a research fellow at the Training and Doctrine Command of the Spanish Army and a NATO Research Fellow. He has been part of several research projects sponsored by the Spanish Army, the Institute "General Gutiérrez Mellado" and the Institut des Hautes Etudes de la Sécurité Intérieure and since December 2004, the AGIS Programme with the Institute National des Hautes Etudes de Securite. He has published several articles on jihadism in Europe and Spain in *Studies in Conflict and Terrorism, Terrorism & Political Violence, International Journal on Intelligence and Counterintelligence,* and *Mediter-*

*ranean Politics.* He is the author of three books in Spanish on terrorism and the theory of war.

CHRISTOPHER MICHAELSEN is a law graduate from the University of Hamburg, Germany, and also holds a Master of Laws (LLM) from the University of Queensland, Australia, specialising in international human rights and security law. In 2003, he joined the Strategic & Defence Studies Centre at the Australian National University in Canberra with a view to submitting a Ph.D thesis in 2007. Chris has worked for the United Nations Department for Disarmament Affairs in New York, the Asian Law Group in Semarang, Indonesia, and Civil Liberties Australia (ACT) in Canberra. In January 2006, he took up the position of Human Rights Officer (Anti-Terrorism) at the Office for Democratic Institutions and Human Rights (ODIHR) of the Organization for Security and Co-operation in Europe (OSCE) in Warsaw, Poland.

MARTIN A. MILLER is professor of Russian history at Duke University. He is the author of *Kropotkin* (1976), *The Russian Revolutionary Exiles* (1986) and *Freud and the Bolsheviks: Psychoanalysis in Imperial Russia and the Soviet Union* (1997) as well as numerous articles on the theory and practice of terrorism in historical perspective. He is currently writing a book analysing the origins of modern terrorism in Russia and Western Europe.

JOHN MUELLER holds the Woody Hayes Chair of National Security Studies, Mershon Center, and is Professor of Political Science, at Ohio State University where he teaches courses in international relations. He is the author of several classic works of political science including *Policy and Opinion in the Gulf War, The Remnants of War* and most recently, *Overblown: How Politicians, the Terrorism Industry and Others Stoke National Security Fears* and many editorial page columns and articles in *The Wall Street Journal, Los Angeles Times, The New Republic, Reason, The Washington Post,* and *The New York Times.* Mueller is a member of the American Academy of Arts and Sciences, has been a John Simon Guggenheim Fellow, and has received grants from the National Science Foundation and the National Endowment for the Humanities. He has also received several teaching prizes.

PETER OBORNE is a contributing editor of *The Spectator* and columnist for the *Daily Mail*. He is the author of *Alastair Campbell, New Labour and the Rise of the Media Class* (1999 and, with Simon Walters, 2004), *A Moral Duty to Act There* (2003), *Basil D'Oliveira: cricket and conspiracy* (2004) and *The Rise of Political Lying* (2005).

ROBERT A. SAUNDERS is an Assistant Professor at the State University of New York at Farmingdale where he teaches courses on globalisation and the history of technology. His research interests include post-communist states, mass media, and minority nationalism. He received his Ph.D from the Division of Global Affairs at Rutgers University, in 2005. He is a regular contributor to *Transitions Online* (TOL) and *Russia in Global Affairs*. His articles have also appeared in *Nationalism & Ethnic Politics, Journal of Albanian Politics, East Asia: An International Quarterly, Global Media and Communication*, and various edited volumes.

JONATHAN STEVENSON is Associate Professor of Strategic Studies in the Strategic Research Department of the Center for Naval Warfare Studies at the US Naval War College. Previously, he was Senior Fellow for Counterterrorism and editor of *Strategic Survey* at the International Institute for Strategic Studies (IISS) in London, and Director of Studies of the IISS–US in Washington in 2004–2005. As a writer and journalist, he covered conflicts in sub-Saharan Africa and Northern Ireland from 1992 to 1999. His work has appeared in a wide range of international affairs journals, including *Foreign Affairs, Foreign Policy, The National Interest*, and *Survival*, and he has written op-eds for the *Financial Times*, the *International Herald Tribune, National Review, The New Republic*, the *New York Times* and *The Wall Street Journal*. Stevenson is author of *We Wrecked the Place: Contemplating an End to the Northern Irish Troubles* (1996), and two monographs: *Counter-terrorism: Containment and Beyond*, (2004); and *Preventing Conflict: The Role of the Bretton Woods Institutions*, Adelphi Paper 336, 2000.

LEONARD WEINBERG is Foundation Professor of Political Science at the University of Nevada and a Senior Fellow at the National Security Studies Center at the University of Haifa. Over the course of his career he has been a Fulbright Senior Research Fellow for Italy, a visiting scholar at UCLA, a guest professor at the University of Florence, Italy and the recipient of an H. F. Guggenheim Foundation grant for the study of political violence. He has also served as a consultant to the United Nations Office for the Prevention of Terrorism. For his work in promoting Christian-Jewish reconciliation Weinberg was a recipient of the 1999 Thornton Peace Prize. His books include *Global Terrorism* (2005), *Political Parties and Terrorist Groups* (2003, with Ami Pedahzur), *Right-Wing Extremism in the Twenty-First Century* (2003, ed. with Peter Merkl), *Religious Fundamentalism and Political Extremism* (2003, ed. With Ami Pedahzur) *The Democratic Experience and Political Violence* (2001, ed. with David Rapoport), *The Emergence of a Euro-American Radical Right* (1998, with Jeffrey Kaplan). He is the senior editor of the journal *Democracy and Security*.

PAUL WILKINSON is Professor of International Relations and Chairman of the Advisory Board of the Centre for the Study of Terrorism and Political Violence (CSTPV) at the University of St Andrews. Prior to his appointment at St Andrews in 1989 he was Professor of International Relations, University of Aberdeen 1979-1989. He was visiting Fellow at Trinity Hall, Cambridge in 1997–1998 and is Honorary Fellow of University of Wales, Swansea. His publications include *Political Terrorism* (1974); *Terrorism and the Liberal State* (1977/1986); *The New Fascists* (1981/1983); *Contemporary Research on Terrorism* (as co-editor, 1987); *Aviation Terrorism and Security* (as co-editor, 1999) and *Terrorism versus Democracy: The Liberal State Response* (2001). He co-authored with Joseph S. Nye Jr. and Yukio Satoh the report to the Trilateral Commission (May 2003) Addressing the New International Terrorism; Prevention, Intervention and Multilateral Co-operation. He served as Adviser to Lord Lloyd of Berwick's Inquiry into Legislation Against Terrorism, and authored volume two of the Research Report for the Inquiry (1996). A revised and expanded edition of his book, *Terrorism Versus Democracy* was published in the summer of 2006.

# 1
# INTRODUCTION

*George Kassimeris*

Early on the morning of 11 March 2004, a bright, spring morning, Luis Garrudo, the doorman of a small block of flats close to the railway station in Alcalá de Henares, a Madrid dormitory town, noticed three men busying themselves around a white Renault van parked across the street. Garrudo's first instinctive thought, as he would later tell the police, was that the men looked like armed robbers; however, it did not make much sense at that time of the morning. At just before 7 a.m. Garrudo walked the 200 metres to the railway station to pick up a copy of *Metro*, a free daily morning paper. By the time he got back, the men had gone. The men Garrudo had seen, young Muslim extremists, equipped with thirteen bombs, had started hopping from carriage to carriage, and from train to train, across platforms packed full of early morning workers, placing thirteen sports rucksacks in four different trains. Each bag contained a mobile phone, a copper detonator, nuts and screws to act as shrapnel, and some twelve kilos of Goma 2 Eco explosives. The bombers targeted four separate trains which passed though Alcalá de Henares between 7.00 a.m. and 7.15. They may have ridden them for the first few stops as the trains headed in towards Madrid's Atocha station, distributing the bombs amongst the packed carriages. The bombs, detonated by the alarms in the mobile phones, started going off at 7.37 a.m. and had wrought their full destruction by 7.43.

The terrorist bombings on *El 11-M*, as the Spaniards call that day, caused the death of 191 people and the injury of another 1,900.

The death toll could have been even higher had three of the thirteen bombs not failed to explode. The bombers, it quickly became apparent, had intended to cause maximum casualties for in some trains those who went to help the wounded from the first bomb were caught by the second or third.

The timing of the attacks—three days before a general election—was carefully chosen by the bombers whose central aim must have been to influence the course of those elections. But even they could not have foreseen the direction events would take over the next three extraordinary days.

Once the bombers struck that Thursday morning, everyone in the country knew that on top of the human misery there would be significant political consequences. With a general election only 72 hours away, the identity of the bombers was crucial. The Partido Popular (PP) right-wing government of José Maria Aznar knew that most people would instinctively point the finger to the Basque separatist movement, ETA. Spain, after all, had been suffering persistent terrorist assaults at the hands of ETA since the 1970s. If the government could successfully put the blame on the Basque movement, there would be a double bonus for the PP since a central plank of the government's election platform was that the Socialist PSOE were 'soft' on ETA terrorism. Yet, the Aznar government must also have known that, given the magnitude and style of the operation, it was highly unlikely that the Basque terrorist group were behind the attack. ETA had never in its 30-year terrorist campaign acted on this scale, or with this degree of arbitrary barbarity.

There is no word in Spanish for 'spin', but what happened next was an audacious exercise in spinning and political manipulation. Following the golden rule that the first impression is what counts and coupled with the slavish support of a compliant state media machine (state television, state radio and most of the press), the Aznar government set about getting their own version of events into the public domain. PP had only three days to avoid the charge that it had attracted the bombers by taking Spain into the Iraq war against the wishes of 90 per cent of the Spanish population. Aznar himself made personal phone calls to the editors of the major national daily newspapers, 'giving assurances in absolute terms' (to use the words of the *El Pais* editor, Jesus Ceberio) that ETA was behind the attacks.[1] At the same time, a motion was forced through the United Nations in New York, blaming the Basque terrorists for the atrocity and Spanish ambassadors worldwide were instructed 'to make the most of every media opportunity encountered to confirm ETA's responsibility'. It worked for 48 hours but not the necessary 72. By the time the Spanish police had arrested three Moroccans with fundamentalist connections, opposition politicians had already started to let it be known that they thought the government was lying in order to win votes. In Spain, as in most Mediterranean countries, demonstrations or any type of political gatherings are illegal the day before an election but on the night before the 2004 election, an angry crowd of more than 5,000 people gathered outside the PP central headquarters in downtown Madrid, chanting, '*Quien ha sido? Quien ha sido?*' (Who was it? Who was it?)

The game for the Aznar government was finally up when, after an anonymous phonecall to a television station, police picked up a videotape in which three machine-gun-toting masked men claimed responsibility for the attack. This is, they said, 'our answer to your collaboration with that criminal Bush and his allies... the answer to the crimes you have committed in the world, in Iraq and Afghanistan.... You want life and we want death.' The delivery of the tape, hours before Spaniards went to vote, meant that nobody who stepped into a polling booth the following day could have any doubt who had attacked Madrid.

José Maria Aznar and his party were voted out of office not because of their support for the war in Iraq, not even because of the bombings, but because they were perceived by the electorate to have

---

1   On the Madrid bombings and the events that followed see Giles Tremlett's chapter 11-M: Morosy Cristianos' in his *Ghosts of Spain: Travels Through a Country's Hidden Past* (London, 2006), pp. 246–80.

been playing politics in response to them. Aznar was voted out of power, the Catalan commentator Rafael Ramos wrote angrily a few days after the election, 'not because of Al-Qaeda and the bombs in Madrid, but because [he] exploited terrorism for political purposes and appealed to the lowest inclinations of the Spanish electorate'.[2] A post-voting poll showed that one in five Spaniards had this uppermost in their minds when they voted. It was enough to win it for the Socialist leader, José Luis Rodriguez Zapatero whose highest ambition a week before had been to limit the size of PP's majority in the new parliament.

Playing politics with terrorism was not, of course, invented by José Maria Aznar and his government. Governments and career politicians have always been tempted to exploit disasters and use them to realise their political objectives. As American commentator David Ignatius once put it: 'There is a temptation that seeps into the souls of even the most righteous politicians and leads them to bend the rules, and eventually the truth, to suit the political needs of the moment.' When it comes to terrorism, a phenomenon that almost always stirs fear and insecurity disproportionate to the actual danger, the temptation for governments to bend the rules and the truth becomes irresistible. Of course, the post-9/11 semi-permanent state of maximum alert in which we now find ourselves has taken things into a new dimension but, as a number of essays in this book show, the exaggeration of the terrorist threat by governments in order to sustain a credible antterrorism narrative, to manipulate public opinion, to push through draconian legislation or even to win elections is not only a post-9/11 phenomenon. Far from it. We have been here before. Governments in many countries, from Putin's Russia and Fujimori's Peru to Italy in the 1970s, have manipulated the threat and fear of terrorism for their own political advantage. So why should 9/11 and 'the war on terror' be any different?

---

2   See Rafael Ramos,'Arrogance, not Bombs, Brought Down Aznar', in the *Independent*, 16 March 2004.

## *The threat of indiscriminate terror*

One of the stranger consequences of early twenty-first century terror-ism and the rise of militant Islam is that it has induced a nostalgia for an earlier kind of terrorist. The replacement of political ideology with religious fanaticism has eroded the self-imposed constraints which limited terrorist violence in the past. In the 1970s and 80s, terrorist factions issued communiqués explaining their political agendas, their demands were clear and their targets were specific and comprehen-sible. In those days, terrorist groups, such as the German Red Army Faction (RAF) and the Italian Red Brigades (BR), engaged in highly selective acts of violence. However radical or revolutionary these groups were, the majority of them were conservative in their opera-tions using a very limited tactical repertoire directed against a narrow set of targets.[3] In that period terrorists wanted, to use Brian Jenkins's often-cited observation, 'a lot of people watching and a lot of people listening and not a lot of people dead'. Now things are different. What we have now is a series of loose, mutually reinforcing and quite separate international networks whose followers combine medieval religious beliefs with modern weaponry and a level of fanaticism that expresses itself primarily in suicide bombings and a willingness to use indiscriminate violence on large scale.

It is not flippant to suggest that Islamist terrorists would inspire less public apprehension if they confined their murderous designs to politicians, diplomats, policemen, judges and soldiers as did the more 'traditional' ideological and ethno-nationalist organisations which dominated the terrorist scene from the 1960s to the 1990s. The double problem with al-Qaeda and its followers is not only that they hate our society's norms and values but also that they refuse to recognise innocents or noncombatants deserving of mercy.[4] Unlike

---

3   See Bruce Hoffman, *Inside Terrorism* (London, 1998), pp.169-80.

4   On al-Qaeda's ideological militancy see Faisal Devji, *Landscapes of the Jihad: Militancy, Morality, Modernity* (London, 2005); see also Jason Burke, *Al-Qaeda: the True Story of Radical Islam* (London, 2004); Olivier Roy, *Globalised Islam: The Search for a new Ummah* (London, 2002).

the terrorist warfare of the past which entailed a certain degree of clarity about identities, in the terror battles of today confusion of identity is not an accident but the principal tactic. There is no clarity about ultimate responsibility and, most alarmingly, no separation of enemy combatants from the general population. The threat of indiscriminate terror, even if our intelligence and police work improves a great deal, will be with us for some time and this makes it all the more important to deal with the root causes of this type of terrorism, rather than simply try to defend against it as we have been doing for quite some time.[5] Western policies since 9/11 have been primarily focused on capturing or killing the jihadis rather than trying to work out what motivates them and why some communities support them.

## A realistic sense of the threat

'At 9:38 a.m., the entire Pentagon shook. I went outside and saw the horrific face of war in the 21st century.' This is how, the former US Secretary of Defense, Donald Rumsfeld, writing in September 2006, on the fifth anniversary of 9/11 for the *Wall Street Journal*, described the event.[6] The fact that from the very start Bush and Rumsfeld had called 9/11 a war must have been precisely the legitimation that the al-Qaeda militants sought. They thought they were at war and wanted to be recognised as warriors; but it was a terrible error on the part of the US administration; to take them at their own estimation. The Americans addressed the threat as if no country had previously faced terrorism. True, the attacks were more deadly; but the use of suicide bombers was nothing more than an intensification of existing tactics elsewhere.

---

5   Lawrence Rosen, 'Homesick Everywhere' in *London Review of Books*, 4 August 2005; see also Christian Caryl, 'Why They Do It' in *The New York Review of Books*, 22 September 2005.

6   Donald Rumsfeld, 'A Force for Good' in *The Wall Street Journal Europe*, 11 September 2006.

Let us be clear about one thing: al-Qaeda did not invent terrorism even though it feels, thanks to the constant 'heightened' state of alert and the international media's 24/7 coverage of the story, as if terrorism actually began on 11 September 2001. However a second's reflection should remind us that terrorism has been a near-permanent feature of our lives for several decades. One has to accept that 9/11 was a deeply traumatic incident but, in retrospect, America's biggest enemy after 9/11 was not bin Laden and his followers but its inability to maintain a realistic sense of the threat they posed. We should not forget that it was before the atrocities of 11-M in Madrid and 7/7 in London had planted 'a catastrophic style of thinking' in key American policymakers that terrorism was seen as supremely evil, the work of dark forces which must be defeated and eradicated at all costs. It was a belief that the British prime minister shared from the start and which he has promoted ever since with the strongest conviction. The belief that the bombers are 'evil' and groups like al-Qaeda and Hamas are 'death cults who are in love with death' may have been psychologically comforting and convenient for the leaders of Britain and America but it has rendered any attempt to understand the 'evil' bombers in a different context a great deal more difficult.

Life since 9/11 may have become, 'that bit more unsettlingly chaotic, that bit more worryingly, lethally uncertain'[7] but that should not prevent us from acknowledging that our lives overall have been largely unchanged by the menace of Islamist terror. This is not to ignore those who have lost their lives or their families, nor is it to advocate complacency about what is arguably going to be a long campaign given the number of jihadi networks al-Qaeda has spawned around the globe. We need, however, to grasp the true scale of the threat and understand that, although it is going to be long-term, it is also smaller than almost anyone will admit. The number of people lost to terrorist atrocities in the West since 9/11 is actually less than a tenth of the death toll in Iraq.

---

7   William Boyd, 'Carry On' in *The International Herald Tribune*, 10 September 2006.

Five years ago, nineteen terrorists hijacked four planes and according to conventional wisdom, changed the course of history. But did September 11, really change the world? 'We cannot yet grasp, by any stretch, all that this means,' wrote the late Hugo Young, one of the most measured and perceptive British political commentators two days after the event; but 'already we start to imagine how it will poison trust, wreck relationships, challenge the world order, and vastly magnify the divide between the enemies and friends of democracy.'[8]

The poisoned trust that Hugo Young prophetically referred to in that piece reached its apogee when it became disturbingly clear that the Blair and Bush administrations, in their attempts to fit the case for an Iraq invasion onto a post-9/11 political framework, had manipulated the evidence about Saddam's weapons of mass destruction, effectively misrepresenting the nature and seriousness of the threat posed by the late Iraqi dictator. In that sense September 11 did change the world since it has now become a place where fact and fiction merge, a world where powerful states like the US create their own realities. When Pulitzer prize-winning author, Ron Suskind, was working on a book about the inner workings of the Bush White House in 2004 he reported the following conversation with a White House aide:

The aide said that guys like me were 'in what we call the reality-based community,' which he defined as people who 'believe that solutions emerged from your judicious study of discernible reality'. I nodded and murmured something about enlightenment principles and empiricism. He cut me off. 'We're are an empire now, and when we act, we create our own reality. And while you're studying that reality—judiciously, as you will, we'll act again, creating other new realities, which you can study too, and that's how things will sort out. We're history's actors... and you, all of you, will be left to just study what we do.'[9]

8  Hugo Young, 'The free world must decide how its values are protected' in the *Guardian*, 13 September 2001.

9  http://www.ronsuskind.com/articles.

It is precisely this irrationally grandiose world-view of international relations which has driven the White House leadership to embark on a campaign to persuade itself, the American people and the rest of the world that a 'long war' (first Iraq and then, most probably, Iran) will somehow eradicate the terrorist threat.[10] In fact, apart from being a massive propaganda gift to militant Islamist extremism, the war in Iraq has led to terrorism on an even bigger scale. 'The Iraq war package (the fiasco and the lies)', as former government analyst, Crispin Black, graphically put it, 'has been to Islamist terror what Prohibition was to the 1920s Mafia in the United States. Our intervention in Iraq, more than any other issue, has given the terrorist recruiters a golden opportunity to get a foothold in the mainstream.'[11]

As the body counts of both soldiers and civilians pile up in the chaotic theatres of the Iraq and the Middle East, perhaps western political leaders should rethink the consequences of war.[12] In Britain, for example, Tony Blair continues to insist at every opportunity that the 7 July bombings, had 'nothing to do' with Iraq. The point the British premier is obviously trying to make is that the real blame for any such atrocity lies with its perpetrators but prevention of the recurrence of a 7/7-style atrocity is only possible by trying to understand how those perpetrators' grievances metastasised into such a lethal cult of suicide and murder.[13] There are very few people on this planet who would devise carnage for the sheer hell of it. They do what they do for a cause. From George Grivas to Ulrike Mainhof and Renato Curcio, to Timothy McVeigh and Osama bin Laden, the history of modern terrorism is filled with groups and individuals who believed

---

10 See Anatol Lieven, *America Right or Wrong: An Anatomy of American Nationalism* (London, 2004), pp. 217-22.

11 Crispin Black writing for the *Independent on Sunday*, 19 November 2006; see also Black's 7/7 *The London Bombs: What Went Wrong* (London, 2005).

12 Thomas E. Ricks, *Fiasco: the American Military Adventure in Iraq* (London, 2006); see also Mark Danner, 'Iraq: the War of the Imagination' in the *New York Review of Books*, 21 December 2006.

13 See Tariq Ali, *Rough Music: Blair, Bombs, Baghdad, London, Terror* (London, 2005).

themselves to be acting in response to intolerable wrongs committed against themselves or others.[14]

## The trouble with hyperbole

Western governments have helped to make al-Qaeda what it is today. Bin Laden and company excel at hyperbole but so do our political elites. It has come to the point where everything we know comes from two sides that both have vested interests in exaggerating the threat posed by al Qaeda: the terrorists themselves and the government agencies that have an interest maintaining the myth of an overwhelmingly dangerous enemy.

One does not need a PhD in counterterrorism studies to realise that all this hyperbole plays directly into the hands of the terrorists. For the most powerful weapon in the terrorist arsenal is fear. A key goal, if not the central one, of terrorist tactics is to undermine confidence in our security and in ourselves, which is why governments—no matter how powerful and well-organised the enemy—should avoid at all costs adding to terrorism's psychological impact. Today we face two dangers: the risk of what jihadist militants might do to us and also the risk of what we might do to our country out of fear. We are, as Martin Amis put it in a review of Lawrence Wright's *The Looming Tower: Al-Qaeda and the Road to 9/11*, 'arriving at an axiom in long-term thinking about international terrorism: the real danger lies not in what it inflicts but in what it provokes.'[15] One of bin Laden's intentions back in 2001 must have been to portray the West as scared, emotionally vulnerable, over-reactive, decadent and hypocritical about liberal values. The West has done a very good job of proving him right. The invasion of Iraq, the images of torture and the widely documented abuse of prisoners at Guantanamo and other

14 See Louise Richardson, *What Terrorists Want: Understanding the Terrorist Threat* (London, 2006); see also Milan Rai, *7/7, the London Bombings, Islam and the Iraq War* (London, 2006).

15 Martin Amis, 'The real conspiracy behind 9/11' in *The Times*, 2 September 2006.

US detention facilities has left the US reviled not only in the Arab world but throughout the West, undercutting the moral authority which is vital for any liberal democracy in dealing effectively with persistent terrorist violence.[16]

A cruel and wicked dictator has been removed in Iraq but the world is less safe because of that. Our actions have created resentment throughout the Middle East and Iraq is now the world centre of terrorist activity.[17] The Egyptian President, Hosni Mubarak, was prescient when he warned in 2003 that the Iraq war would spawn '100 new bin Ladens' even though bin Laden, has become by now a strategic irrelevance in the fight against terrorism. Bin Laden, wherever he is hiding, is not directing operations, but his ability to elude his potential captors has provided the inspiration and example for a new generation of terrorists who have never been to his training camps in Afghanistan and whose only connection to al-Qaeda is a shared desire to lash out at the West.

None of this was inevitable. Western political leaders, who should know better, have been playing a very dangerous and, in the end, counter-productive game. The decision to respond to the 11 September attacks with a global crusade was a choice based on certain ideological assumptions and strategic goals.[18] Iraq had little to do with the war on terror until the Bush administration decided to invade it. There were numerous other means by which the West might have responded to the attacks that did not require abuse and torture camps, restrictions on civil liberties, the creation of a permanent state of emergency or a war built on a series of myths, secrets and fiction.

---

16 Lewis Lapham, *Theater of War: in Wwhich the Republic Becomes an Empire* (New York, 2003); Stephen Grey, *Ghost Plane: the Inside Story of the CIA's Secret Rendition Programme* (London, 2006).

17 Robert Fisk, *The Great War for Civilisation: the Conquest of the Middle East* (London, 2006), pp.1234-54.

18 See Matthew Carr, *Unknown Soldiers: How Terrorism Transformed the Modern World* (London, 2006), pp.322-8; see Simon Jenkins, 'Lies, damn lies' a review of Bob Woodward's *State of Denial: Bush at War, Part III* in *The Sunday Times*, 10 July 2006.

The real war on terror ought to be fought by means of effective police work and intelligence and a genuine hearts and minds campaign to separate the terrorists from the communities where they derive their support.

The White House and Downing Street mantras of '9/11 changes everything' and 'the rules of the game have changed' began as an explanation and a justification but were rapidly hijacked by political leaders whose main priority was to turn terrorism into a divisive choice between order and chaos. The American president and the British prime minister have spent half a decade exploiting bin Laden and al-Qaeda for their political ends, terrifying their electorates with new and bloodcurdling threats and deliberately confusing the personal with the political and the political with national security. There never was 'a terrorist threat' to western civilisation or democracy, only to western lives and property.[19] Such a threat becomes systemic only when democracy loses its confidence and when its leaders exploit public fear for political ends. As a *Guardian* editorial put it on the fifth anniversary of 9/11, 'the man in the cave [that is bin Laden] and the man in the White House must not drown out voices of reason with their inflammatory talk of clashing civilizations. Terrorism must be fought—but kept in perspective.'[20]

In a terrorist emergency such as 9/11 or 7/7, when our lives may be in danger, we have no option but to trust our political leaders to act quickly and decisively to protect public safety. Insecurity can take many forms, but nothing else plays quite so sharply on a civilian population's sense of vulnerability as random, deliberate terrorist violence so, in a time of crisis, the public need to believe they are being told the truth and, even more crucially, that their government is acting in good faith. Regrettably, at a time when we need to trust our government, many of us do not. In Britain, where this introductory chapter is being written, a rising number of people have become

19 For a diametrically opposite view see Paul Berman, *Terrorism and Liberalism* (New York, 2003).
20 'Bleak Horizons' in the *Guardian*, 9 September 2006.

sceptical about what they are told[21]—and who can blame them? They remember that the intelligence used to make the case for invading Iraq was shamefully inaccurate and/or doctored. They remember the tanks parked outside Heathrow airport, the 'ricin plot' that didn't add up to a row of beans, the Forest Gate police fiasco etc. When a government's warnings on such a serious issue as terrorism are viewed with suspicion there is a fundamental problem. Not only because it generates public cynicism but also because it risks devaluing the victories that have been achieved in bringing real terrorists to justice.

The principal aim of the chapters in this collection is to argue that the situation is far from irredeemable. Yet, if the early decades of the twenty-first century are not to become a permanent state of emergency in which manipulated societies are frightened into anti-terrorist hysteria, it is imperative that our political elites regain a sense of perspective. For one day, like all wars, even 'the war on terror' will come to an end and when it does, 'we will find ourselves still living in fear: not of terrorism, or radical Islam, but of the domestic rulers that fear has left behind'.[22] Exaggerating the terrorist threat for political purposes eventually creates more problems than it solves and damages the very liberty and democratic culture that the terrorists seek to destroy. It will take years for Spain, described recently by Antonio Munoz-Molina, as 'a dismal battleground where lies and slander reached an appalling level of viciousness,'[23] to recover from the events of March 11 and José Maria Aznar's lamentable attempts to play politics with the identity of the bombers.

It is now more than five years since George W. Bush launched America on a global crusade to 'rid the world of evil'. Much of the rest of the world lost faith some time ago in his vision of America as the world's leader—with Britain as the deputy leader—of freedom

---

21  See John Tulloch, *One Day in July: Experiencing 7/ 7* (London, 2006); see also 'People are definitely sceptical in the *Guardian*, 16 August 2006.

22  Corey Robin, *Fear: the History of a Political Idea* (Oxford, 2004), p.25.

23  Antonio Munoz-Molina, 'Hush, memory' in *The New York Times*, 10 September 2006.

and democracy battling against enemies variously described as terrorists, criminals, evildoers and Islamofascists.[24] Yet only now are the Americans beginning to doubt the mental construct of 11 September as a 'war' framed the Bush administration's reaction.

History will be harsh in its judgements of both the Bush and Blair administrations but the question remains—where do we go from here? It is unlikely that we will witness any dramatic policy U-turns in the method of dealing with the terrrorist threat until the current occupants of the White House and 10 Downing Street leave the stage. One has to hope that their successors will have learned the lesson that when you are confronted with a terrorist problem you do not, to use the metaphor of George Grivas (who led terrorist attacks against British rule in Cyprus in the 1950s), send tanks to catch field mice. A cat always does the job better.

---

24 David Runciman, *The Politics of Good Intentions: History, Fear and Hypocrisy in the New World Order* (Oxford, 2006); see also John Brady Kiesling, *Diplomacy Lessons: Realism for an Unloved Superpower* (Washington, DC 2006).

# 2

# TERRORISM: 'THE GREAT GAME'

## Martin A. Miller

"Trying to understand is not to justify; not trying to understand is unjustifiable."

Samia Serageldin

To co-join the terms 'terrorism' and 'play' might at first seem to be inappropriate if not inaccurate. Playing in the form of a game involves learning a distinct and known set of rules by which the players must abide. Most of us discover how to play games as children in situations in which the rules to be learned and accepted take place in a family context of enjoyment and relaxation. Our safety is an unquestioned assumption. The worst consequences to befall us in playing the game would be to vicariously fall into bankruptcy, prison or, if one includes more recent video games, even suffer the virtual loss of life. Regardless of who wins, once the game is over the rules are suspended we feel satisfied, and we return to 'life' where we operate, supposedly, under another and, indeed, different set of rules.

Terrorism involves actual violence, which is employed to achieve specific objectives that in most cases are political in content. It is a phenomenon, as it will be argued here, that operates according to its own set of rules with players very actively participating. Terrorism has its own logic, planning, tactics, strategy, and outcome risk assessments. As horrible as the violence is, the phenomenon of terrorism is neither irrational nor unpredictable. Further, terrorists are usually

15

representative members of the political and social order rather than lunatics in office or gang leaders in power.[1]

There is a large literature on the subject of terrorism, but it is usually interpreted as a clandestine anti-government current organised from below. Absent from these studies is the role of the state or a view of the government as one of the key players in the violent game. At the same time, there is a separate literature concerned with the violence of the state, but these scholars are concerned primarily with either the holocaust of the Nazi era or the death squads conducting 'dirty wars' in Latin America.[2]

In my view, terrorism is the result of an interactive dynamic between agencies of states and sectors of society that seek to resolve political problems by resorting to tactics of violence. Governments are willing to sacrifice liberties and risk their legitimacy in their attempt to neutralise or destroy what they perceive as a threat to 'national security' while social groups from below, dedicated to the use of terrorist techniques, are committed to forms of what they regard as heroic martyrdom to achieve their objectives of demoralising or destroying the state's ability to function. Because such groups claim to obey 'higher laws,' they too have little interest in preserving what they perceive as the false liberty of a democratic order based on a legal system they despise. In both cases, the political violence employed is distinguished in the minds of its proponents from ordinary civil crimes such as homicides by virtue of its appeal for justification and legitimacy. Terrorists believe that they are rectifying an untenable and unjust reality. Their targets always carry symbolic value, and,

1  On the 1960s, Peter H. Merkl, *Political Violence and Terror* (Berkeley, 1986), and Donatella della Porta, 'Left Wing Terrorism in Italy,' in Martha Crenshaw ed., *Terrorism in Context* (University Park, 1995), pp. 105-59, have argued for the rationalism of terrorism. For an opposing view, see Jerrold M. Post, 'Terrorist Psycho-Logic: Terrorist Behavior as a Product of Psychological Forces,' Walter Reich, ed., *Origins of Terrorism* (Baltimore, 1998), pp. 25-40.

2  See, e.g., Ervin Staub, *The Roots of Evil: the Origins of Genocide and Other Group Violence* (Cambridge, 1989), and Patricia Marchak, *Reigns of Terror* (Montreal, 2003).

although they are compelled to act in secret, they must make public the rationale for their violence, however deceitful their reasons may be. Indeed, their ability to sustain their violent activities is, to a significant degree, rooted in the success of this medium of communication. It is important to note that the media can be manipulated either by an authoritarian government literally in control of its airwaves and cyberspace or by radical groups in society who are covered wholesale by the independent reporters of the 'free press' in a more democratic polity. In either case, the mobilisation of public opinion for support or complicity is crucial.

This interpretation challenges the more traditional view that terrorists provoke governments, who act in self-defence when deciding to employ tactics of violence.[3] The overlooked aspect of the history of terrorism over the last century is that there are always two kinds of players, and as often as not, the state has been the provoking agent. When the state is authoritarian, the reliance on weapons of terror is fairly obvious, and forms the core of the category of 'terrorism from above.' In democratic societies, 'terrorism from below' is more common. This is true not only because the violence is more possible in free societies than under repressive regimes but because of the very nature of democracy. For terrorists attacking a parliamentary state, their assumption is that all sectors of the 'ruling classes' are responsible for the policies of the government since they elected them to office for that purpose. Hence, they are 'legitimate' targets since they are perceived to be willingly complicit enforcers of the objectionable aspects of the social and political order against which the terrorists are at war.

Both the state and radical groups committed to violence have interests they seek to protect and visions of the future that they demand to be realised. Though less obvious, and despite protestations to the contrary, all agents of political violence, from above or below, gain a measure of satisfaction by playing politics with terrorism and

---

3   See the discussion of this problem in Peter Alan Sproat, "Can the State be Terrorist?" *Terrorism*, v. 14, 1991, pp. 19-29.

from abiding by the rules of this 'Great Game.' The state's interests historically have been chiefly the preservation of power and legitimate authority, notwithstanding the public claims about protecting citizens' well-being and sponsoring economic policies that promise progress and development for both the government and the society. All governments consider their first duty to be defence against external and internal enemies. The state reserves the right to exercise its monopoly on (or control over) weapons of violence against the declared enemy when that antagonist poses a serious threat, which may be real or constructed. Aside from actual interstate warfare, governments have used their power violently against their own citizens systematically (the 'dirty war' in Argentina in the 1980s or the Nazi persecution of non-Aryans in Germany during the 1930s) or episodically (the US assault on Native Americans in the 1830s or Stalin's purges in 1937–8).

Radical groups from below have also played politics with violence. Their interests have been focused on utilising acts of terrorism in order to destabilise, demoralise, threaten or overthrow the established government or regime under whose authority they experience unacceptable injustice. They wantonly challenge the prevailing legal system, declare it unethical, and appeal to higher forms of justice, whether religious or secular-utopian in nature. Their goals are, inter alia, the expulsion of a foreign power from occupying their land, the purification of defiled sacred sites, or the realization of a future social order that will create conditions of liberty and equality once the present regime is abolished. Essentially, terrorists continue to utilise the ancient arguments of pre-modern tyrannicide theorists going back to Aristotle, who sought to define conditions of despotism in order to justify using violence, as a last resort, to bring it to an end.[4]

In both cases, employing the tactics of terrorism is justified by appeals to legitimacy and, at the same time, is intended to create

---

4   See Martin A. Miller, "The Intellectual Origins of Modern Terrorism in Europe," in Martha Crenshaw (ed.), *Terrorism in Context* (University Park, 1995), especially pp. 29-30.

an atmosphere of fear and intimidation which in turn opens up additional playing fields. The officials of the state, perceiving themselves to be under attack, damage their own principles by restricting the liberties of their citizens in the guise of protecting them and by engaging in the repression of perceived enemies from within. Similarly, radical terrorist groups take advantage of every opportunity, particularly when it comes to abusing laws designed to protect them. Indeed, these groups will seek to provoke the government into further repression, thereby reducing society's freedoms further as the state responds in kind, in order to demonstrate their claim that the regime is indeed despotic.

In this way, each side becomes more deeply involved in mobilising resources and manpower to expand, not limit, the use of violence, and to extend the framework of justification. Each side believes that it alone will emerge as the winner at the end as they seek to out-anticipate one another with regard to planning tactics. Most importantly, each side psychologically needs the other to continue to play the violent 'Great Game'. Solitaire will not work as a model or in reality. The terrorist must have an active, willing antagonist. Finally, the claims to victimisation fall on contested ground since both the perpetrators and the targets of the violence, whether from state or society, will portray themselves in the role of having been the object, never the agent, of attack; their terrorism is always justified defence.

## Two kinds of terrorism in historical context

Walter Benjamin was able to present us with the crucial issues to solve when he asked 'whether violence, as a principle, could be a moral means to just ends,' and if great human problems can be solved only with violence.[5] To which we might add the question: who has the right to political violence and what criteria explain the legitimacy of this right? The past offers guidance toward answers. In this section, I will examine historical case studies of the two main forms of

---

5   Walter Benjamin, *Reflections* (New York, 1978), pp. 277, 293.

terrorism. Although each is presented in its appropriate historical context, the connection between that past and our own present problems with terrorism and political game playing will become evident in the discussion.

## 1. France in the 1890s

In what remains as perhaps the single most horrendous act of violence by any European government against its own citizens prior to the Nazi era Holocaust, the French army was ordered to put an end to the Commune of Paris in June, 1871. The members of the Commune had seized the city hall in Paris in March to protest the surrender of the French army at the conclusion of the Franco-Prussian War. The situation was further complicated by the collapse of the Imperial government of Napoleon III, leading to a political vacuum that produced a wide spectrum of factions, from monarchists to socialists, seeking control over the nature of the new regime. Within two months, the Commune was transformed into a decree-issuing administration with socialist influences that the French authorities, under the leadership of the conservative Adolphe Thiers regarded as an intolerable threat to its legitimacy. In a fortnight, using some of the most advanced weaponry then in existence, the soldiers slaughtered between 30,000 and 40,000 French communards in and around their headquarters at the Hotel de Ville. Hundreds of others associated with the Commune were either imprisoned or forced into exile. The long commemorative wall in the Paris cemetery Pére Lachaise with the known names of the dead is all that remains of the massacre.[6]

For the generation coming of age in the 1870s and 1880s, the combination of the creation of the German Reich through violence in successful warfare and the French government's responsibility for the brutal destruction of the Paris Commune brought the power of the modern state into focus. And particularly for those who believed

---

6    For a recent discussion of the impact of the Commune, see Alexander Varias, *Paris and the Anarchists: Aesthetes and Subversives during the Fin de Siécle* (New York, 1996).

that a defence against the state's capacity for violence was more necessary than ever before, the ideology of anarchism offered an attrac-
tive alternative. Many communards and those sympathetic with their
cause went into exile, forming political groups, parties and organisations, and created the historical memory of the Paris Commune
that became a crucial part of the ideology of the growing socialist
movement. Peter Kropotkin, who would later succeed Bakunin as
the leading anarchist theoretician, claims in his memoirs that the
foundational inspiration for his conversion to anarchism was the
experience he had with communard exile Benoit Malon and other
members of the Jura Federation in the mountain retreats of Switzerland in 1872, when the rage and blood of the Paris Commune was
still quite fresh.[7]

In 1886, two attempts were made on the life of the German emper-
or in the name of anarchism, inaugurating a relentless and worldwide
assault on government leaders which was dedicated to avenging the
martyred communards and to the destruction of the violent capacity
of the state. During the next decades, until the outbreak of World
War I, more heads of state were either assassinated or wounded in
attempts on their lives than at any other time in modern European
history. The list includes kings, emperors, presidents and prime
ministers of France, Italy, Germany, Spain and the United States.
Governments, proclaiming that they were acting in response to un-
provoked assault and in defence against an obvious threat, instituted
legislation limiting the liberty of their citizens as well as emergency
laws against 'nihilists', the term of choice for that era to describe
terrorism from below. The anarchists seemed to be everywhere and
nowhere, across and within national borders, operating individually
or in small cells.[8] Despite extensive co-operation among police forces
and the sharing of intelligence from state ministries, the combat

---

7   Jean Maitron, *Le Mouvement Anarchist en France* (Paris, 1975), pp. 56-66;
    Martin A. Miller, *Kropotkin* (Chicago, 1976), pp.72-85.
8   James Joll, 'Terrorism and Propaganda by the Deed', *The Anarchists*
    (Cambridge, MA, 1980), pp. 99-129.

went on, each side claiming their own virtue and eventual victory. There are no records of calls to negotiate. Instead, each side appealed for recruits and support, justifying their acts of violence. They eagerly adopted their roles as players in the Great Game.

Also in this period between the 1890s and the outbreak of World War I, the zone of battle between the state and the anarchists widened significantly as an insidious new current emerged. So long as the combatants were confined to the agents of the state and their enemies below, most ordinary citizens felt they had little to fear. This 'era of attentats' came to public attention on February 9, 1878 when a bomb blew up during a funeral commemoration for the Italian ruler, Victor Emanuel II. In October of that year, an unsuccessful attempt was made on the life of his successor, Umberto I in Naples. Within the next months, bombs were thrown into demonstrations led by monarchist groups by shadowy figures whose actions were accompanied by cries of 'long live the Republic,' and 'avenge the Commune'. That same year, two separate attempts were made on the life of the German Kaiser. Although they claimed to be acting on behalf of the cause of anarchism, there remains doubt as to their actual affiliation with any anarchist party. Significantly, both the Italian and German governments responded to these events by rushing through anti-socialist acts stripping citizens in both countries of liberties, jailing suspects in large numbers and shutting down newspapers, printing presses and publishing houses believed to be associated with anarchists and 'commune socialists'. Often these tactics turned against the state; the growing anarchist movement gained more adherents and sympathisers in this time period in part as a consequence of the intolerance and repression shown by the governments. The media continued to become more deeply involved in the zone of combat; mainstream newspapers and magazines tended to reflect the attitudes of the state, portraying the anarchist terrorists as maniacal, irrational and even mentally ill extremists outside the bounds of civilised behavior, while the anarchist papers painted the state in similar colours and defended the assailants from below as heroic warriors defending the exploited underclass and preparing for utopian future order.[9]

Alongside the continuing escalation of assaults on heads of state, the new trend appeared, seemingly out of the blue, in 1882 when someone threw a bomb into a well patronised music hall in Lyons; an anarchist named Cyvogt was arrested but it is not clear from the evidence that he was the perpetrator. This was followed by a far more publicised act of violence in 1886 when Charles Gallo dropped a crude bomb and fired shots from the visitors' balcony of the Paris stock exchange into the trading area below on the main floor. At his trial, he spoke proudly of the influence of 'anarchist doctrine.' The tempo picked up in the early 1890s with a series of bombings of apartment buildings in Paris where members of the French judiciary lived. The police discovered that these attacks had been committed by an anarchist militant, Ravachol, who was caught, tried and executed. Further acts of revenge followed as the government began arresting people associated with anarchist newspapers. In Spain, similar terrorist acts, now being referred to as 'propaganda by the deed,' were carried out. After an incident in which a bomb was thrown at a general who had been involved in the sentencing of several Spanish anarchists in 1891, anarchist Santiago Salvador took revenge against the state by exploding a bomb in a Madrid theatre in which at least 20 people were killed.

Undoubtedly the single worst act, which unalterably changed the terrain of political violence by breaking down all remaining borders of the conflict, was committed by the anarchist Emile Henry when he left a bomb in the crowded restaurant of a busy railway station in 1894 at midday. Henry was arrested and executed after proclaiming to the world at his trial that he acted on behalf of the 'innocent victims of the state' who are left to wither and die in poverty.[10] His

---

9   See Edward James Erikson, Jr, *The Anarchist Disorder: The Psychopathology of Terrorism in Late Nineteenth Century France*, (PhD dissertation, University of Iowa, December 1998).

10  Maitron, op. cit., pp. 206-50.

attack was a premeditated tactical assault on the ruling class of that unjust state, the bourgeoisie who took the trains to work and their families who saw them off and greeted them upon return. For him, they were as responsible for the exploitation of the underclass as were the representatives they elected to power in the National Assembly.

Henry's act of unprecedented act of violence against civilians was also motivated by private revenge. His father, a communard, had escaped into exile in Spain, where Emile was born, and had been sentenced to death in absentia by the government of the new French republic. According to a source cited by historian Richard Sonn, Emile Henry's mother apparently cried out that her husband had been avenged when she was told of her son's responsibility for the railway restaurant bombing in Paris.[11]

A point of no return had been reached. Just as the French government's decision to murder thousands of its own citizens in 1871 at the Paris Commune established a precedent, the anarchists of the 1890s also ended the long-standing rules of political violence that had limited the enemy to the head of state. Although assassinations continued on both sides (the police hunted down suspected bombers while attentats against rulers went on), a new element had been added which would become the defining feature of modern terrorism—namely, the inclusion of the whole civil order in the struggle. The definitions of the enemies of the state and the enemies of the people were stretched to include not merely individuals in positions of leadership but entire abstract categories of complicit participants. This was particularly true in a democratic republic like France, where the leaders were elected to power by those privileged to vote, and who were actively supported by the elite sector of society engaged in capitalist economic development, investment and profit-making enterprises. Governments, meanwhile, expanded their own lenses as they used political authority in the service of stifling terrorism. In 1919, the Congress of the United States, arguably the most demo-

11 Richard D. Sonn, *Anarchism and Cultural Politics in Fin de Siécle France* (London, 1989), p. 246.

cratic polity in the western world, passed the Alien Act which permitted the deportation of more than 11,000 legal immigrants who were tainted by association with socialist, communist or anarchist organizations and publications. Among this vast list one finds the name of Emma Goldman, who was deported to Soviet Russia, in part for her refusal to disavow an earlier justification of the assassination of President William McKinley by an anarchist sympathiser.

## 2. The trajectory of Russian terrorism before the 1917 revolution

In Russia, events proceeded along somewhat different lines despite the fact that the conflicted and interdependent relationship between the state and the disaffected sectors of society were similar to the Western European situation described above. Russian terrorism was far more deadly, more extensive and, at the same time, more traditional in its orientation than that of the anarchists who chose political violence in Western Europe. Russian revolutionaries were the originators of the sophisticated, underground political party. Because of the illegality of all political parties in an autocratic regime, all opposition to the government's policies had to be conducted in the context of a powerful surveillance operated by the state's secret national police force with its broad authority to arrest and condemn suspects across the realm.

Another facet distinguishing the development of Russian terrorism is the role played by exiles. Throughout the nineteenth century, Russians critical of the autocracy found it necessary to abandon their country and move to Geneva, Paris and London in order to carry out their anti-government activities. By the end of the century, thousands of exiles had crowded into immigrant neighbourhoods in these European capitals where they established their own printing presses and trusted routes of access to smuggle their banned books, newspapers and pamphlets to St. Petersburg, Moscow, Kiev and other cities across the country.[12] Although freer while abroad than they could possibly have been at home, even there they were not beyond the reach of the autocracy. The tsar recognized the danger posed by the exiles and sought permission from the French government to allow agents of the Russian national police (known until 1881 as the Third Section of His Majesty's Imperial Chancery and after 1881 as the *Okhrana*) to conduct activities against the exiles in Paris. Permission was granted, which led to a number of surveillance operations and acts of terrorism. Some of the more sensational of these acts were the blowing up of bookstores and printing presses operated by the exiles in Paris.[13]

The main drama, however, was at home. The trajectory of terrorism in Russia went through a spectacular evolution within a very short time span. The frustrated generation of the 1860s finally took action against the censorious nature of the regime, which still had no legal national parliament, political parties, independent media or organisations of labourers. If there was a single precipitating cause for the sudden upturn of violence, it was disappointment over the legislation issued by Emperor Alexander II between 1861 and 1864. These 'Great Reforms' did finally abolish the detested and humiliating institution of serfdom, and also reshaped the army and established the framework for a modern judicial system. Nevertheless, criticism began almost immediately after the decrees were made public. Opponents pointed out that the conditions were such that little change would actually take place. The 'freed' former serfs were to continue to live in the same humiliating situation under the control of their landlords for a decade until terms could be worked out to compensate the gentry for their losses in manpower on their estates. Moreover, the critics predicted that because these peasants could not actually take possession of land themselves until they had paid off the cost over years that could stretch into a lifetime, the injustices of the social

---

12  Martin A. Miller, *The Russian Revolutionary Emigres, 1825–1870* (Baltimore, 1986).

13  Fredric S. Zuckerman, *The Tsarist Secret Police Abroad* (New York, 2003).

structure would endure rather than change for the better for the vast majority of the country's agriculturally dependent population.

The rage of the opposition emerged initially in pamphlets and broadsides that appeared on the streets of St. Petersburg promising 'rivers of blood' from the axes of peasants still denied the benefits of liberty.[14] In 1866, Dmitry Karakozov, a member of a small radical group calling itself Hell, attempted to assassinate the emperor in broad daylight during a public ceremony. He seems to have assumed the existence of a repressed collective hostility among the peasantry against the regime; when he was wrestled to the ground by the peasants in whose name he fired at the tsar, he cried out, according to the contemporary police report, 'fools, I did this for you!'[15]

The fantasy among the radical intelligentsia, who were situated primarily in the large cities with a flourishing youth culture that had moved beyond the values of their parents, revolved around the notion that the peasantry was waiting for their leadership and inspiration in order to move toward full scale rebellion against the state. During the next decade, the Russian revolutionary underground and the repressive police policies continued to grow. A small group of conspirators at Moscow University in 1869 murdered a member of the circle who had decided not to take part in the planned assassination of the tsar. Sergei Nechaev, the leader of the group who admired Karakozov, fled to Switzerland where he composed the foundational document in the history of Russian terrorism, 'The Catechism of a Revolutionary'. Though only several pages in length, Nechaev's 'Catechism' combines a pitiless description of the professional, full time terrorist for the first time together with a comprehensive hit list of

---

14 James H. Billington, *Fire in the Minds of Men: Origins of the Revolutionary Faith* (New York, 1980), pp. 394-5. An important role in stimulating the opposition had been played by literature, which was the only forum for the public criticism of the autocracy and serfdom. The influence of Ivan Turgenev's *Fathers and Sons* (1861) and Nikolai Chernyshevskii's *What is to be Done?* on this generation was extraordinary.

15 A. I. Ushakov, *Politicheskaia politsiia i politicheskii terrorizm v Rossii* (Moscow, 2001), pp. 27-8.

their targets.[16] The government, acting quickly and with resolve, ordered the arrest of a large number of students who were put on trial. In the absence of damning evidence, most were acquitted.

In the 1870s, the violence intensified as various currents of political anxiety fed into one another. One of the most important was the reaction in Russia to the events of the Paris Commune. The tsar and his cabinet of ministers kept a close watch on the affair and, though they were relieved that the threat against legitimate authority had been suppressed, there remained a pervasive fear of what Catherine the Great, in reference to the French Revolution of 1789, had called 'the French madness' spreading to Russian society. The mainstream press, represented by the widely read newspaper *Moskovskie Vedomosti (Moscow News)* and the popular journal *Russkii Vestnik (Russian Herald)* were filled with reports on the dangers of the Commune to the legitimate government, reflecting the position of the tsarist officialdom. On the other side of the divide, critics of the Russian regime identified with the communards whom they portrayed as socialist martyrs. Some of the most influential members of the enlarging radical movement in Russia, including Michael Bakunin and Peter Lavrov, wrote with engaging enthusiasm on behalf of the struggle of the communards against the state.[17]

After the failure of a radical underground party to awaken the rural peasantry to criticism of the regime and rebellion in 1874, hundreds of students were arrested. In 1877, 193 of them were tried, convicted and sentenced to a variety of punishments, including exile and hard labour in Siberia. Those who remained at large formed another group, called The People's Will, but this time the commitment was to outright terrorism. Tightly organised around an executive committee of a dozen members in St. Petersburg, the party managed to assassinate a number of high ranking officials in 1879 - 1880.

---

16 The document can be found in Philip Pomper, *Sergei Nechaev* (New Brunswick, 1979), pp. 90-4.

17 For a comprehensive study, see Boris S. Itenberg, *Rossiia I Parizhskaia Kommuna* (Moscow, 1971).

They climaxed their campaign of violence with the assassination of Emperor Alexander II on 1 March 1881, which sent shock waves throughout the courts of Europe. The expected peasant rising did not materialise, and most of the members of the party were arrested, tried and the leaders executed. Still, The People's Will set an important precedent which would soon haunt governments and societies around the world. In spite of all the intelligence at the disposal of the government and a network of police informers, the organisers of The People's Will had managed to create the western world's first professional terrorist organisation, which became a model for terrorist groups of the future.[18]

Things were to get far worse. After a decade of crackdown by the state in which censorship was expanded and university autonomy was severely limited, the violence renewed, reaching levels never before seen. In 1901, the Russian Socialist Revolutionary Party was formed outside of the country, committing itself to fomenting a peasant revolution. A faction of that party agreed to concentrate exclusively on terrorism, consciously following in the violent footsteps imprinted first by The People's Will. The casualty statistics are shocking. Propelled by the year-long revolution which broke out in 1905 in St. Petersburg and spread across the country in the ensuing months, the terrorists managed to claim responsibility for between 7,000 and 9,000 killed or seriously wounded, of whom at least 4,000 were assassinated officials of the government, in the period between 1905 and 1907.[19] The targets were carefully chosen. As one commentator put it, wearing any kind of uniform was asking to be shot.

Once more the expected rising of the masses did not occur, and the state responded ruthlessly. Once again, there were no calls for rapprochement or discussion. Each side preferred, and indeed, to a large extent, needed to fight the war. And, once more, both the

---

18  Norman M. Naimark, 'Terrorism and the Fall of Imperial Russia,' *Terrorism and Political Violence*, v. 2, no. 2, 1990, pp. 171-92.

19  See Anna Geifman, *Thou Shalt Kill: Revolutionary Terrorism in Russia, 1894–1917* (Princeton, 1993), pp. 21, 264, n. 59.

government and the radical organisations (anarchist groups and other parties were also involved in the terrorism, but to a lesser extent) played politics for their own ends. Submitting to the rules they themselves had established for the game of violence, both claimed they were acting in collective self defence, and that the violence was a last resort after all other options had failed. Both promised that victory would bring security and freedom, and, by working together against each other, they guaranteed that such conditions would be impossible to realise.

## How to end the game?

To return to the problem raised by Walter Benjamin, it may be useful to try to distinguish perceptions from realities. As the two case studies analysed above have shown, both government officials from above and radical organisations from below have acted on the basis of unequivocal commitments to the ethics of political violence. Thus, in the arena of perceptions, terrorist tactics have been used in a similar manner by two utterly antagonistic camps, each of whom needs the other to justify the use of the violence. Benjamin was seeking to confront a deeper issue—namely whether there is a realistic basis for a moral understanding of the use of political violence. His approach to an answer involved distinguishing the 'law-making' capacity of strategically employed political violence. In his view, if the violence produced legal outcomes (constitutions, treaties and negotiated settlements) acceptable to the responsible parties, there might in fact be such a reality-based justification.[20]

Hannah Arendt also devoted serious thought to these issues. Recalling Max Weber's definition of the state as the centralised institutionalisation of legitimate violence for the purpose of ordering human relations in society, Arendt argued the necessity of distinguishing the term 'power' from 'violence.' For her, the former was legitimate, arising from the voluntary choice by members of a society

---

20 Walter Benjamin, op. cit. pp. 283-4. See also J. Angelo Corlett, *Terrorism: A Philosophical Analysis* (Dordrecht, 2003), pp. 112-44.

to invest in a representative form of authority, while the latter was illegitimate because it was a coercive and unjustifiable form of authority.[21] Can we take this one step further by asking whether there can be forms of 'just violence' or even justifiable terrorism in the same way scholars argue there can be 'just wars'?[22] There is no doubt that states have been responsible for far greater numbers of casualties than insurgent groups throughout their history, so the answer cannot lie in statistics alone.[23]

Terrorism is actually the tactical by-product of unresolved issues that the parties involved refuse to recognize and address directly. One scholar who has tried to broaden our understanding of the ethical issues of terrorism is Ted Honderich. By linking the quotidian conditions of inequality with the goals of the perpetrators of violence, he has shown us the undercurrents of rage that often motivate terrorists and their rationalisations for having to resort to extreme measures. We will be forced to continue either to fear or be complicit with acts of political violence, he concludes, until we learn to face and rectify 'the abysmal wretchedness of daily life for the world's majority.'[24] This is not a problem of which social class the proponents of violence come from; it is about the horror of preventable death, disease, unbearable poverty, racism and ethnic intolerance, and immoral conditions of inequality that dominate the planet because they are tacitly acceptable to those fortunate enough to have avoided them.

Indeed, in both of the case studies analysed here, echoes of these cries can be found. The tsarist government in Russia systematically neglected the vast social inequities of the country's population. Russia's problematic context was that the autocracy did not permit

---

21 Hannah Arendt, *On Violence* (New York, 1970), pp. 50-6.

22 Michael Walzer, *Just and Unjust Wars: a Moral Argument with Historical Illustrations* (New York, 2000).

23 See Bruce Campbell and Arthur Brenner eds, *Death Squads in Global Perspective* (New York, 2000) and the comprehensive statistics compiled in R. J. Rummel, *Death by Government* (London, 1994).

24 Ted Honderich, *Terrorism for Humanity: Inquiries in Political Philosophy*, (London, 2003).

political parties, workers' organisations or an open press in which reform policies could be discussed and debated. Violence thus became the option of choice *faux de mieux* for both the state and for the opposition, each claiming this mode as necessary to defend its own priorities. In France, a new republic was established on the smoldering ruins of the Commune massacre. The conservative government was committed to limiting the role of the socialists, blamed for the disaster in 1871, while the left opposition found itself confronting what it perceived to be an *état manqué*, a despotic democracy run by a reactionary elite. For them, the only solution seemed to be to adopt the worldview of the anarchists and to seek violently to eliminate the rulers in charge together with those in the society who chose and supported them.

How did it end, and what meaning might that have for the terrorism of the twenty-first century? All games must come to an end, and the periods of high intensity terrorism in France and Russia discussed here also reached their denouements. In both cases, the players experienced a sense of exhaustion as their goals slipped further away from their grasp of the most determined advocates of violence. In addition, participants not in the centre of the tactical planning actually settled for something less than absolute victory, weakening the overall operation. The most important factor, however, was that despite the fact that their terrorisms were different in terms of symbolic targets and modes of organisation, in both countries the end came not through the triumph of either the state or the insurgents, but because another significant force came into play-the rise of a militant workers' movement-which assumed a preminent status across the combat zones that simultaneously attracted recruits and distracted others from their obsessions with the tactics of political violence.

In France, Fernand Pelloutier's skill in convincing factory workers to join the fledgling General Confederation of Labour in Paris was echoed in Georges Sorel's 1909 treatise, *Reflections on Violence*. Sorel made the case for prioritising industrial violence as a means of generating a collective identity among the working class that, he predicted, would lead to a huge and paralysing strike that would damage the state and bring the proletariat to positions of power. In the years before the outbreak of the First World War, increasing numbers of people who previously would have been attracted to the anarchist movement, and perhaps to its involvement with political violence, instead gravitated into the ranks of the labour federations.[25]

The terrorists of the Socialist Revolutionary Party found themselves faced with a similar historical moment. After thousands of victims, and a year of revolution culminating in a devastating general strike in Moscow in October 1905, the tsarist regime still reigned, and the peasants remained a largely illiterate and exploited underclass as yet unrecognised as citizens of a modern state. Working class organisations appeared in Russia as they did in France, but in an entirely unique manner. The government organised unions for industrial workers in a number of cities and towns with the active participation of the police in an effort to compete with a rising socialist movement and to head off further recruitment to the terrorist cells already in existence.[26] In April 1912, amidst rising strikes around the country, a group of workers were fired from their positions at a gold mining site in the Siberian Lena river area. Army troops had to be called in to stop the walkout of workers who refused to return to their jobs unless all were rehired, and fired on the crowd killing between 100 and 200 of the unarmed miners. This act of state violence, reported in the press, was a shock to the public and brought waves of widespread sympathy to the victims and significant disillusionment and criticism toward the government. By the time the Russians entered the Great War two summers later, more than a million workers were participating in factory strikes according to government statistics, and terrorism had come to a halt.

Historical episodes of terrorist conflict between states and societies have, of course, led to outcomes other than the two case studies

---

25 Jean Maitron, op.cit. pp. 258-61, 265-9.

26 Jeremiah Schneiderman, *Sergei Zubatov and Revolutionary Marxism: the Struggle for the Working Class in Tsarist Russia* (Ithaca, 1976).

discussed above. In some instances, violent regimes have been over-thrown or overtaken by events in which their capacity to rule by fear and punish with violence was brought to a conclusion by a variety of means, including global war (the Nazis), domestic elections (Chile after Pinochet) and internal collapse (USSR). From below, violent insurgent groups have been overcome by police force (Baader-Mein-hoff in West Germany) and fatally weakened by the loss of popular support combined with an amnesty offered by the government (the Red Brigades in Italy). In some instances, victory was claimed whether it was deserved (the FLN in Algeria) or questionable (the US Weather-Underground organisation). In yet other cases, terrorist movements 'succeeded' by virtue of being flexible enough to transform themselves from paramilitary groups into parliamentary organizations (the IRA and the PLO), willing to accept the responsibilities of political participation in government. The destiny of the conflict between al-Qaeda and the international alliance of governments arrayed against it remains to be seen, but it is likely that it will eventually follow one of the above scenarios.[27]

Meanwhile, the 'Great Game' goes on relentlessly. As one cycle winds down, another takes off, and the acts of outrageous violence continue to be perpetrated and justified. Media coverage, which becomes part of the partisan conflict, demonstrates that instead of one side speaking to the other, it is as though the blind are talking to the deaf. Judging from the lessons of history, we may have to conclude that terrorism will never entirely cease to threaten our lives, but its power to inflict damage may substantially decrease when the real issues that drive the rage behind the violence are forthrightly addressed, and nonviolent proposals are placed on the table as the only viable solutions. The urge to annihilate often rests on an insecure foundation

---

27 The constituency, ideology and motivation of suicide bombers worldwide between the years 1980 and 2003 have been studied by Robert A. Pape in his recent book, *Dying to Win: the Strategic Logic of Suicide Terrorism* (New York, 2005). His research shows, contrary to much current opinion, that Islamic terrorism is primarily driven by secular and anti-state interests. See also 'For Jihadist, Read Anarchist,' *The Economist*, 18 August 2005.

of fearing annihilation, just as aggressive hostility and arrogance can be a cover for deeply rooted personal uncertainties and ambivalence: but the degree to which these drives are fantasies or realities can only be comprehended once open dialogue ensues. Jacques Derrida, in his fascinating reflections on the World Trade Center disaster with Jürgen Habermas, mentioned that it may be 'too early' really to talk about 9/11 because of the great passion it evokes both for those who suffered the tragedy and for the larger number of people who vicariously lived through it as a traumatic event.[28] Until we can, the 'Great Game' will move on like a juggernaut, devouring the virtuous and the demonic indiscriminately as required by all the players.

---

28 Giovanna Borradori, *Philosophy in a Time of Terror: Dialogues with Jürgen Habermas and Jacques Derrida* (Chicago, 2003). Derrida was attempting to make the important distinction between having a generalized discussion as opposed to analytically understanding a problem. He had his doubts only about the latter.

3

# THE ALDO MORO MURDER CASE AS POLITICS

*Richard Drake*

The kidnapping of Aldo Moro and the killing of his five-man security guard in Rome on 16 March 1978 plunged Italy into national shock. Moro had been the principal Italian political leader for nearly twenty years. Made secretary of the hegemonic Christian Democratic Party (DC) in 1959, he subsequently served as prime minister from 1963 to 1968 and twice more between 1974 and 1976. At the moment of his kidnapping, he was president of the party. In the mid-1970s, he had been the principal architect of a historic compromise with the Communist Party (PCI), which since 1947 had been excluded from participating in the Italian government. Fearing that the rising incidence of terrorism since the 1969 Piazza Fontana bombing in Milan threatened the country's democratic institutions, he had persuaded the Christian Democrats to accept the support of the increasingly moderate Communist Party, on the grounds that it no longer posed a revolutionary threat. His assessment of the PCI echoed that of the extra-parliamentary left, an ideologically differentiated mass of groups still committed to the idea of a communist revolution. The Red Brigades, emerging from the most extreme sector of the extraparliamentary left, offered themselves as a replacement for the now pro-establishment PCI. With their kidnapping of Moro, they aimed at destroying this establishment in the name of Marx and Lenin.

For the next fifty-four days, the Red Brigades held Moro captive in the 'People's Prison.' They offered to free him in exchange for thirteen imprisoned terrorists. An agonising debate unfolded in the country over the wisdom of negotiating with the Red Brigades. Proponents of *fermezza*, or firmness, argued that dealing with terrorists in any way would inevitably encourage more acts of terrorism. The *trattative*, or negotiation side, countered that human life mattered more than an abstract concern for the state. Almost all the political parties and national newspapers supported the government policy of firmness. Their reasoning prevailed. Amidst dissension in their own ranks, on 9 May the Red Brigades made good their threat to kill Moro. Charges and counter-charges about the political manipulation of Moro's murder case have haunted Italian politics ever since.

*Conspiracy theories*

Conspiracy theories in the case quickly surfaced. Just a few months after the murder, Leonardo Sciascia charged in *L'affaire Moro* that the government had played politics with Moro's kidnapping. One of Italy's most distinguished novelists and social critics, he had belonged to the Communist Party and at the time of the kidnapping served as a Radical member of Parliament. His book, reissued in English in 2004 by the prestigious New York Review of Books publishing house, has been a central reference point for conspiracy theorists. For example, in a 2001 book that boasts of being 'the first work of history about the Moro kidnapping,' Marco Clementi writes: 'Insofar as the facts occurred, there is not much to add to the words of Sciascia…'.

Sciascia, who in 1974 had written a satirical portrait of Moro in *Todo Modo*, began *L'affaire Moro* with a chronology of the kidnapping. He presented the extreme ineptitude of the police search as a defining moment of the Italian state's futility. By earnestly requesting negotiations and by writing letters voluminously in the People's Prison, Moro doubtless had hoped to give the authorities time to find him. They failed him utterly. In his despair, Moro raised the question that Sciascia turned into an indictment of the government: did his 'friends' really want him to come back alive? In a letter to Benigno Zaccagnini, his close ally and DC party secretary, he felt obliged to write that if he were not freed in a prisoner exchange, 'you yourselves will have wished it and I can say, without rancor, that Party and individuals alike will be held responsible for the inevitable consequences.' As the weeks passed, Moro became more direct in his accusations against the Christian Democrats: 'Can you really agree in wanting my death for a so-called reason of state...?' Agreeing with Moro, Sciascia assigned ultimate responsibility for the crime of the Red Brigades to the government, although he did so without identifying any particular malefactors. Subsequent conspiracy theorists would be much more graphic in their indictments than Sciascia was.

A member of the commission created by parliament to investigate the kidnapping and murder of Moro, Sciascia filed a minority report in 1983. In this document, he added to the list of charges presented in *L'affaire Moro*. More than ever, he found it simply incredible that so many mistakes of omission and commission could have occurred during the 'useless and misguided' manhunt. The number of missed or neglected leads defied the laws of probability. In the first of the Moro trials, which had ended earlier that year, the judges had concluded that the Italian police were 'psychologically and materially unprepared to confront emergency situations of these dimensions.' Sciascia thought otherwise: 'The general opinion voiced by officials and politicians that the State was unprepared for such an attack cannot be accepted without demur.' The police had long known about the seriousness of the Red Brigade threat, had accumulated much intelligence on it, and had identified many members of the terrorist group: 'But the fact is that such advantages were put to no use.' Why not?

Sciascia primarily gave a cultural answer to his own question. He thought that Moro had died in large part because of a state fecklessness derived from the Italian national character. The major premise of his argument about the Italian character went essentially like this: to do something well is not as important as to be perceived to be doing something well. Accordingly, the government wanted most of all to create a dazzling effect in its search for Moro. Thousands of policemen milling around Rome gave the impression of a mighty effort, for all of its practical uselessness: 'the need for display prevailed over professionalism and diligent investigation'. The government could not be bothered with basic intelligence work and its co-ordination. He contended that only a political, psychological, and psychoanalytical explanation could penetrate to the deepest truths of the tragedy. This kind of emergency, for which only the most practical problem-solving skills would be adequate, always brought out the worst in the excessively imaginative Italian people. Yet, as a tantalising supplement to his reflections on how national character traits undermined the government's effort, on the last page of the report he mentioned what to many constituted the heart of the Moro murder case: 'the imperceptible waning of any eagerness to find Aldo Moro.'

Sergio Flamigni's *Tela del ragno* may be taken as representative of the vast Moro conspiracy literature in its extreme form. A Communist deputy on the parliamentary commission investigating the Moro kidnapping and murder case, he, too, began by enumerating the many failures of the police search. Unlike Sciascia, however, he did not present any kind of cultural explanation for them. He thought that Moro had been betrayed by a conspiracy of deviant politicians, police officials, and military men. He had also served on the Parliamentary Commission investigating the secret Masonic lodge known as Propaganda 2 (P2). Licio Gelli, its leader and a notorious right-winger with important contacts in Washington, had succeeded in placing a network of men loyal to his organisation in the police and intelligence services. On behalf of Gelli's political agenda, these P2 operatives derailed the Moro manhunt. Their 'mistakes' occurred by design: 'In the secret rooms of power, men of State with the most sensitive [*delicatissimi*] offices (heads of the secret services, heads of the armed services, officials in charge of the investigation) were at the service not of the country's republican institutions, but of 'venerable Masonic masters', who sent investigators down one blind alley after another. They wanted Moro to die and to use his death as an excuse to establish an authoritarian regime.

Flamigni further charged that the American government, through Gelli's contacts with it, had played a villainous role in the Moro tragedy. Henry Kissinger had opposed Moro's historic compromise with the PCI, as well as his pro-Palestinian stand on issues dealing with the Middle East. Although the kidnapping occurred during the Carter administration, Flamigni contended that Kissinger's baleful anti-communist and pro-Israel influence remained powerful in Washington through his protégés who continued to occupy key positions in the State Department. For the United States, Israel, and P2, Flamigni asserted, Moro's death would be welcome. Moreover, he thought that the Red Brigades 'had been "infiltrated," conditioned, and utilised' by reactionaries in the government and their allies abroad. For this part of his indictment, he cited the testimony of Red Brigade founding father Alberto Franceschini, who believed that the organizer of the Moro kidnapping, Mario Moretti, worked as a police spy. All along, a collusive relationship existed between the 'piloted' Red Brigades and elements of the State apparatus. Flamigni thought that in all probability an actual 'pact' existed between them.

## Defending the Italian government

Many variations of the conspiracy theory exist in the Moro murder case. Together they form the dominant view of the case in Italy. The opposition to them began to form during the kidnapping itself, in response to Moro's grave charges from the People's Prison against the Christian Democrats. His Christian Democratic colleagues and their allies in the firmness front argued that in one way or another—through torture or psychological pressure or the censoring of information coming into the People's Prison as well as of the outgoing letters—Moro lacked the freedom to speak his true mind: 'Moro is no longer Moro,' the saying went at the time. His accusations, therefore, counted for nothing. In other words, the proponents of firmness accused those who wanted to use Moro's letters as an indictment against the government of playing politics with the kidnapping.

The Moro murder trials that began in 1982 and continued into the 1990s ended in judgments that exculpated the government from the charges of the conspiracy theorists. In the sentence for the first trial, the judges complained that the 'interminable series of discussions' about conspiracies could only be interpreted as a sign of immaturity in Italian public life.[1] The government had not exaggerated the terrorist threat. Italian democracy had been at genuine risk as a result of the Red Brigade terror campaign. Moreover, the government had done its best to find and to liberate Moro: 'Not one piece of evidence, not even circumstantial evidence, not one page of the trial [record] authorizes the [conspiracy] hypothesis.'[2]

In subsequent judicial proceedings, witnesses and judges repeatedly denied that any connections or contacts existed between the Red Brigades and secret service organizations or right-wing plotters. For example, Franco Bonisoli, an ex-terrorist witness, in a 6 October 1985 *Corriere della Sera* interview that was included in the court records for a 1987 trial described the conspiracy theories as "improbable stupidities that have never found even the smallest support in reality... they can only be classified as a form of gossip."[3] In the investigative preliminaries for the final trial in the case, Judge Rosario Priore specifically challenged Sergio Flamigni's conspiracy theory book, *La tela del ragno*. Writing in August 1990, the judge asserted that all the main points in the Moro case now could be established, especially that conspiracy theories lacked judicial credibility. The police investigation did not give rise to a single serious legal concern, in his ruling. As for P2, he could find no proof at all or even a trace of reasonable presumption of any irregularity.[4]

---

1  Sentenza nel procedimento penale, Moro 1 e bis,' Corte di Assise di Roma, vol. 2, pt. 5, I mtivi della sentenza, p. 908.

2  Ibid., p. 914.

3  Richard Drake, *The Aldo Moro Murder Case* (Cambridge, MA, 1995), p. 180.

4  Ibid., pp. 206-9.

## *The Moro prison testament*

Just two months after Judge Priore's findings in the case, workmen in Milan discovered a cache of Moro letters and testimony from the People's Prison. Suddenly, the judge's seemingly definitive summary seemed obsolete. With the publication of the newly discovered Moro papers, the conspiracy theories took on new life. Once again, Moro's prison writings got the controversy rolling. He castigated all the foremost chiefs of the Christian Democratic party for their corruption and cynicism. They had been false friends and treacherous colleagues. He wondered if they wanted his death 'almost as a solution for all the problems of the country.'[5] He condemned the Christian Democrats as his real executioners. These heartless partisans of firmness had led him 'to certain death.' As always, they had taken their cue from the United States, which thought of Italy as part of its empire. Moro's resistance to American directives regarding the Italian Communist party and unquestioning support for Israel in the Middle East had landed him on Washington's enemies list. In *La tela del ragno*, Flamigni had pointed to Henry Kissinger's enmity toward Moro as an explanation for America's probable responsibility in his death. Now Moro's prison writings appeared to confirm the conspiracy school's anti-American indictment. The Communist party secretary, Achille Occhetto, spoke for many in the aftermath of the publicity about the Moro papers when he declared that the kidnappers had been mere pawns "piloted" by secret service agencies both domestic and foreign.[6]

Christian Democrats and former Red Brigadists made common cause against critics like Occhetto, who saw in the Moro papers new and confirming evidence in support of conspiracy theories. Giulio Andreotti, the prime minister during the kidnapping, spoke for the

---

5  Vincenzo Vasile, "Dodici anni fa aveva scritto, 'Tutto questo ricomparirà'," *l'Unità*, 23 October 1990, p. 12. This Communist newspaper published virtually all of the Moro papers.

6  Concita De Gregorio, "Occhetto: 'Br pilotate nel rapimento Moro'," *La Repubblica*, 15 December 1990.

Christian Democrats. He ridiculed the idea that Moro's denunciations of the party could be taken as a serious expression of what he actually believed. Facts contravened all the fierce criticisms of the party in the so-called Moro 'testament.' In and out of office, he had led the party for more than two decades. It simply made no sense to believe in the validity of a self-destructive political critique authored by an obviously terrorized man. All the revelations in the Moro papers about Christian Democratic complicity in CIA plots, now being greeted breathlessly by the left, had been such staple fare for so long in Italian public life that the Red Brigades did not even bother to report them in 1978. They themselves, as numerous trial witnesses had testified, perceived their interrogation of Moro to have resulted in nothing worthwhile. Yet, Andreotti complained, these clearly established facts could not prevent the ongoing political manipulation of the Moro tragedy. As for Moro's ferocious denunciations in the People's Prison of him personally, Andreotti defied anyone to produce a single document indicating that he had held these views prior to 16 March 1978. Moreover, why would Moro personally have asked Andreotti to head the national unity government of that year, if he were such a sinister figure?[7]

Mario Moretti also found himself on the defensive in the fall of 1990. Why, indeed, had he not made use of Moro's damaging confessions about the collusion among the CIA, NATO, and the Italian secret services? One of the founders of the Red Brigades, Alberto Franceschini, who had been in prison at the time of the kidnapping, thought that Moretti must have been a 'spy.'[8] Moretti responded to such accusations by repeating, in effect, Andreotti's point about the routine nature of Moro's revelations. These were 'secrets' of State that every communist in Italy knew full well. They did not have to be discovered in the People's Prison. Nevertheless, conspiracy theories

---

7  Eugenio Scalfari, 'Interroghiamo Andreotti a domanda risponde,' *La Repubblica*, 19 October 1990.

8  Rocco Tolfa, 'Caccia ai manovratori,' *Il Sabato*, 15 December 1990.

involving now both the government and the Red Brigades completely eclipsed the sober-minded judicial interpretation of Judge Priore. The courtroom phase of the fourth and final trial began in late 1991. Against a tumultuous background of historic events involving the end of the Cold War, the demise of the Italian political party system including the dissolution of both the PCI and the DC, the protracted government corruption scandal known as Tangentopoli, and the sensational investigation into Andreotti's alleged ties with the Mafia, Moro quater proceeded to its conclusion. The judges handed down their sentence on 1 December 1994. New facts had emerged concerning the personnel involved in the kidnapping and the routine of Moro's life in the People's Prison. The judges claimed, though, that the previous trials had established the main outlines of the case, most notably that the Red Brigades, not the government, bore responsibility for the kidnapping and murders. In reconstructing 'these mournful events,' they expressly rejected conspiracy theories.[9]

## Parliamentary commission reports

The investigations of two parliamentary commissions coincided with the early trials in the Moro murder case. The judges in the trials took the reports of these commissions into account. The members of the commissions split along party lines in rendering majority and minority reports. The majority report from the Moro Commission emphasized the absence of "secure evidence" in support of any conspiracy theory.[10] "Insufficient diligence" could not be interpreted as proof of a plot by supposedly treasonous police and government officials. In short, the government had done its best to rescue Moro. The Socialists, who had broken with the government's firmness policy during the kidnapping, filed a minority report in which they expressed

---

9  Sentenza nel procedimento penale, Moro quater, 1ˢᵗ Corte di Assise di Roma, 1 December 1994, p. 56.

10  *Relazione della Commissione Parlamentare d'Inchiesta*, vol. 1, 'Relazione di Maggioranza,' p. 87.

their doubts about the integrity of the search for Moro. Too many troubling circumstances in Moro's kidnapping and death raised the legitimate suspicion of foul play by the police. The Socialists also rejected the majority report's confident assertion about the absence of "international support" in the Moro tragedy.[11] Other minority reports, including the one by Leonardo Sciascia recounted earlier, raised similar concerns about the official explanation of Moro's kidnapping and murder.

Nothing did more to perpetuate the belief in conspiracy than the Parliamentary Commission reports on Propaganda 2. Tina Anselmi, a friend and supporter of Moro in the Christian Democratic party, authored the majority report. She emphasized "the significance of the presence of numerous *piduisti* [members of P2] in positions of exalted responsibility during that period."[12] Many of the highest police, military, and secret service officers involved in the Moro manhunt belonged to P2. The hatred that Licio Gelli bore toward Moro for his opening to the Communists would explain why these officers would have been motivated by "another order of considerations" besides saving Moro.[13] The Radical party minority report of Deputy Massimo Teodori went even further in attacking what he called the P2-corroded government. P2, he contended, had evolved as a natural consequence of thirty years of Christian Democratic misrule. Although "certain proof" did not exist, he thought that P2 criminally had undermined the search for Moro.[14] The repeated failures of the manhunt pointed toward an "objective opposed to the stated objective," the manipulation of the Moro kidnapping for right-wing po-

---

11 Ibid., Relazione di minoranza dei deputati Luigi Covatta e Claudio Martelli e dei senatori Paolo Barsacchi e Libero Della Briotta (gruppo parlamentare del PSI), p. 50.

12 *Relazione della Commissione Parlamentare d'Inchiesta sulla Loggia Massonica P2*, 'Relazione di Maggioranza,' doc. 23, #2 (Rome 1984), Section II, 'I collegamenti con l'eversione, pt. 3 "L'affare Moro,"' p. 103.

13 Ibid., p. 104.

14 Ibid., 'Relazione di Minoranza dell'Onorevole Massimo Teodori," doc. 23, pt. 1 'Prassi: la vera azione della P2', ch. 5 'Moro-Andreotti-P2,' p. 69.

litical ends. Moro's death had to be seen against the deep background of the country's right-wing politics, by then thoroughly penetrated and controlled by P2 and through that lodge by the most politically retrograde elements in Washington. For most Italians the truth of the Moro case lay somewhere between the moderate conspiracy view of Anselmi and the extreme conspiracy view of Teodori.

## Films and the Moro case

Popular films played an important part in reinforcing the view that the government had played politics with the Moro murder case. *Il caso Moro*, directed by Giuseppe Ferrara and starring the internationally acclaimed actor Gian Maria Volonté as Moro, premiered on 13 November 1986. Ferrara had made numerous documentaries and had specialized in films about controversial episodes in contemporary Italian history. Volonté earlier had played Moro in Elio Petri's screen version of Leonardo Sciascia's *Todo Modo*. In Ferrara's film, his co-screenwriter Robert Katz recycled the conspiracy theory that he had presented in a book, *Days of Wrath. The Ordeal of Aldo Moro: the Kidnapping, the Execution, the Aftermath* (1980). He portrayed Moro as a victim of assorted right-wing plotters in and out of the government. The film resulted in controversy along predictable lines, with the Christian Democrats taking the lead in denouncing it as transparent left-wing propaganda.[15] Even some PSI critics who had opposed the government's firmness policy thought that *Il caso Moro* ignored the complexity of history in favor of rank partisanship.[16] In the aftermath of the P2 Commission reports, however, many who had supported firmness were prepared to accept the film's conspiracy thesis. Certainly in the public at large conspiracies of the kind shown in *Il caso Moro* continued to find widespread support.

Renzo Martinelli's *Piazza delle Cinque Lune* premiered on 8 May 2003, the twenty-fifth anniversary of Moro's death. Martinelli also

---

15 For the screenplay and the controversy surrounding the film, see Armenia Balducci, Giuseppe Ferrara, and Robert Katz, *Il caso Moro* (Naples, 1987).

16 Ugo Intini, 'Il caso Moro,' *Mondo operaio*, 1 (January 1987).

came to feature films with a background in documentaries. With Sergio Flamigni as his chief consultant, he presented the Moro murder case as a tissue of conspiracies. The Red Brigades served as mere pawns in a much larger game of subversion controlled ultimately by the CIA, which plotted to eliminate Moro in order to block his opening to the Communists. The former terrorist, Alberto Franceschini, professed himself to have been overcome with emotion while watching the film. He agreed completely with its thesis about government conspiracies in the case. In further agreement with the film, he repeated his earlier accusation that Moretti had to have been a plant for the secret services.[17] Only with Moretti acting as their accomplice could the kidnapping have turned out the way it did, in Moro's death, which the secret services wanted, and in the otherwise inexplicable failure to use any of the damaging revelations from the interrogation in the People's Prison.

Government spokesmen dismissed the film as disinformation of the left. Francesco Cossiga, the Minister of Interior in 1978, thought that the accusation of Franceschini against Moretti, 'this Gothic construction,' belonged to the realm of political fantasy.[18] Judge Priore also dismissed Franceschini's remarks about Moretti as baseless and once again took a stand on the principle that judgments in the Moro case must be based 'only on what is proved.'[19]

A few months later, in September 2003, a very different kind of film about the Moro case appeared, Marco Bellocchio's *Buongiorno, notte.* A director as well-known for his extreme left-wing politics as for brilliantly original motion pictures, Bellocchio enjoyed enormous international prestige as one of the great contemporary masters of the Italian cinema. His films, beginning with an extraordinarily success-

---

17  Giovanni Bianconi, 'Ma va, Moretti era un infiltrato, Cia e Kgb dietro il caso Moro', *Corriere della sera*, 21 May 2003.

18  Lorenzo Fuccaro, 'Moretti spia? Tesi da ex Pci, gli do la mia solidarietà,' *Corriere della sera*, 22 May 2003.

19  Paolo Mieli, 'Dov'è la prova che Moretti sia un figlio di Yalta?,' *Corriere della sera*, 24 May 2003.

ful debut, *I pugni in tasca* (1965), had won the most coveted awards in the European cinema. Throughout his career he had targeted Italian establishment institutions for their corruption and futility. From such a director connoisseurs of conspiracy in the Moro case anticipated a political exposé of surpassing artistic ingenuity.

Bellocchio surprised his fans with a film described by many critics as remarkably understated. In an interview on the day of the premiere, he declared: 'I don't know if it [Moro's death] was the fault of the KGB, the CIA, or P2, and I am not interested in establishing the truth of the matter.'[20] He claimed to have set out in this film solely to depict daily life in the People's Prison, not to discover new facts in the case or to promote conspiracy theories. The personal drama of Anna Laura Braghetti, one of Moro's jailers and the author with Paola Tavella of *Il prigioniero*, provided the film's main story line.[21] The country's leading newspaper, the *Corriere della sera*, reported that *Buongiorno, notte* produced 'a hurricane of positive reviews.'

Adriana Faranda, one of the key Red Brigade leaders during the kidnapping, counted herself among Bellocchio's most appreciative viewers. She thought that he completely understood the psychology of the terrorists inside the People's Prison: 'Bellocchio has put the Red Brigades on the psychoanalyst's couch.'[22] Both the psychology and the ideology of the Red Brigades explained their taking of Moro. They believed in the imminence of revolution and thought that Moro's abduction could bring it to pass. She did not exclude the possibility of 'external manipulation' of the kidnapping, but Bellocchio had succeeded to an astonishing degree in showing how 'that

20  Maurizio Pirro, 'Ho solo raccontato la psicologia dei terroristi', *Corriere della sera*, 5 September 2003.

21  Anna Laura Braghetti and Paola Tavella, *Il prigioniero* (Milan, 2003). The book deals with the Moro kidnapping as its central subject, but Braghetti also comments in a highly illuminating way about the process through which, 'in a gradual approach, step by step,' she evolved from being an ordinary participant in the extra-parliamentary left movement to membership in the Red Brigades, p. 19.

22  Luca Talese, 'Avrebbero potuto prenderci,' *Il Giornale*, 9 September 2003.

crime was born and developed inside the Red Brigades.' Although she continued to believe that had the police been completely serious in their search they could have found the Red Brigades, people needed to be reminded of what Bellocchio had driven home in his film: 'We the Red Brigades, certainly not the secret services, killed Moro.'

Prospero Gallinari, another one of Moro's jailers and Braghetti's lover at the time of the kidnapping, emphasized the film's weak points, above all the scene in which before killing Moro the terrorists make the sign of the cross. This kind of 'grotesque' smudging of the facts obscured the organization's 100 percent Marxist-Leninist character, which only in Hollywood or in Hollywood on the Tiber could be portrayed with such brazen indifference toward the historical truth.[23] The Red Brigades, insofar as Gallinari knew, included no Catholic believers in their ranks.

Not caught up in the hurricane of positive reviews either, Giulio Andreotti thought that Bellocchio's film belied his reassuring words. One scene in particular disturbed the former prime minister, where he was shown to be giving firmness-driven instructions to Pope Paul VI on how the Vatican should handle the kidnapping. Andreotti detected Flamigni's influence in the filming of this scene. Such a tell-tale manipulation of the tragedy revealed the substantially conspiracy-minded agenda of the director. Andreotti protested that a genuine attempt had been made to rescue Moro and that in the frightening uncertainties of the time firmness seemed to the overwhelming majority of government and party leaders to be the most promising strategy for finding him and maintaining political unity. About that strategy he ruefully but unapologetically observed: 'We paid a high price, but [without firmness] we would have paid an even higher one.'[24]

---

23  Pirro, 'Ho solo raccontato…,' op. cit.
24  Luca Talese, "Andreotti: 'Autorizzai il Vaticano a pagare un riscatto per Moro'," *Il Giornale*, 11 September 2003.

Francesco Merlo, a gadfly journalist of left-wing orientation writing in the *Corriere della sera*, denounced the film as a sham from beginning to end. He complained that in an unacceptably licentious way, Bellocchio had transformed the Red Brigadists from the ideologically besotted killers they were into idealists of the most exalted New Age sensibilities. In search of the good society, they appeared on screen to be wrestling heroically with their consciences over the tragic necessity of killing Moro. Andreotti, the Pope, and the PCI appear to be suffering from no inner turmoil. With the Red Brigadists exculpated for dramatic purposes, the role of villain went by default to the firmness front. The portrayal of 'Chiara' (Anna Laura Braghetti) threw the entire film into a fatal moral confusion, according to Merlo. Supposedly conscience-stricken at the time of the Moro kidnapping, this terrorist with a bleeding heart two years later killed Professor Vittorio Bachelet 'like a dog' outside his classroom at the University of Rome.[25] In her memoir, *Il prigioniero*, Braghetti describes this murder. She pumped eleven bullets into him as part of the Red Brigade campaign in the winter of 1980 'to strike the heart of the State.'[26] As the vice-president of the Superior Council of the Magistracy, Bachelet was an ideal target for them. Fleeing the scene of bloody mayhem outside the recently renamed Aula Moro, she felt 'a sense of absolute emptiness.'[27] Nevertheless, still in the grip of Marxist-Leninist ideological fervor, she went on participating fully in the murderous campaign of the Red Brigades, furnishing surveillance reports on Judge Girolamo Minervini for his killers in March 1980 and numerous other acts of this kind, right up to the time of her arrest in May of that year. As the police handcuffed her in a Rome bar, she and other Red Brigadists were in the act of planning the murder of the head procurator in Rome, Giovanni De Matteo. Moreover, she admits to having killed or to having participated in

---

25 Francesco Merlo, 'I brigatisti e Moro, sogni finti e tragiche realtà,' *Corriere della sera*, 11 September 2003.

26 Braghetti and Tavella, *Il prigioniero*, p. 130.

27 Ibid., p. 131.

the killing of two policemen at a 1979 shootout in Rome's Piazza Nicosia. She did these things because of her revolutionary faith: 'Simply, I believed.'[28]

What crisis of conscience might she have been going through in the Bachelet murder, Merlo asks? One had to wonder why we did not get films of this comprehending variety about Nazi murderers and torturers. Instead of playing the part that Bellocchio designed for Braghetti, as our moral guide regarding the ethical significance of the Moro case, Merlo wanted her and all the other deluded Red Brigade maniacs to relegate themselves to 'a cultural mortuary' and begin to make it possible for the country to forget the misery that in fanatical pursuit of will-o'-the-wisps they had brought to so many families. In a *Corriere della sera* roundtable discussion of the film, Bellocchio recalled his shock at the time of the Moro kidnapping, and he described the Red Brigades as 'mad and stupid.'[29] Critics like Merlo, however, complained that this negative image of the Red Brigades did not come through at all in the film.

## The Vladimiro Satta rebuttal to the conspiracy theories

Between the premiere of *Piazza delle Cinque Lune* in May 2003 and that of *Buongiorno, notte* in September of that year, Vladimiro Satta published a major anti-conspiracy theory book, *Odissea nel caso Moro*. A précis of the book had appeared in the November-December 2002 issue of the *Nuova Storia Contemporanea*. A researcher on Parliament's Commissione Stragi (Commission on Massacres), Satta based his interpretation of the case on a careful analysis of that body's gigantic collection of documentary evidence. The documents simply did not support the commonly held view that he had died as a result of 'obscure plots ordered by mysterious entities that guided or at the very least exploited the Red Brigades.'[30] In all of the documentation

---

28  Ibid., p. 182.

29  Paolo Franchi, 'Moro, simbolo di una tragedia irrisolta...', *Corriere della sera*, 18 September 2003.

30  Vladimiro Satta, 'I misteri del 'Caso Moro',' *Nuova Storia Contemporanea*,

generated by the Commissione Stragi, Satta could find no reason to question the version of the case handed down by the courts. No evidence existed to confirm the theory that the CIA or the Warsaw Pact nations had influenced the kidnapping in any way. In one of the conspiracy theories, Czechoslovakia was supposed to have provided support for the Red Brigades, but research in that government's archives, made possible by the collapse of communism at the end of the Cold War, had produced nothing. Ballyhooed claims about the state secrets that Moro had turned over to the Red Brigades as another of the reasons for secret service skullduggery in the case also turned out to be empty. Satta's research confirmed the testimony of several witnesses in the trials, that Moro had given the Red Brigades nothing of importance. About accusations against the police for their alleged wrongdoing during the manhunt, he noted that due to a complete absence of legal proof not a single official ever had been indicted.

Satta turned to contemporary Italian terrorism, in order to put the Moro case in proper context. After more than a ten-year hiatus, the Red Brigades had returned to terrorize the country by murdering two economists, Massimo D'Antona on 20 May 1999 and Marco Biagi on 19 March 2002. Though led by a new generation, the Red Brigadists of today identify completely with the revolutionary aims and ideology of their predecessors in the 1970s. They provided a detailed explanation of why they killed D'Antona and Biagi, who worked for the government on labor issues. D'Antona for the 'leftist' prime minister Massimo D'Alema and Biagi for the 'rightist' prime minister Silvio Berlusconi had proposed reforms that would subjugate Italy's workers to the conditions of the increasingly globalized market. Claiming to act in the name of 'the Marxist conception of the imperialism of the State,' the Red Brigades insisted that such experts had to die in order to protect the suffering proletariat.[31]

---

vol. 6, no. 6, November-December 2002.

31 'Documento di Rivendicazione Iniziativa Br,' www.caserta24ore.it, March 2002.

Satta reasoned that the recent Red Brigade murders as well as the 11 September 2001 attacks on the United States should have made clear that the prevention of terrorism is never easy or a given, 'not even when the criminal preparations give off warning signals far more clear than those of the Red Brigades in organizing the attempt against Moro.' Conspiracy theories in the Moro case, 'as prevalent as they are groundless,' have done nothing to help us understand what actually happened. They have only succeeded in distracting us from the historical truth. We should look to the magistrates' reconstruction of the case: 'The mosaic assembled during the course of the judicial proceedings is incomplete, but the missing pieces... seem marginal.' Although there will be more revelations in the future, they will not significantly modify our current understanding of the individuals responsible for the crime and their motives.

*Odissea nel caso Moro*, Satta's book on the case, takes the form of a systematic critique of Flamigni, the most frequently cited name in the index, save Moretti and Moro himself. All of the missed leads, misplaced evidence, and investigative failures on which Flamigni bases his conspiracy theory, Satta places in the context of Italy's 654 kidnappings from 1969 to 1990.[32] The police succeeded in rescuing eighty-six of these victims. Of the twelve Red Brigade kidnap victims, only two of them gained liberation as a result of successful police work. Satta argues that even in normal times the police had a poor record in solving crimes of kidnapping, and in 1978, with the secret services in the midst of reorganization, the government was 'without its eyes and ears,' as one official informed the Commission on Massacres.[33] Here Satta echoes Severino Santiapichi, the presiding judge in the first Moro trial. He observed that an abiding weakness of the conspiracy theories in this case concerned the unfounded belief that the police could have rescued Moro had they so desired.[34] In fact, the performance of the police in the Moro kidnapping conformed to

---

32 Satta, *Odissea nel caso Moro* (Rome, 2003), p. 143.

33 Ibid., p. 170.

34 Drake, *The Aldo Moro Murder Case*, op. cit., pp. 79–80.

the general character of their exertions in such crimes. It would have been much more surprising had they succeeded in freeing Moro.

When Satta's book appeared in the spring of 2003, he told an interviewer that the tide of public opinion showed most welcome signs of turning against the conspiracy theories: 'I was pleasantly surprised by the fact that the coming of this sad anniversary [the twenty-fifth] did not give rise, as I thought it would, to a festival of conspiracy mongering.'[35] Even a publication as prone in the past to invoking conspiracies as the extra-parliamentary left-wing *Manifesto* had begun to criticize them for their lack of intellectual honesty. This newspaper had given *Piazza delle Cinque Lune* a negative review, a judgment with which Satta entirely agreed. For too long such paranoid fantasies had passed for historical analysis in Italy. All the evidence in the case, he declared in a 16 January 2004 interview, pointed to the sole culpability of the Red Brigadists, who had killed Moro in the hope of provoking the crisis of the hated Christian Democratic regime: 'That the Red Brigades acted alone seems to me a proven fact.'[36] A giant cloud of dust had been raised to conceal these central facts, but 'there are no great mysteries in the case... [and] there never have been any.'

Satta furnished an example of what he meant by further revelations, in a 2005 article for the *Nuova Storia Contemporanea* on the Church's attempts to gain Moro's release. Pope Paul VI's concern for Moro, whom he had known very well for more than forty years, had taken the form of active intervention by the Vatican. With the consent of the government, Church officials sought to establish contact with the Red Brigadists, in order to offer them ransom money for Moro. Satta interviewed Monsignor Fabio Fabbri who possessed first-hand knowledge of the episode. He had been the chief assistant to Monsignor Cesare Curioni, the Church's negotiator in

---

35 Paolo Mieli, 'Caso Moro, campane a morto per la dietrologia,' *Corriere della sera*, 18 May 2003.

36 Marco Imarisio, 'Può chiarire i dubbi sui due in moto in via Fani,' *Corriere della sera*, 16 January 2004.

the attempted exchange of money for the prisoner. Using Fabbri's testimony in conjunction with earlier statements about the matter, Satta concluded that the Church never came close to success in its aspirations. The Red Brigades wanted political recognition from the government, not money from the Church. To have taken money would have made them look like common criminals. In any case, Monsignor Curioni never established direct contact with the Red Brigades. Fabbri's testimony and other evidence as well led Satta to think that the interlocutors of Monsignor Curioni either were thieves hoping to gain the ransom for themselves or individuals not belonging to the Red Brigades but who might have been able to establish contact with them. Satta's main conclusion concerns the genuineness of the Church's effort to bring Moro home alive. On the basis of the historical evidence, he rejects the view, shared by Moro himself with the conspiracy theorists, that the Church did little or nothing to help him. About the ongoing recriminations between the firmness and negotiations parties in the Moro debates, Satta reflects that neither one should be demonized: 'both options had their respectable reasons, even if they were destined to be in conflict with each other.'[37]

## The Agostino Giovagnoli rebuttal to the conspiracy theories

Agostino Giovagnoli's *Il caso Moro: Una tragedia repubblicana* appeared early in 2005 as well. This professor of contemporary history at the Catholic University of Milan also cast doubt upon the plausibility of the conspiracy theories. In one respect, he took a more moderate view of them than Satta did. Giovagnoli conceded that some mysteries continued to haunt the Moro case. Not everything about it could be explained convincingly. Regarding the massacre and kidnapping of 16 March 1978, for example, he thought that many questions still awaited exhaustive and persuasive answers. Nevertheless, 'an exces-

---

37  Vladimiro Satta, 'Caso Moro: le vie della Chiesa. Una testimonianza sulle trattative per la liberazione del leader Dc,' *Nuova Storia Contemporanea*, vol. 9, no. 2, March-April 2005.

sive insistence on the mysteries... had produced distorting effects.'[38] The obsession of conspiracy theorists with the hidden actors in the drama had resulted in the neglect of the real actors, particularly the central role of the Red Brigades. Accordingly, he set out to establish what could be said with certainty about the most sensational political kidnapping and murder in modern Italian history.

Giovagnoli dealt summarily with the conspiracy theory books and films: 'Despite the many formulated accusations..., convincing proof has not emerged that a part of the political class deliberately chose to derail the manhunt in order to bring about the death of the kidnap victim.'[39] Based on his own original research in party meeting minutes and other primary source documents, as well as on the previous work of other historians, he contended that the Red Brigades bore sole responsibility for Moro's death. Their own communications made clear what they hoped to accomplish: the destruction of the Christian Democratic establishment through a communist revolution. They expressed themselves in the classic revolutionary language of Marxist-Leninism and thought of their group as the true advocates of this ideology now that the Communist party had become a pillar of the Christian Democratic establishment through the historic compromise. A statistically small but influential extra-parliamentary left-wing culture in the universities and the factories had the same revolutionary aspiration as the Red Brigades, who wanted to galvanize this segment of public opinion into action. Throughout the kidnapping the Red Brigades made their moves on the basis of a principle enunciated in Lenin's *State and Revolution*, one of their favorite and most frequently cited books: in moments of revolution, communists revolutionize. No self-respecting Marxist-Leninist could doubt that in the current horrendous firestorm of imperialist exploitation a revolutionary moment had struck. The Red Brigades professed to be

---

38  Agostino Giovagnoli, *Il caso Moro: Una tragedia repubblicana* (Bologna, 2005), p. 9.

39  Ibid., p. 15.

following the Leninist dictum, to unify the revolutionary movement and to construct the fighting communist party.

The Red Brigades miscalculated. Their kidnapping of Moro did produce a rise in the organization's enlistments, as testimony in the subsequent trials revealed, but on the whole the extra-parliamentary left stayed home. *Lotta continua*, the leading extra-parliamentary left-wing newspaper, disavowed the Red Brigades with the slogan, 'neither with the Red Brigades nor with the State.' Their inability to say what they were for in this crisis underscored a serious problem for the future of the extra-parliamentary left, which in the highly representative case of *Lotta continua* gradually abandoned revolutionary politics in favor of a generically progressive agenda. Moreover, the Red Brigades discovered during the kidnapping that the granite foundation of their ideological belief system, the 'revolutionary masses,' did not exist in Italy. Giovagnoli reports that popular demonstrations in support of the government genuinely shocked the Red Brigades. For the next few years, they continued to kill and to maim, but in retrospect the murder of Moro produced permanent ruptures within the organization and isolated it from the rest of the extra-parliamentary left movement.

Giovagnoli presents the defeat of the Red Brigades as a vindication of the government's firmness policy. He gives the government credit for sound judgment based on what it knew at the time. Following the shocking slaughter of Moro's security team, the Red Brigades appeared to be 'an invincible force,' in Andreotti's image of them.[40] To have negotiated would have undermined the one point of near unanimity among the political parties and, therefore, increased the vulnerability of the government to a coordinated campaign of terrorism. During the kidnapping, the Red Brigades engaged in other acts of terrorism as well, always trying to force the government into a fatal misstep. Giovagnoli essentially agrees with Andreotti, while applauding all the sincere efforts to save Moro, for they, too,

---

40  Talese, "Andreotti: 'Autorizzai il Vaticano a pagare un riscatto per Moro'," op. cit.

contributed to the isolation and defeat of the terrorists. 'Democratic firmness,' a term that Giovagnoli himself puts in quotation marks, turned out to be good for everyone, except Moro.[41]

Giovagnoli's argument about the wisdom of the government's actions in the light of what was known at the time seems unexceptionable.[42] What we know now about the Red Brigades, however, has compelled many previous supporters of firmness to question the wisdom of this strategy. The collapse of the Soviet Union, the end of the Cold War, the virtual disappearance of Marxist-Leninism as a serious alternative to Western democracy, the feebleness of Red Brigadism's resurgence early in the twenty-first century—and its swift and seemingly complete defeat—provide the historical context for Italian terrorism that Andreotti lacked in 1978. In this context, it is clear that the Red Brigades belonged to the twilight phase of the country's long fascination with revolutionary communism. Despite all the human wreckage and heartbreak that the Red Brigades caused, they had the same nearly blank future in Italy that revolutionary communism had in Europe generally. Andreotti made the right decision, knowing what he knew. Knowing what we know, we can second-guess him, but only in an abstract retrospective way, not in the concrete historical terms of that terrible moment.

To question firmness in the way we have is not even to touch on the much-debated principle of negotiating with terrorists at all. Insofar as this debate is concerned, the deadly outcome of the Moro case and its long aftermath reinforced in Italy the side advocating the saving of human lives as an absolute good before which abstract concerns about alleged threats to the State's integrity and about encouragement of more terrorist acts in the future must retreat. The national reaction to the Moro case helps us to understand the Italian willingness in the Iraq War, in sharp contrast to American policy, to pay ransom to the insurgents for the release of kidnap victims.

---

41  Giovagnoli, *Il caso Moro*, p. 260.

42  For a similar interpretation, see Drake, *The Aldo Moro Murder Case*, op. cit., p. 260.

## *The political manipulation of the Aldo Moro case*

In a bitter denunciation of how the United States played politics with terrorism after the attacks of 11 September 2001, Anatol Lieven writes: 'The Bush administration and the Republican Party... in fact moved with ruthless speed to capitalize on the national emergency to strengthen their domestic political position and push their domestic agendas.'[43] Did the Italian government act in a similar way after Moro's kidnapping? Certainly the Italians, like the Americans, wasted little time in enacting special anti-terrorism measures. For the first time in the history of the Italian republic, military men took over traditionally civilian offices; people suspected of terrorism could be detained by order of a magistrate and interrogated without the presence of a lawyer; the imposition of life sentences—the maximum penalty in Italy—became much more common; and the government suspended or drastically cut back laws preventing unreasonable search and seizure. The most extreme of these special measures concerned the law of repentant terrorists. Designed to elicit testimony against unrepentant terrorists still in the field, this law raised a host of constitutional issues about hearsay evidence and special sentencing provisions, even for murderers, who turned state's evidence. As a practical measure, though, it resulted in the arrest of dozens of terrorists and contributed significantly to the defeat of the Red Brigades.

Far from protesting against these measures, the Italian people welcomed them. They had become terrified as a result of the more than ten-year period of unremitting violence by extremist groups. Unlike the attack of the radical Islamic group al-Qaeda in the United States, Moro's kidnapping and murder came on top of literally thousands of terrorist acts in Italy. Given a choice between order and anarchy, the Italians did what Lord Acton said any people would do in such circumstances: they chose order and turned to the men who would give it to them. Even five years later, 36 percent of people

---

43 Anatol Lieven, *America Right or Wrong: an Anatomy of American Nationalism* (London, 2004), p. 23.

in a highly respected national poll chose contemporary terrorism as the most important Italian historical development of the past half century. Only 16.6 per cent chose fascism, 14 per cent Italy's transformation from an agricultural society into an industrialized one, and 12 per cent the country's liberation in World War II. All the other historical developments cited, including the uninterrupted forty-year reign of the Christian Democratic party, stood at single digits in the poll.[44] Also in contrast to the United States, Italy did not try to link terrorism to anything else, such as a completely unrelated war in Iraq. The Italian government kept its focus entirely on the real enemy, the domestic subversive groups, that the populace as a whole feared and opposed. To the large-scale support of the people for the government's anti-terrorism campaign may be ascribed the principal reason for the defeat of the Red Brigades. No substitute exists for this kind of support in vanquishing terrorism.

Historical research clears the Italian government of the charge that it played politics with the Moro murder case, in the sense of Lieven's blast against American policies in the war on terror. The same cannot be said for the promoters of conspiracy theories. For them the principal villains in the Moro tragedy are not his Red Brigade killers, but the Christian Democrats, who, in the words of a reviewer of Sciascia's recently reissued *Moro Affair*, 'did not want Moro to come back alive.'[45] Complex psychological, political, and intellectual reasons explain why such wholly unsubstantiated theories find devout believers across a broad spectrum of public opinion in Italy.[46] In terms of human psychology, great crimes inevitably draw many people to conspiracy theories, as in the American response to

---

44 Giovanni Valentini, 'E Garibaldi batte Mussolini,' *La Repubblica*, 8 February 1984. Monitorskopea conducted the poll for *La Repubblica*.

45 Frederika Randall, 'Fear and Loathing in Italy,' *The Nation*, 28 March 2005. See the response of Richard Drake to this review, in 'Letters,' *The Nation*, 13 June 2005.

46 See Drake, 'Why the Moro Trials Have Not Settled the Aldo Moro Murder Case: a Problem in Political and Intellectual History,' *The Journal of Modern History*, vol. 73, no. 2, June 2001.

John Kennedy's assassination, which, against all evidence, continues to inspire speculation about the plots of shadowy figures and hidden powers. The Italian response to the Moro murder, though belonging in the same general psychological category, exhibits a peculiarly vivid coloring due to the country's unstable political structures and to a judicial system that inspires very little confidence.[47] The agitations of the present take place against a historical backdrop of lost wars, foreign invasions, and domestic treachery. Machiavelli's birthplace is not an accident of history.

Renato Curcio, a founder of the Red Brigades, and three other members of the organization touched on the political and intellectual reasons behind the prevailing belief in conspiracy theories. In 1987, they asserted that many people wanted to forget the connections that existed between the Red Brigades and their many supporters on the extra-parliamentary left. Red Brigadism had been "entirely within 'the critical practice' of that state of things [quello stato di cose] that vast and varied class strata had developed in a thousand forms."[48] Contrary to the protestations of many influential opinion-makers who once had belonged to the extra-parliamentary left, the Red Brigades did not have a history separate from that of the widespread culture of revolutionary Marxism. They all had played at the same game of revolution. The need to obscure the ultimate cause of his death, in the culture of revolutionary Marxism, continues to be the primary force behind the political manipulation of the Moro murder case.

---

47  Sergio Zavoli analyzes the manifold problems of the Italian judicial system, in *Ma quale giustizia* (Rome, 1997).

48  Piero Bertolazzi, Renato Curcio, Maurizio Ianelli, and Mario Moretti, 'Occorre una soluzione politica per tutti,' *Il Manifesto*, 5-6 April 1987.

# 4

# PLAYING POLITICS WITH TERROR: THE CASE OF FUJIMORI'S PERU

## *Jo-Marie Burt*

When Alberto Fujimori assumed the presidency of Peru in 1990, he faced tremendous political and economic challenges. A political outsider who had no real political party to draw upon in forming his government, Fujimori faced a restless military, two insurgent movements, rampant hyperinflation, and broad social discontent. His promises of gradual economic reform were dropped after advisors urged him to adopt tough austerity measures, and he soon fully embraced the neo-liberal economic model he questioned during the presidential campaign. Fujimori's belt-tightening measures brought inflation under control, and his promise to resume payments of Peru's debt to foreign creditors won him allies in the international financial institutions and in the US government as well as much-needed infusions of cash. But Peruvians remained sceptical: the recession was not abating, violence was escalating to the point that observers began speaking of the possibility of an insurgent victory, and the government seemed rudderless.

Fortune shifted for Fujimori after he announced the closing of Congress and the suspension of the 1979 Constitution on 5 April 1992. The so-called autogolpe, which was backed by the armed forces, met with immediate popular approval. Exhausted after a decade of violence and economic crisis, and disillusioned with political party elites and their failures to resolve these crises, 80 per cent of Peruvians voiced their support for Fujimori's bold move. Such emergency measures were necessary, he argued, to rout out corruption, deal with narcotrafficking, and eliminate subversion. 'Chaos, corruption and the failure of some fundamental institutions such as the legislative branch and the judiciary to identify with the great national interests block the country's reconstruction effort and the development of government,' Fujimori said in his April 5 address to the nation.[1] Fujimori proclaimed a 'Government of National Reconstruction,' and assured citizens that within three years the insurgent movements would be eliminated.

Yet violence continued unabated. The Communist Party of Peru, also known as Sendero Luminoso or Shining Path, a Maoist-inspired insurgency that had declared a 'prolonged popular war' against the Peruvian state, launched a series of violent campaigns in Lima, the capital city, which unnerved Peruvians of all social classes. Fujimori's popularity once again began to decline.[2] Calls began to be heard in the halls of the US government for increasing US intervention in Peru to prevent a Sendero victory.[3]

On 12 September 1992, things changed dramatically for Fujimori: Abimael Guzmán, Sendero's principal leader, ideologue and strategist, was arrested along with three of his top commanders. Fujimori's popularity again soared.[4] Peruvians breathed a sigh of relief, hopeful that this might signify the end of years of violence and instability. There was also hope that Peru would return to the democratic fold with elections for a new legislative body, which Fujimori begrudgingly agreed to after international condemnation

---

1  As cited, Agence France Press, 6 April 1992.

2  Fujimori's approval ratings soared after the *autogolpe*, to 82 per cent, but dropped to 56 per cent in early September. Data from the Lima polling firm Apoyo.

3  For example, see the statement by Assistant Secretary of State for Inter-American Affairs Bernard Aronson before the US Congress (Subcommittee on Western Hemisphere Affairs) on 12 March 1992.

4  According to Apoyo's polls, Fujimori's popularity increased to 74 per cent after Guzmán's arrest.

63

of the autogolpe threatened Peru's standing with the international financial community.

This was not to be, however. Rather than build on this very substantial success in the counter-insurgency war to bring an end to the internal conflict—which had cost an estimated 30,000 lives[5] and damages in the billions of dollars—and to re-establish democratic governance in Peru, Fujimori and his allies instead politicised the terrorist threat in order to consolidate an authoritarian political project and perpetuate their hold on power. This chapter will explore the mechanisms used by the Fujimori regime as it played politics with terror, and will analyse the negative consequences of this for Peruvian democracy, human rights, and for the 'war against subversion' itself.

The chapter begins with a brief analysis of the single-most important event in the government's counter-insurgency strategy: the arrest of Guzmán. It analyzes how Guzmán's arrest became the centrepiece of an official discourse asserting the virtues of the Fujimori regime's authoritarian politics and the triumph of the Peruvian Armed Forces over subversion. This discourse was deployed frequently over the course of the 1990s to reassert the regime's power at moments of crisis, to win electoral contests, and to intimidate opponents.

The chapter then examines four specific instances in which the Fujimori regime manipulated the terrorist threat for political purposes to illustrate the mechanisms at work and to tease out their political consequences. First, it analyses the regime's manipulation of Sendero's call for peace talks with the government to bolster its campaign to get voter approval for a new constitution hand-tailored to allow Fujimori a second term in office. Second, it examines how the regime exaggerated the 'resurgent' terrorist threat and deployed

---

5   This was the figure of victims of politically motivated violence used at this time. The Peruvian Truth and Reconciliation Commission (CVR), using statistical projection methods, calculates that the actual number of persons killed in the period between 1980 and 2000 due to political causes was 69,280. CVR, *Informe Final* (Lima, 2003). Available online at www.cverdad. org.pe.

a massive counterinsurgency operation (Operation Aries) to bolster Fujimori's bid for re-election in the 1995 presidential elections. Operation Aries was a spectacular and bloody propaganda effort aimed at reiterating the importance of Fujimori's leadership in the war on terror and the regime's stop-at-nothing campaign to eliminate the vestiges of terrorism, all in the context of securing five more years in office for President Fujimori.

The chapter then analyses the takeover of the Japanese Ambassador's residence by a column of the Tupac Amaru Revolutionary Movement, or MRTA, and the surprising role the four-month hostage crisis played in buttressing the regime's anti-terrorism discourse and its justification of heavy-handed measures, despite the fact that political violence had diminished significantly by 1996. As a result, civil liberties remained severely constrained as the regime argued the necessity of maintaining states of emergency and the continued use of military courts to try terrorism cases. The final example focuses on the growing opposition to Fujimori's authoritarian tactics after 1997 and particularly on his unconstitutional bid for a third term in 2000. During this period, the regime continued to play politics with terror by asserting a latent threat of terrorism and seeking to link legitimate social protest and opposition activity with illicit terrorist organisations in an effort discredit all opponents and maintain power.

## *The discursive power of victory: the triumph over subversion*

Without a doubt the arrest on 12 September 1992 of Abimael Guzmán, the principal leader and ideologue of Sendero Luminoso, marked a decisive victory for the Fujimori government. The man who had eluded government capture for more than a decade and whose aura of invincibility created a mystique around his movement and its so-called revolutionary war was now behind bars. The arrest of Guzmán provided the regime with crucial political capital, as Peruvians believed that this might bring an end to political violence and some return to normalcy in their lives. It also helped restore legitimacy to the state, which was crucial for the regime's larger project of reasserting the power of the state over society.[6]

Foucauldian analyses of discourse suggest that discursive formations do not simply reflect power relations; they fundamentally constitute relations of domination, power and control. Through discursive formations, elites assert state power and control over social groups, and these relations of domination are reinforced by political and social practices that reiterate the claims embedded in elite discourse. Departing from such a premise, this brief analysis of the discourse deployed in the aftermath of Guzmán's arrest illustrates the way the Fujimori regime's discourse constituted power in Peru by ascribing victory to the Peruvian armed forces, blaming Sendero and the MRTA for all 30,000 deaths committed during the internal conflict, and affirming the efficacy of the regime's authoritarian practices in defeating the insurgency. The arrest of Guzmán and the putative 'triumph over subversion' was central to construction of an official historical narrative of Peru's internal conflict that portrayed the armed forces as the defenders of legality and honour, and ascribed responsibility for the violence to Sendero and the MRTA.[7]

In this official history, Shining Path and the MRTA are responsible for each of the 30,000 deaths that occurred over the course of the conflict.[8] Human rights violations committed by the armed forces and the national police, which constitute one-third to one-half of the total victims of politically motivated deaths, are effaced from this

6  Philip Mauceri, *State Under Siege: Development and Policy Making in Peru* (Oxford, 1996); Jo-Marie Burt, 'State-making Against Democracy: the Case of Fujimori's Peru,' in J. Burt and P. Mauceri, eds, *Politics in the Andes: Identity, Conflict, Reform* (Pittsburgh, 2004), pp. 247-68.

7  This section draws on Jo-Marie Burt, 'Unsettled Accounts: Militarisation and Memory in Postwar Peru,' *NACLA Report on the Americas*, 32:2 ,1998, pp. 35-41. See also Carlos Iván Degregori, *La Década de la antipolítica: Auge y huida de Alberto Fujimori y Alberto Montesinos* (Lima, 2000), and CVR, for a discussion of the regime's effort to create a '*memoria salvadora*' to assert an official version of events, eliminate rivals, and retain power.

8  See note 5 on the question of the number of victims of Peru's internal conflict.

narrative.[9] Any act of violence or human rights crime committed by the military is portrayed as an act of self-defence against the 'terrorist scourge.' This notion—that the army bears no responsibility for any crimes it might have committed in the war against terrorism—was taken to its logical extreme in 1995, when the pro-government majority in Congress passed an amnesty law that not only guaranteed impunity for members of the police and armed forces who committed human rights violations between 1980 and 1995, but also set free those few who had previously been convicted of such crimes. 'The logic of the military,' according to Susana Villarán, former president of the Lima-based National Co-ordinator for Human Rights, 'is that the armed forces defeated the enemy and that society should be grateful.'[10]

The moral superiority of the armed forces was thus constructed discursively; any criticism of the military was considered as tantamount to treason, establishing a 'with us or against us' mentality that did not bode well for national reconciliation or the restoration of democratic liberties in Peru. It may be difficult to imagine dialogue with a group such as Sendero Luminoso that had made a point in several published documents of rejecting any possibility of negotiating with the 'bureaucratic capitalist state'. Yet by rejecting a discourse of reconciliation and instead prioritising one of conflict and polarisation, the regime created a categorical imperative that made it virtually impossible to consider any approach to defeating terrorism and bringing the conflict to a close beyond a strictly military one, in

9   During the 1990s, human rights groups calculated that state security forces committed about one-half of all politically motivated killings. (Author interview, Susana Villarán, former president of the Coordinadora Nacional de Derechos Humanos, Lima, 23 June 1998.) See also the annual reports by the Coordinadora on the human rights situation in Peru: Coordinadora Nacional de Derechos Humanos, *Informe anual de la situación de derechos humanos*, Lima (various years). The CVR's *Final Report* (Ibid.) reflects a smaller percentage of overall killings attributed to the state security forces, about 30 percent. This calculation is based on the universe of testimonies received by the CVR during its two-year investigation.

10   Author interview, Susana Villarán, Lima, 23 June 1998.

which victory was decided on the battlefield and negotiations (and the concessions they inherently involved) were viewed as dangerous and even treasonable. This reflected the regime's unwillingness to recognise the collective trauma that had engulfed the Peruvian nation since the early 1980s in which both the state and the insurgent groups, particularly Sendero Luminoso, were complicit. Recast as a morality play in which Fujimori and the military were the saviours and Sendero and the MRTA the villains, negotiations of any sort were written out of the realm of possibility. With insurgents discursively excluded from the nation, any effort to establish the grounds for collective coexistence were denied. The polarising logic that defined Peru during the 1980s and early 1990s was thus reinforced rather than deconstructed in the interests of establishing a long-lasting peace; indeed, the regime perpetuated this polarisation in order to justify its continued iron-fisted rule, its evisceration of democracy, and its indefinite hold on power.

Also central to the regime's discourse was the assertion, made frequently by Fujimori and his allies, that Guzmán's arrest was the direct result of the autogolpe and the concentration of power that it entailed. Just a few months after Guzmán's arrest, for example, Fujimori stated: 'It would have been irresponsible to not consummate the autogolpe [since it] permitted us successfully to wage the battle against terrorism, combat corruption within the judiciary and deepen neoliberal reforms.'[11] This idea would be reiterated with frequency. Just after his re-election in 1995, Fujimori continued to cultivate an image of himself as a decisive leader and of his authoritarian practices as a historical necessity: 'What Peru needed was order, discipline, the principle of authority, good management—and an iron fist against terrorism.'[12] Fujimori juxtaposed his policy successes with the past failings of civilian politicians, and he frequently referred to the political system he inherited as a 'party-ocracy' to suggest that political

---

11 As cited from major Lima newspapers, DESCO Database, 31 March 1993.

12 As quoted in *The San Francisco Chronicle*, 11 April 1995.

parties ruled in their own self-interest rather than on behalf of those who elected them: 'My government is the product of rejection, of Peru's fatigue from frivolity, corruption and inefficiency of the traditional political class.... [T]he people who voted for me are tired and weary of this false Peru.'[13] The efficacy of the regime's authoritarian methods was thus constructed discursively, first in contrast to the inefficacy of civilian politicians, and second by affirming that such methods had borne fruit, evidenced by the arrest of Guzmán and the subsequent decline in political violence. Such discursive formations in turn helped constitute popular approval for Fujimori and his authoritarian methods.[14]

In fact, Guzmán's arrest had little to do with the centralisation of power and political repression associated with the autogolpe. The 'arrest of the century' was the result of years of laborious intelligence gathering by a special police unit, Dincote,[15] under the leadership of Police General Antonio Ketín Vidal. Not a shot was fired in the course of the arrest. In short time numerous other top leaders were arrested, and several organisational structures, including the important Socorro Popular, which operated in Lima, were dismantled.[16]

---

13  As quoted in *The Dallas Morning News*, 28 Nov 1993, p. B5.

14  Explanations of support for Fujimori centre on the regime's policy successes (Julio Carrion, 'La popularidad de Fujimori en Tiempos Ordinarios, 1993-1997,' in F. Tuesta Soldevilla, ed., *El juego político: Fujimori, la oposición y las reglas* (Lima, 1998) as well as its provision of material goods in exchange for votes (Kenneth Roberts, 'Neoliberalism and the Transformation of Populism in Latin America: The Peruvian Case,' *World Politics*, 48, 1995, pp. 82-116). These are significant variables yet they do not reflect the ways in which state power and official discourse may constitute—or in the words of Chomsky and Herman, manufacture—consent. See Noam Chomsky and Edward S. Herman, *Manufacturing Consent: A Political Economy of the Mass Media* (New York, 1988). For how discourse helped constitute consent in Fujimori's Peru, see Jo-Marie Burt, 'Quien habla es terrorista: The Political Use of Fear in Fujimori's Peru,' *Latin American Research Review*, 41:3, 2006.

15  Dirección Nacional Contra el Terrorismo.

16  Only six top leaders of Shining Path had been arrested prior to Guzmán's capture in September 1992. Three leaders, Elena Iparraguirre, Laura

The arrest, in other words, had little to do with the centralisation of power in the hands of the executive, or the blank cheque granted to the armed forces in waging counterinsurgency warfare after the 5 April coup. It had everything to do with good old-fashioned detective work, and it occurred squarely in the context of democratic procedures.[17]

But emphasising the work of Dincote would have ill-suited the Fujimori regime's larger project, which was to justify the autogolpe and the regime's authoritarian measures. To this end, a political struggle over the authorship of the 'arrest of the century' ensued, as Vidal's role was minimised and Fujimori and his top advisor, Vladimiro Montesinos, claimed credit for the arrest.[18] Montesinos was reportedly furious at Vidal for refusing to hand over Guzmán to him at the National Intelligence Service (SIN). Shortly thereafter, Dincote was dismantled and Vidal promoted to a position of utter irrelevance. In their effort to establish authorship of the capture of Guzmán, Fujimori and Montesinos effectively eliminated one of the most effective instruments against subversion within the state apparatus.

This was a stunning turn of events, for there is no doubt that such instruments were central to allowing the Peruvian state to finally obtain the strategic advantage in the counterinsurgency war. During the 1980s, counterinsurgency had been turned over to the armed forces by elected governments. The result was ineffective military campaigns that targeted civilians indiscriminately, resulting in massacres, forced disappearances, torture, and other human

---

Zambrana Padilla, and María Pantoja, were arrested with Guzmán on the evening of 12 September. Fourteen top Shining Path leaders had been captured as of May 1998. *Reporte Especial*, 85, May 1998, p. 10.

17 The same could not be said for the trial proceedings, which were held in secret by hooded military judges and violated basic due process procedures. In 2004, the Inter-American Commission on Human Rights passed a resolution calling on the Peruvian government to hold new trials that respect due process.

18 Fujimori himself was unaware of the imminent raid against the Shining Path's top leader—he was off fishing in the Amazon on the day Guzmán was arrested. *Sí* (Lima, 14 September 1992).

rights violations, as well as frequent conflicts between military and civilian leaders, particularly when massacres or other rights violations became public knowledge.[19] Human Rights Watch and the Peruvian Truth and Reconciliation Commission both referred to this as an 'abdication' of democratic responsibility by civilian elites.[20] The failure of this policy was measured in the rising toll of dead, the expansion of Sendero activity throughout the country, and growing distance between citizens and a state marked by deteriorating institutional coherence that had lost effective control over significant parts of its national territory. These failures spurred strategic sectors within the armed forces to re-evaluate counterinsurgency policy by the end of the decade. Most significantly, plans were put in place in the final years of the government of Alan García (1985-90) to shift the focus to intelligence gathering with the aim of decapitating the insurgencies. It was reasoned that since Sendero was a fundamentally hierarchical organisation centred around the charisma and vision of Guzmán, bringing down the leadership would effectively cripple the insurgency—a highly appropriate strategy, as was borne out after Guzmán's arrest. Also key to this redesign of counterinsurgency policy was an effort to gain peasant support for the state, first by reducing indiscriminate violence (though targeted killings and disappearances continued), and second by trying to build alliances with peasants and the urban poor—'winning the hearts and minds' of the civilian population—through civil defence patrols (rondas campesinas), civic action programmemes, and other development initiatives. These shifts isolated Sendero from their logistical support base, and helped exacerbate the growing divisions between Sendero and some sectors of the rural peasantry, much of which allied itself with the

---

19  In his first year in office, Alan García (1985-90) attempted to assert civilian control over the military and punish human rights violations. This was resisted by the military and eventually abandoned by the García regime in the context of other mounting crises.

20  Human Rights Watch, *Abdicating Democratic Authority: Human Rights in Peru* (New York, 1984); CVR, Ibid.

military to protect itself from Sendero's growing violence.[21] It was these shifts in counterinsurgency policy that can be largely credited with the eventual isolation of Sendero in the countryside, and with the arrest of Guzmán rather than the centralisation of power that followed the autogolpe.[22]

The arrest of Guzmán did not become a basis for promoting effective detective work and intelligence gathering as the key elements of counterinsurgency policy, which could presumably have contributed to fully dismantling the insurgency, but rather was used to assert the efficacy of the Fujimori regime's centralisation of power and other heavy-handed tactics and of Fujimori himself as the indispensable leader. It would become a central part of the discursive formation establishing a causal relationship between the government's repressive and authoritarian tactics and effective counter-insurgency policy. Establishing the efficacy of the coup was crucial to the larger project of consolidating the civic-military government that had been put in place with the April 1992 autogolpe.[23] It permitted the regime to push through neo-liberal reforms, including a rapid privatisation programmeme, with relative ease, and it legitimated the preponder-

---

21  See Carlos Iván Degregori, 'Harvesting Storms: Peasant Rondas and the Defeat of Sendero Luminoso,' in S. Stern (ed.), *Shining and Other Paths: War and Society in Peru, 1980-1995* (Durham, 1998), pp. 128-57.

22  For an early analysis of these shifts, see Carlos Iván Degregori and Carlos Rivera, *Fuerzas Armadas, Subversion y Democracia: 1980-1993,* Documento de Trabajo 53, (Lima, 1993). The *Final Report* of the CVR provides an extensive analysis of the shifts in counterinsurgency policy from 1980 to 2000 (CVR, Ibid.).

23  Though the Fujimori regime was forced to allow a new legislative body to be formed in 1992, which in turn wrote a new constitution, this new institutional structure did not mark Peru's return to the democratic fold, as some international policy makers and scholars suggested. In fact, this restructuring permitted the Fujimori regime to establish a democratic façade on a fundamentally authoritarian system controlled by the executive branch in collaboration with the armed forces. See Fernando Rospigliosi, *Las fuerzas armadas y el 5 de abril. La percepción de la amenaza subversive como una motivación golpista.* Documento de Trabajo 73 (Lima, 1996); Burt, 1998, Ibid; and CVR, Ibid..

ant role of the military in politics, while at the same time permitting the extension of military control over society. Even as the threat of subversion dwindled, the government argued for the necessity of keeping in place its highly draconian anti-terrorist legislation, which led to hundreds, perhaps thousands, of innocents being arbitrary detained, tried and convicted without due process;[24] emergency measures such as state of emergency decrees, which covered one-third of the national territory and half the population depriving citizens in these areas of their full civil and political rights, and often placed the military in positions of political authority,[25]created a climate of fear and intimidation that inhibited the expression of dissent or organised opposition.[26]

Rather than building on its successes in the war against subversion, the Fujimori regime sought to politicise these successes to guarantee its permanence in power. It failed to build upon these successes to eliminate the remaining vestiges of Sendero either through specific military actions or through broader policies of national reconciliation. In effect, by failing to fully defeat Sendero, the regime could point to the continued existence of Sendero—by way of occasional armed actions touted as a 'resurgence' of the 'terrorist threat'—to continue to justify its authoritarian practices and its permanent hold on power.

*Peace talks: pacification or propaganda?*

One year after Guzmán's arrest, the government aired a series of videos showing a presumably repentant Guzmán asking the government to engage in peace talks and criticising at-large Sendero leaders who continued to engage in guerrilla warfare. This seemed an abrupt and even unbelievable volte-face for the man who, during a press conference two weeks after his capture, asserted that his arrest was no more

---

24 Ernesto de la Jara, *Memoria y batalla en nombre de los inocentes. Perú 1992-2001* (Lima, 2001).

25 CVR, Ibid.

26 Burt, 2006, Ibid.

than 'a stone along the path' to victory and defiantly proclaimed the inevitability of the triumph of his revolution. Most observers doubted the sincerity of Guzmán's peace proposal, and many wondered what the logic behind it was given that he was already in prison and his movement had been strategically defeated. Yet a second letter appeared, and then another from other high-ranking members of Sendero backing Guzmán's proposal. What was the logic behind the letters, and why did the government permit the videos to be publicly aired on national television? Why did the government immediately reject Guzmán's offer? And how could Guzmán's seeming capitulation just a year after he ordered his organisation to continue the armed struggle be explained?

It became clear rather quickly that this was a thinly-veiled propaganda effort in the context of a referendum to be held on a new constitution proposed by Fujimori's allies in Congress. Because of external pressure in the wake of the 5 April autogolpe, Fujimori felt compelled to backtrack from his authoritarian project, but he did so on his terms. The legislative branch was restored, but it was now a unicameral congress that was much easier for the executive to control; indeed, Fujimori's party, Cambio 90-Nueva Mayoría, easily dominated the new institution, which many criticised as a rubber-stamp congress.[27] This new legislative body was charged with writing a new constitution. It was to help secure the passage of this new Magna Carta, which unlike its predecessor would allow for one successive re-election, thus permitting Fujimori to run for a second term in 1995, that Guzmán's letters were made public by the regime. By allowing Guzmán to propose peace talks, then firmly rejecting such a proposal based on his government's 'no negotiations' policy with terrorists, Fujimori could revisit his government's success in the

---

27 Several opposition parties, including APRA and Acción Popular, refused to present candidates in the congressional elections as a form of protesting the fact that this simply legitimised the autogolpe and the reorganisation of power under Fujimori, while allowing him to create a more pliant legislative body.

war against terror, reaffirm the efficacy of its hard-line policies, and bolster his public imagine just before the vote was due.

In two letters to Fujimori written in September and October 1993, Guzmán, recognising Fujimori as the Peruvian head of state, requested peace talks to end the war. In his letters, Guzmán admitted that Fujimori's government had successfully reconstructed the Peruvian state and acknowledged the significance of his capture for the Maoist organisation as far more than just 'a stone along the path.'[28] Shortly thereafter, four of Shining Path's principal leaders, including Osmán Morote, wrote (from prison) another letter to Fujimori backing Guzmán's petition for peace talks.[29] While neither of Guzmán's letters spoke of a ceasefire, this letter called on the organisation's cadre to avoid engaging in 'desperate, adventurous actions...that would undermine and impede the implementation of the proposed Peace Agreement,' and that such actions 'should be prevented and denounced firmly and immediately.'[30]

The writing of the letters, particularly that of the Morote group, could only have occurred with logistical support from the regime, since they were all in prison—some, like Guzmán and Iparraguirre, in the Naval Base in Callao and others, such as Morote, in the high security Yanomayo prison in the remote highlands of Puno. It can

---

28 The first letter, dated 15 September 1993, was written by Abimael Guzmán and his second-in-command, Elena Iparraguirre, from the Callao Naval Base and directed to 'Señor Ingeniero Alberto Fujimori Fujimori, Presidente de la República.' The second letter, dated 6 October 1993, signed again by Guzmán and Iparraguirre, is more extensive in laying out the leaders' arguments for proposing a peace agreement. It was not publicly revealed, however, until late October, to coincide with the 31 October referendum on the newly drafted constitution.

29 Vladimiro Montesinos, de facto head of the National Intelligence Service, reportedly facilitated communication between the top Sendero leaders within the prisons. Some, such as Osmán Morote, were even flown in from Puno to participate in discussions with other Sendero leaders and to present this letter in a video, also aired on national television.

30 'En nueva carta, cúpula senderista pide detener los atentados,' *Expreso*, 30 October, 1993, pp. 1-2; 'Sendero llama a militantes a no caer en acciones desesperados y provocadores,' *La República*, 30 October 1993, pp. 1-3.

therefore be deduced that the Fujimori regime actively solicited Guzmán's public request for peace talks that might have been used as a way of dismantling the remnants of Sendero and bringing a close to the years of violence. However, Fujimori's public response to the letters was to reject Guzmán's request for peace talks. In response, Fujimori stated: '[My administration] is not a government of compromise. I have declared total war on the Shining Path and the MRTA'.[31]

Fujimori's opponents immediately charged the regime with utilising Guzmán's letters to help buttress support for his constitution. Guzmán's second letter and the 'letter of support' were made public just days before the 31 October referendum on the new constitution. There was substantial opposition to the proposed charter, not only because it would permit Fujimori to seek re-election. Opposition emerged to its reinstatement of the death penalty, particularly by the Catholic Church and human rights organisations, and to its undermining of social protections established in the previous constitution, particularly job stability. Moreover, though Fujimori's allies had easily won majority control of the unicameral Congress established in November 1992, municipal elections in January 1993 did not go so well for pro-government candidates, raising concerns within the regime about the referendum vote on the proposed constitution.

In reference to Guzmán's statements seemingly praising the 'objective successes' of Fujimori's counterinsurgency plan, Congressman Julio Castro of the Democratic Left stated: 'It appears that Guzman has come to be the main promoter in the campaign for the 'yes' vote.'[32] Indeed, polls registered that voters were more inclined to vote in favour of the constitution after Guzmán's letters were made public, followed by Fujimori's stern admonition: '[A]s President of the Republic, I am sending [Guzmán] the message that there will

---

31 As quoted in Andrew Katel, 'Peru's President Rejects Surprise Rebel Peace Offer,' The Associated Press, 1 October 1993.
32 United Press International, 12 October 1993.

be no negotiations and he should direct his followers to surrender.'[33] According to a poll taken immediately after one of the videos was shown on October 10, 59 per cent said they intended to vote in favour of the referendum while 31 per cent said they would vote against it, an approval rating ten percentage points higher than in a previous poll taken two weeks earlier.[34] Reviving Fujimori's image as the man the defeated terrorism was thus a strategy to help win votes. In the end, Fujimori's hand-tailored constitution was approved, but only by a slim majority.[35]

Clearly there was also a strategic dimension to the public airing of the letters and the videos: to provoke a division within Sendero Luminoso and to encourage mass desertions among the rank-and-file. Government strategists believed that Guzmán's 'capitulation' would not only discredit him in the eyes of his followers, but would also generate fatal divisions within the organisation's once-monolithic ranks, which in turn would demoralise middle- and lower-level cadres and lead them to abandon the armed struggle. Given the intense personality cult around the figure of Guzmán, government strategists reasoned that this would deal the fatal blow they needed to fulfil Fujimori's promise of liquidating Sendero by 1995. This strategy seemed to be working when the Sendero leadership that remained at large—headed by Oscar Ramírez Durand, a.k.a. 'Comrade Feliciano,' the third-ranking leader of the organisation at the time of Guzmán's arrest and head of the Popular Guerrilla Army—refused to accept the letters as valid, labelling them a 'sinister and underhanded farce' mounted by the government and the National Intelligence Service (SIN).[36] Ramírez Durand, who had reorganised the Central Com-

---

33  Agence France Press, 11 October 1993.

34  *Latin America Weekly Report,* WR-93-42, 28 October 1993, p. 495.

35  The vote in favour was 52.3 per cent versus 47.7 against, with nine per cent of the votes blank or nullified. Fernando Tuesta, *Perú Político en Cifra* (Lima, 1994), p. 129.

36  See, for example, 'El Silencio de los corderos,' and 'Pronunciamiento: ¡Unir al pueblo en defensa de la jefatura, contra la dictadura genocida vendepatria!', in *El Diario Internacional* 23, April 1994, pp. 2-3 and 14-16 respectively. See

mittee within a few months of Guzmán's arrest, was still following Guzmán's directive from the prisons in 1992 to continue the popular war, and he vowed to continue doing so.[37]

Guzmán was not simply caving in to government demands in order to receive certain privileges in prison (though these he did receive, including conjugal visits from his lover and second-in-command, Elena Iparraguirre), as many observers suggested at the time. A handwritten manuscript authored by Guzmán casts light on his about-face.[38] The document reveals that Guzmán's intention was not to end the war peacefully and integrate Shining Path into Peru's political system along the lines of the M-19 in Colombia or the FMLN in El Salvador. In this document, Guzmán does not renounce the armed struggle; rather, he states, quoting Mao: 'war is the highest form of class struggle,' and affirms that Communism is the only destiny for humanity. 'It is inexorable, the principal tendency is revolution,' he argues, but instead of speaking in years, he speaks in decades. According to Guzmán, the 'ideological and political offensive of imperialism'—capitalist restructuring and the application of neoliberal policies worldwide—is 'transitory,' and by the year 2000 it will become clear that imperialism is in 'slow agony'. Hence, he claims, the task for all revolutionaries is to 'struggle for the future great wave of world revolution' which will emerge between 2010 and 2060.

Guzmán's call for peace talks was also based on his conviction that the leadership of any revolutionary movement takes precedence over all other variables. Reflecting his belief in the Leninist principle of the centrality of the vanguard party, Guzmán acknowledges that his arrest represents a fundamental blow to his organisation. Since he

---

also 'Abajo la patraña contrarrevolucionaria. Gloria a los heroes del pueblo,' of the Comité de Familiares de Presos Políticos Prisioneros de Guerra y Desaparecidos del Perú, February 1994.

37 "Feliciano acuerda seguir 'guerra popular'," *La República*, 28 April 1994, pp. 19-21.

38 'Asumir y Combatir por la Nueva Gran Decisión y Definición' (October 1993). Partially reprinted in *La República*, 23 January 1994. This author had full access to the hand-written document.

was no longer able to direct Sendero according to the 'correct political line', there was no possibility of developing the popular war, only 'maintaining it'. These objective facts prompted the party leadership to adopt 'a new and great decision' to pursue a peace agreement.[39] Guzmán goes on to criticise Feliciano: 'The leadership outside [the prisons] does not analyze the new problems, the new direction.' Guzmán still maintains that 'War is politics with the spilling of blood,' but under these new conditions, it is time for 'politics [which] is war without the spilling of blood'.[40]

Guzmán was playing his own game of chess, trying to take advantage of the opportunity provided by the government to direct an orderly retreat of his forces so that they would be better prepared to regroup in the future, when conditions were more favourable.[41] In hindsight, Guzmán seems to have achieved his goal at least partially. After bitter divisions within the Maoist organisation over Guzmán's call for peace talks, today most of the group's remaining militants now support Guzmán and his call for engaging in 'politics without the spilling of blood'. While many key cadres remain imprisoned, there is clear evidence of a recomposition of Sendero Luminoso

---

39  Ibid.

40  Ibid. Other internal documents apparently authored by Guzmán to explain his new political line to his comrades in prison further elaborated his reasoning. The state, he argued, had met the three essential challenges necessary for its reconstitution: (1) establishing the economic basis of the capitalist-bureaucratic state; (2) restructuring of the state, culminating in the 1993 Constitution; and (3) military victory over Shining Path, i.e., the capture of the organisation's leadership. These documents include 'Luchar por un Acuerdo de Paz y Sentar Bases para el II Congreso' (November 1993) and 'Unirse más bregando decididamente en luchar por un Acuerdo de Paz y sentar bases, defender y combatir' (October 1994).

41  The government did not publicise a third letter in which Guzmán conditioned his participation in peace talks and a declaration of a ceasefire on the government making a similar pledge to a ceasefire. For a further analysis of the shifts in Sendero's strategy in this period, see Jo-Marie Burt and José López Ricci, 'Shining Path after Guzmán.' *NACLA Report on the Americas*, 28:3, 1994, pp. 6-10 and Isaías Rojas Pérez, 'Sendero(s) Luminoso(s): Guerra de supervivencia,' *ideéle*, 82-83, 1995, pp. 98-105.

in some parts of the country, where they are engaged in a political strategy not dissimilar from the strategy deployed by the insurgents in the 1970s, prior to the declaration of armed revolution, of building grassroots support among dissatisfied segments of the population. Interviews with Shining Path leaders in the Women's Prison in Chorrillos in 2002 confirms the organisation's commitment to a political struggle of long duration.[42]

Playing politics with terror achieved short-term political gains for the Fujimori regime, both in terms of shoring up support for its candidates and programmemes during election time, and in terms of maintaining popular consent or at least tolerance for the regime's authoritarian practices. But playing politics with terror implied two fatal flaws. First, the regime's emphasis on the victory of the armed forces over Sendero created a categorical imperative for a military victory, rather than any kind of negotiated solution to the conflict. This required an almost exclusive focus on a military-organisational level that made it difficult if not impossible to address the insurgency on a political level. In such a militarised counterinsurgency policy, the only way to bring about an end to the political violence was the military destruction of Shining Path. By categorically refusing to negotiate with guerrillas—a centerpiece of the regime's attempt to win political support for its 'heavy-handed' approach to subversion—the government cut itself off from pursuing political solutions to bring the war to a close, leaving little room to pursue policies to incorporate former guerrillas into political and social life to ensure that those who repented did not rejoin guerrilla forces or other criminal organisations. Ongoing violence—by both the state, in its effort to completely eliminate the vestiges of the insurgent movements, and by insurgents, who had little incentive to do anything but continue fighting—was the inevitable result. In this no-man's-land of perpetual warfare, the Fujimori regime was content to reproduce its triumphalistic discourse to perpetuate itself in power indefinitely.

---

42 These interviews took place in December 2002 in the context of research carried out for the Peruvian Truth and Reconciliation Commission.

This brings us to the second flaw: the total defeat of the insurgency does not appear to have been the regime's priority, for a latent threat of a Sendero resurgence would allow it to continue to justify its authoritarian measures indefinitely—its anti-terrorist legislation; military control over more than a third of the national territory through state of emergency decrees that denied civil and political liberties to nearly half the population; its centralisation of power in the hands of the executive and its dismantling of democratic checks and balances—all of which were crucial to preventing opposition groups from articulating themselves in the public sphere and hence to maintaining the regime's hold on power. In other words, success in the counter-insurgency war became subordinate to the Fujimori regime's determination to perpetuate itself in power. Thus the epistolary episode was intended to strengthen the image of Fujimori as an iron-fisted leader who refused to negotiate with terrorists in an effort to secure votes in the upcoming referendum on his new constitution, which in turn was part of a broader plan to ensure the regime's continuation in power. Politics trumped security policy, though the ultimate result was to allow a recomposition of the Sendero leadership and the articulation of a new political strategy that continues to structure Sendero's activities today.[43] In this context, we can better understand the paradox of Operation Aries, which exaggerated the terrorist threat in order to bolster Fujimori's image as the 'saviour' of the nation to help his campaign for re-election in 1995.

*Exaggerating the terrorist threat: Operation Aries and the imperative of re-election*

On 5 April 1995—three years to the day from Fujimori's autogolpe—the armed forces launched a massive campaign of aerial bombardment and military occupation of the left bank of the Huallaga river, where, according to the government, Sendero columns were attempting to

---

43 Jo-Marie Burt, 'Plotting Fear: The Uses of Terror in Peru,' *NACLA Report on the Americas* 28:6, 2005, pp. 32-37.

regroup after the strategic defeat of the organisation with the capture of Abimael Guzmán in September 1992. According to the Peruvian Truth and Reconciliation Commission, the massive operation represents a paradox, since the strength of Sendero in the area was not that significant, and because the military had presumably previously established its control over this zone as part of its campaign to re-establish state authority throughout the national territory and isolate Sendero Luminoso.[44] The paradox is explained by examining the political context in which the operation was carried out: with presidential elections scheduled the following year, and the regime seeking to secure a second term for Fujimori, it became necessary again to highlight the image of President Fujimori as the man who saved the country from the terrorist scourge.

Fujimori had long asserted that by 1995 he would eliminate all vestiges of the two insurgencies wreaking havoc on Peru. Especially after the arrest of Guzmán, such promises formed a central part of the regime's discourse asserting its triumph over subversion. Yet because of the regime's refusal to address the insurgency politically, small columns of the organisation remained active in remote parts of the country. The regime thus determined that the time was right to launch a 'final offensive' against these remaining groups: such a military operation would presumably secure the organisation's final demise while also providing significant political capital to Fujimori in the context of the upcoming elections. Media coverage of the military campaign revealed, however, the extent to which this was less about destroying the last vestiges of terrorism than it was an attempt to revive the image of Fujimori (and the armed forces) as the destroyer of terrorism.

Sendero had long ago established a presence in the Huallaga, the epicenter of the drug trade, by offering protection to coca growers

---

44 This account of Operation Aries and its aftermath is drawn from a factfinding mission by human rights groups as reported in Coordinadora Nacional de Derechos Humanos, *Que no vuelva el horror* (Lima, 1994); and CVR, Ibid.

from government eradication programmemes, abusive police and drug-traffickers, and through imposition of strict guides of moral behaviour. But the disarray of the organisation in the aftermath of Guzmán's arrest led to a weakening of the group's presence in the Huallaga, though clearly some columns remained active. As noted above, the Fujimori regime's desire to capitalise on its image as being 'tough on terror' for political purposes created a categorical imperative in which negotiations of any kind with terrorists was unacceptable. With political solutions to pacification thus blocked, the only solution left was the military destruction of the remaining vestiges of Sendero Luminoso. In an early formulation of this strategy, Fujimori publicly proclaimed: 'There will be no refuge left because we are going to put a grip on Sendero Luminoso from Mazamari, Satipo, Pucallpa and Atalaya and corner the guerrillas.... We are going to have a little Vietnam War here.'[45] The guerrillas, he added, would be crushed by the end of his term in 1995.[46]

In early 1994, Fujimori personally instructed the armed forces to launch a 'final mission' presumably to defeat Sendero once and for all. Known as 'Operation Aries', it was touted in the pro-government press as the last push in the war against subversion. Yet the contradictory nature of the military operation was evident in press articles that portrayed Sendero as disarticulated yet highlighted that eliminating the insurgency was a priority for the Fujimori government. There is clear evidence that the army also exaggerated the size of the Sendero column in the area; intelligence reports suggested the insurgents had 100-180 uniformed fighters, but Army General Nicolás Hermoza de Bari Ríos claimed that there were at least 450. The press also portrayed the two forces as engaged on virtually equal terms in terms of armament, munitions, training and so forth, but in fact the army had aerial support and vastly superior weaponry.[47]

---

45 'Peru chief pledges to wipe out guerrillas,' *The Record* (Toronto Star Newspapers), Oct. 26, 1993, p. E14.

46 Ibid.

47 CVR, Ibid.

A few weeks after Operation Aries was launched, the Coordinadora Nacional de Derechos Humanos, the country's leading human rights organisation, visited the area and reported the massive violation of human rights by the military, questioning both the efficacy and the necessity of the campaign. The Coordinadora charged that the aerial bombardment campaigns, scorched earth tactics, torture, rape, and extrajudicial executions that occurred in the context of Operation Aries represented a dramatic and unexplainable shift back to the 'dirty war' strategies of the early 1980s, in which the military failed to distinguish between civilians and insurgents, and engaged in indiscriminate violence against innocents resulting in massive human rights violations, including the deaths of at least thirty-six civilians, among them women and children.[48] The pro-government daily *Expreso* excoriated the human rights group, suggesting it was providing cover to the enemy.[49] Later, the pro-government Congress passed a motion condemning the Coordinadora for disseminating 'negative reports about the behaviour of the armed forces.'[50]

Operation Aries was less a carefully designed strategy to eliminate the last vestiges of Sendero than a propaganda campaign cooked up by regime strategists—with extremely high costs in terms of loss of human life—to portray President Fujimori as a determined leader who would spare no effort to deal Sendero the final and ultimate blow in order to bolster his image in the context of the upcoming elections. Needless to say, Fujimori won re-election in 1995 handily. Playing politics with terror seemed to bear tremendous fruits in terms of winning elections, but in its effects on democracy, human rights and effective counterinsurgency, the results were less than sanguine. The threat represented by the remnants of Sendero Luminoso in the Huallaga was greatly exaggerated to justify a military campaign

48  Coordinadora Nacional de Derechos Humanos, *Informe anual de la situación de derechos humanos* (Lima, 1994).

49  As cited in CVR, Ibid.

50  Human Rights Watch, *Peru: Human Rights Developments* (New York, 1995).

that would once again highlight the determination of Fujimori as a leader. The result was massive violations of human rights, and when human rights groups brought these violations to light, they were accused by the regime of propagating misinformation, further contributing to the climate of fear and intimidation and eroding spaces for public dissent of regime practices and policies. Indeed, at the end of 1994, though political violence was substantially on the decline, nearly 50 per cent of the population continued to live under a state of emergency in which four key constitutional guarantees remained suspended, including individual freedom; freedom of movement; freedom of association; and freedom from unreasonable search and seizure.[51] Finally, Operation Aries did not accomplish what it set out to do: eliminate the final vestiges of Sendero Luminoso. Counterinsurgency policy was being used to maintain military control over society by exaggerating the terrorist threat, as well as to win elections.

## The 1996 hostage crisis: or how power reproduces itself even when in crisis

In December 1996, a small Cuban-inspired guerrilla movement, the Tupac Amaru Revolutionary Movement (MRTA), burst into the residence of the Japanese ambassador to Peru, taking hostage more than 500 people who were attending an exclusive cocktail party. Hostages included the mother of then-President Alberto Fujimori as well as his brother Santiago, long considered one of his most influential advisors. The US ambassador to Peru was also among the hostages. Initial negotiations allowed for the timely release of women and the elderly, but 72 hostages remained inside the compound for four gruelling months.

The hostage crisis came at a difficult moment for the Fujimori regime. After two solid years of economic growth in 1994 and 1995 (which contributed to Fujimori's re-election in 1995), the economy was slowing down and job creation remained stagnant, causing a de-

---

51 Coordinadora, Ibid.

cline in President Fujimori's popularity ratings by mid-1996.[52] At the same time, Fujimori had long since declared the insurgencies defeated. While it was acknowledged that some remnants of Sendero Luminoso remained at large, the regime took great pride in the presumed total elimination of the MRTA. The MRTA takeover revealed a massive security breach that belied the government's claim to successful counterinsurgency. Indeed, early reports that the government had intelligence that the MRTA was regrouping but had failed to respond adequately revealed the extent to which the politicisation of the counterinsurgency war had compromised national security.

The regime's situation was complicated further by the difficulties it faced in ensuring a third term for President Fujimori given the constitutional limit of only one consecutive term in office. The 1993 municipal elections, in which the pro-government candidate, Jaime Yoshiyama, lost to incumbent mayor Ricardo Belmont, revealed that there was no natural successor to Fujimori and that Fujimori's popularity was not easily transferable to another candidate. A third term for Fujimori was thus essential to assure continuity in the implementation of a wide-ranging programmeme of neo-liberal economic reform as well as immunity from prosecution for members of the armed forces accused of human rights violations in the context of the counterinsurgency war against Sendero and the MRTA. Though it was not widely perceived as such at the time, it was also necessary in order that those profiting privately from their positions in power within the regime could continue to amass wealth and avoid prosecution. Securing a third term had legal complications the regime felt satisfied it could overcome given its near-total control over the legislature and judiciary, but as the victories of the early 1990s faded from view, Peruvians began to focus on more mundane concerns, particularly continued unemployment and stagnant wages. Fujimori's declining popularity might jeopardise the entire project.

---

52 Gross domestic product was an impressive 14 percent in 1994, but only six percent in 1995 and an anemic two per cent in 1996.

Yet the Fujimori regime was able to snatch victory from the jaws of defeat. The MRTA hostage crisis allowed the regime to put the security issue back on the agenda, an arena where it could arguably claim some success. It gave Fujimori another opportunity discursively to affirm his role as a tough, efficient leader in the fight against terrorism, while demonising terrorists as delinquents with little concern for human life as evidenced by taking of civilian hostages. Foucouldian analyses of power suggest that breaches in the discourse and practice of hegemony may in fact serve to reinforce domination by allowing elites to reproduce the language and discourse of power even as it is being challenged. In this case, the MRTA hostage crisis presented Fujimori and his allies with a massive political crisis that profoundly questioned the government's claim to have defeated terrorism in Peru. Yet it also created a context in which the regime could redeploy its discourse of domination. The MRTA's taking of hostages evidenced, once again, the terrorist nature of such groups; only firm, decisive measures could stop them now and in the future. It also demonstrated that terrorism continued to be a serious threat to peace and stability in Peru, allowing the regime to reassert its justification for its past use of heavy-handed measures, and their continued use in the future. The MRTA takeover thus gave the Fujimori regime an opportunity discursively to assert the continued necessity of its decisive if heavy-handed measures.

This discourse was further bolstered after the military assault on the compound to rescue the hostages on 27 April 1997, which was widely viewed as a success. Government authority was re-established, and loss of life was minimal: one hostage and two army commandos perished in the rescue operation, though all 14 rebels were killed, several allegedly after having surrendered. In widely publicised video footage, Fujimori could be seen walking up the stairs of the compound, the dead bodies of the rebels splayed on the stairway, with a look of grim satisfaction at having eliminated the terrorists who held seventy-two people—and his government—hostage for four long months. Support for Fujimori increased from 38 to 67 per cent after the raid.[53]

Operation 'Chavin de Huantar' was billed as a success both nationally and internationally, reinforcing the regime's discourse of the efficacy of iron-fisted measures against terrorist subversion. Fujimori proudly asserted his leading role in this newest defeat against terrorism: 'I was in permanent contact with the intelligence service. We knew perfectly the location of the terrorists and the majority of the hostages.' He then gave the signal to launch the assault.[54] Fujimori also ventured to criticise those within the Japanese government who favoured peaceful negotiations with the rebels and even offered to pay ransom money to secure the release of their dignitaries, as 'cowardice.'[55] In effect, the regime was able to have it both ways: even as it affirmed discursively its triumph over terrorism, it was also able to use the hostage crisis as evidence that the terrorist threat remained real and that its iron-fisted measures were the only counterweight to the all-too-real possibility of a full-blown resurgence of terrorist activity. Indeed, once the hostage crisis was over, Fujimori again asserted the efficacy of his heavy-handed measures: 'terrorism had infiltrated everything.... [the autogolpe was necessary to establish] true democracy in Peru.'[56] In Fouculdian fashion, even when challenged power was able to reproduce itself.

The four long months of the hostage crisis also helped draw attention away from the growing contradictions within the Fujimori regime. Aside from popular discontent over the economy and questions about the re-election process, there was growing evidence of friction within the regime's supporters. Some of the regime's former allies in the business community were growing skittish over the regime's continued centralisation of power and its brutality, as evidenced by

---

53 Tom Fennell, 'Rescue in Lima: A bold assault sends a message to terrorists,' *Canadian Business and Current Affairs*, 110:18, May 5, 1997, pp. 38–41.

54 Ibid.

55 Ibid.

56 As cited in *La República*, DESCO Database, May 27, 1996.

increasingly negative editorials in the Lima daily *El Comercio*, long associated with the business elite.[57] One of the regime's staunchest allies, Baruch Ivcher, owner of Channel Two Television, began airing stories revealing the regime's criminal and corrupt behaviour.[58] Particularly damaging were the stories documenting the discovery of the dismembered body of former army intelligence agent Mariella Barreto and the brutal torture of another, Leonor La Rosa. Barreto was allegedly the lover of the top commander of the Colina Group death squad, Major Santiago Rivas, and both women were presumably brutalised for having leaked information to the press about the regime's misdeeds. Channel Two also ran stories documenting the government's extensive telephone espionage conducted against the political opposition, as well as Montesinos's inexplicably high income. The government mounted a campaign accusing Ivcher, who was a naturalised Peruvian citizen, of engaging in arms smuggling and treason, and in July he was stripped of his Peruvian citizenship and ownership of his television station. Also, in January, a ruling by the Constitutional Tribunal on the law passed by Congress that enabled Fujimori to run for a third term in office was declared unconstitutional, revealing that the regime's control over the judiciary was

---

57 *El Comercio* also criticised the November 26, 1996 arrest of retired Army General Rodolfo Robles, an outspoken critic of the government's human rights record and the growing power of the SIN. Robles was arrested after he alleged that the SIN had bombed a television station in the provincial town of Puno; he was charged before a military court with insubordination, insulting a superior officer, and defamation of the armed forces. Broad criticism of the arrest forced Fujimori to promise Robles would be released even if found guilty, which was viewed as a rift in his relations with the military. Robles was freed on Dec. 7, 1996. See Maxwell Cameron, 'Arrest of retired general detonates civil-military rift in Peru,' *NACLA Report on the Americas*, 30:4, 1997, p. 2.

58 Ivcher's station had been bombed in 1991 by Sendero Luminoso, leading him to be very supportive of Fujimori and his counterinsurgency policy. Yet he apparently grew wary of the immense power being accrued by Fujimori's top advisor, Vladimiro Montesinos, whose corrupt and criminal practices he viewed as undermining Fujimori's successful government. See Sally Bowen, *The Fujimori File: Peru and Its President 1990-2000* (Lima, 2000).

not as tight as had been supposed. The three dissenting judges were subjected to a campaign of intimidation. A week after the military raid on the Japanese Ambassador's compound, Congress voted to remove the judges from their posts, a move that was clearly beyond the scope of congressional authority.

In effect, the MRTA crisis put the security issue back on the public agenda, giving Fujimori another opportunity to affirm his role as a tough, efficient leader against terrorism. The regime's publicists ably ducked criticism of the security breach itself and instead emphasised the terrorist nature of the hostage taking, and then the successful military rescue operation. Ironically, the hostage crisis also allowed the regime discursively to affirm the notion that terrorism—which it has presumably eliminated—was an ever-present danger and that its heavy-handed approach was necessary to keep it in check. The dangerous trends demonstrated by the Ivcher affair, the killing and torture of regime defectors, and the congressional violation of judicial autonomy in the pursuit of assuring Fujimori's third term as president, were lost in the campaign asserting the regime's triumph over terrorism. The fortification of this discourse would become central in the late 1990s in the context of a growing opposition movement to Fujimori's unconstitutional bid for a third term and the regime's need to discredit and intimidate opposition groups.

A final point is worth mentioning here. The hostage crisis could have conceivably been used by the Fujimori regime as an opportunity to find a lasting political solution to the conflict at least with the MRTA. As Carlos Tapia, a terrorism expert who was later appointed a member of the Truth and Reconciliation Commission, wrote shortly after the military assault:

'[T]he state could have committed itself to discuss the freeing of the MRTA prisoners, not as a concession in exchange for the freedom of the hostages, but as an act in favor of national reconciliation and to affirm its will to consolidate the peace. And it would do so precisely in light of its responsibilities in terms of national security. But with one condition: that the MRTA demonstrate its willingness to abandon the armed struggle.'[59]

The logic of the regime's 'get-tough on terrorism' policy prevented such a path from even being considered. Total military victory over the MRTA was the only solution given the categorical imperatives the regime had established based on its logic of victor's justice.[60] Indeed, the hostage crisis itself revealed the consequences of the regime's failure to find a political solution to the internal conflict. The MRTA action, while bold, did not represent a resurgence of the MRTA, but rather a desperate act on the part of the leadership that remained at large to address some of the problems associated with their defeat, such as the harsh prison regime the organisation's political prisoners (along with their imprisoned Sendero counterparts) had been forced to endure since the 1992 autogolpe. With no possibility of peaceful negotiations with the regime to address such issues, MRTA leaders such as Néstor Cerpa Cartolini, who masterminded the takeover, perceived they had little option but resort to such acts of violence.

## With us or against us: terrorism and the contested election of 2000

The hostage rescue operation gave the Fujimori regime some breathing room to paper over the consequences of growing opposition to its authoritarian project and emerging fissures within its power base. But as time went on, these contradictions continued to deepen. In particular, its authoritarian tactics, human rights violations, and willingness to go to any lengths to assure Fujimori a third term in office, continued to fuel opposition, presenting new challenges to

---

59 Carlos Tapia, 'La oportunidad perdida,' *QueHacer* 106, March/April 1997.

60 The website of the Peruvian armed forces portrays Operation 'Chavin de Huantar' as a complete military victory and evidence of the virtues of not negotiating with terrorists. 'Chavin de Huantar. Lección de Unión y Corage al Servicio el Perú,' http://www.ejercito.mil.pe/destacados/chavin/chavin.htm. Accessed on Oct. 17, 2005.

the regime's staying power.[61] The regime's spin-doctors deployed a series of strategies, including espionage and intimidation, to keep this emerging opposition in check. Portraying critics of the regime as terrorist sympathisers became another tactic used to keep the opposition off-balance. This was made possible by the gradual extension of government control over the principal print and electronic media outlets, which were used to accuse opposition movements and leaders of having pro-terrorist sympathies. The regime was now playing politics with terrorism in a different sense: it had to do more than simply relive the regime's successes on the counterinsurgency front to bolster its support among voters; now it had to heighten the use of fear and intimidation, and attempt to associate opposition movements with terrorism, in an effort to discredit the opposition and keep its hold on power.

Opposition to the Fujimori regime was very limited during his first administration, but the first signs of an organised opposition emerged in 1997 in response to the dismissal of the Constitutional Tribunal judges. Repression and fear quelled the protests, but led diverse opposition groups—university students, human rights organisations, civil society groups such as Democratic Forum, and opposition legislators—to forge an alliance to challenge the law authorising Fujimori to run for a third term through a referendum. If the proper number of signatures could be attained, the law would be submitted to a vote and could be overturned, and Fujimori would be unable to

---

61 O'Donnell noted long ago the inherent problem of legitimacy facing authoritarian regimes (Guillermo O'Donnell, 'Tensions in the Bureaucratic-Authoritarian State and the Question of Democracy,' in D. Collier (ed.), *The New Authoritarianism in Latin America* (Princeton, 1979), pp. 285-318. The particularity of the Fujimori regime was its need to maintain the façade of democratic rule because its attempt to rule in outright dictatorial fashion (the 1992 *autogolpe*) was met by international condemnation, especially from the United States. While Washington had long supported dictatorships and military regimes in Latin America, policy shifts in the 1980s led to a disavowal of such tactics and promotion of 'free markets and free elections'. Thus international politics imposed constraints on the Fujimori regime's authoritarian project and thus imposed the need to retain a legal façade. See Rospigliosi, Ibid., and Burt, 1998, Ibid.

stand in the 2000 elections. After nearly a year, the opposition had successfully obtained more than a million signatures. Yet the pro-government majority in Congress conspired to vet the referendum. Protests were met with fierce repression.

But in dialectic fashion, regime violence and repression, and its continued abuse of authority, became fodder fuelling the opposition. By 1999, human rights groups, university students, democratic groups like Democratic Forum, and opposition legislators had begun to articulate an ethical stance against the Fujimori regime's authoritarian practices and abuse of authority. The recuperation of democracy became the framing device the opposition used to establish as broad-based a movement as possible.[62] This was a small and largely middle class movement, but it challenged the legal basis of Fujimori's 'relentless pursuit of re-election'[63] and thus created the crucial public space to question the legitimacy of the regime and its tactics that would later ignite a broader opposition movement in the context of the fraudulent electoral process in 2000.[64]

Central to this was the declining significance of both MRTA and the Shining Path, particularly when measured by numbers of acts of political violence. It became less convincing for the Fujimori regime to continue playing up the threat of a terrorist resurgence to reap political benefits. In this context, authoritarian measures, once considered justified in the context of the war against Sendero Luminoso,

---

62 On the importance of framing for social movement mobilization, see Sidney Tarrow, *Power in Movement: Social Movements, Collective Action and Politics* (Cambridge, 1994).

63 This is borrowed from the title of an article by Coletta Youngers, 'Fujimori's Relentless Pursuit of Re-election,' *NACLA Report on the Americas*, 33:4, 1999, pp. 6-10.

64 For an analysis of the opposition to the 2000 electoral process see Catherine Conaghan, *Making and Unmaking Authoritarian Peru: Re-election, Resistance and Regime Transition*. The North-South Agenda Papers 47. Miami, 2001. On the evolution of the human rights movement, its shifting focus on democracy by the late 1990s, and the role it played in the opposition movement, see Coletta Youngers, *Violencia política y sociedad civil en el Perú. Historia de la Coordinadora Nacional de Derechos Humanos* (Lima, 2003).

were increasingly viewed by at least some segments of civil society as no longer so.[65] A subtle shift was underway, as the fear of terrorism gave way to indignation that the regime was manipulating people's fear of terrorism to maintain an autocratic and corrupt system in power.

In the context of this emerging opposition, the regime once again played the terrorism card, manipulating fear and using intimidation tactics to beat back the opposition. Two broad strategies can be distinguished in this period. First, the regime sought to again affirm its successes on the counterinsurgency front. For example, it clearly exaggerated the importance of captures of Sendero leaders who remained at large, which served to remind citizens of the latent terrorist threat as well as of the regime's diligence in combatting terrorism. But it also sought to portray these captures as the diligent work of the armed forces and the SIN, which was not the case.

On November 1, 1998, a local TV news programme presented images of Comrade Rita, who it reported had been arrested after being turned in by her subordinates. The following day, however, Fujimori held a press conference stating that Rita's capture was the result of a military operation led by the armed forces and the SIN. A week later, a news programme aired what it claimed was footage of the heroic capture of Rita by state security forces, followed by interviews with army officials relating details of the operation. In fact, it was a montage designed to simulate a military victory against the remnants of Sendero Luminoso. An investigative report published a few days later in *La República* presented evidence supporting the first version of the story: Rita had been arrested not because of a military operation but because her comrades turned her in. In essence, the regime—and its media collaborators—were fabricating a military 'victory' to bolster its image as a relentless fighter of terrorism.[66]

---

65  See Burt, 2006.

66  Fernando Rospigliosi, *El arte del engaño: Las relaciones entre los militares y la prensa* (Lima, 2000). As Rospigliosi notes, this was not a case of government manipulation of the media but of active media collaboration in the preparation

A similar show was mounted in July of the following year with the capture of Feliciano, a.k.a. Oscar Ramírez Durand, the presumed leader of Sendero Rojo, the faction of the insurgent movement that rejected Guzmán's call for peace talks and continued to pursue revolutionary struggle. Feliciano was arrested by a police officer, but the official version was that he was overcome in a military operation led by the armed forces and the SIN with support of the police. Critics charged the regime with manipulating the arrest of Feliciano for electoral purposes, but also with asserting a version of history that ascribed the victory over terrorism to the army and the intelligence services,[67] much like the attempt to attribute Guzmán's arrest to the work of Montesinos and the SIN rather than police general Ketín Vidal's Dincote.[68]

The publicity mounted over the arrests of Rita and Feliciano allowed the regime to affirm simultaneously the persistence of the terrorist threat and its successes in countering that threat. The case of Feliciano was particularly important in light of the upcoming 2000 elections since it again allowed the regime to emphasise its counterinsurgency successes and Fujimori's image as saviour of the nation.[69]

The second strategy deployed by the regime in this period was to undermine the credibility of the opposition by associating it with terrorism. This affected the social movements that were emerging to contest the regime's authoritarian policies and its human rights abuses, as well as leaders of the democratic opposition who were challenging the regime in elections. This took place in the context of the regime's establishment of virtually complete control over the electronic and print media through a vast web of extortion and influ-

---

of disinformation. The numerous videotapes documenting Montesinos's interactions with many of Peru's top media moguls have confirmed this.

67  Carlos Iván Degregori, 'La captura de Feliciano y la batalla por la memoria,' *ideele*, 1999, p. 31.

68  For an analysis of other types of disinformation and manipulation of public opinion used by the regime between 1997 and 2000, see Rospigliosi, Ibid.

69  Ibid. See also Degregori, 2000, Ibid.

ence peddling managed by Montesinos.[70] While some of the print media was able to maintain independence, as was the case with *La República* and *El Comercio*, for example, virtually all the electronic media came under governmental control. One important exception was Canal N, which aired only on Cable TV and was accessible only to those who paid for it. The yellow press that emerged in this period was largely the creation of the SIN. It is also important to note that journalists who maintained their independence and ran stories critical of the regime were often the object of intimidation and death threats.

Fujimori's two key contenders in the upcoming 2000 elections were Alberto Andrade, whose two terms as mayor of Lima had established him as a competent and efficient administrator, and Luis Castañeda Lossio, architect of the successful reform of the national social security system. The regime deployed massive propaganda campaigns to discredit both leaders in the eyes of the public. This campaign had multiple dimensions, including character assassination;[71] here we shall focus on the manipulation of the terrorism issue. The regime's spin-doctors relentlessly portrayed both opposition leaders as "soft" on terrorism or as virtual terrorist sympathisers. When Castañeda Lossio suggested that the Fujimori government should heed the ruling of the Inter-American Court on Human Rights, which called for new trials for four Chileans linked to the MRTA, since the military trials convicting them had denied them any semblance of due process, he was accused of being pro-terrorist. Headlines from *El Chino* on September 29, 1999 read: "Chilean terrorists supported Castañeda Lossio. He has promised to impose their demands on the country" and on October 15, 1999: "For Castañeda Lossio the terrorists are not our enemies. They must have new trials, 10,000 greenbacks and

70  On government control over the media, see Degregori, Ibid.; Rospigliosi, Ibid.; and CVR, Ibid.
71  See Degregori, Ibid.

much comprehension."[72] After several months of such mud slinging, the regime had effectively neutralised both candidates.

It was in this context that Alejandro Toledo emerged as a viable opposition candidate. He had barely registered on public opinion polls in 1999, but as popular opposition grew in the context of mounting evidence of the electoral fraud, Toledo's popularity surged. Had it not been for massive protests, careful documentation of the electoral fraud underway by election watchdog groups such as Transparencia and the Coordinadora, and the presence of international observers, Fujimori might have got away with his plan to assure victory in the first round by obtaining a majority vote. In effect the regime was forced to agree to a second-round vote pitting Toledo against Fujimori. In the two months between the first and second rounds, the regime deployed a similar strategy to discredit Toledo: character assassination and portraying Toledo as pro-terrorist. One headline in the yellow press suggests the nature of this campaign: 'Toledismo continues its campaign of electoral sabotage. In the style of Sendero Luminoso, Peru Posible seeks to impede elections with a spiral of violence.'[73] Racist allusions were made to Toledo as a 'cholo' (a racial category referring to persons of indigenous background who live in the city) who 'incites savagery'.[74] The regime's discourse blatantly played upon the racial-class ordering of the terrorist 'other' that had long dominated popular culture and political discourse in Peru, in which Sendero was associated with 'savage' 'Indians' and 'cholos.'[75]

The regime used similar tactics to associate social movement protests with terrorism. Participants in the protests against the regime's quashing of the referendum on 30 September 1998, were portrayed in the pro-government media as 'savages', and 'beasts', insinuating

---

72  As cited, Ibid., p. 159.

73  *Referendum*, May 23, 2000 as cited, Ibid., p. 174.

74  *La Chuchi*, May 30, 2000 as cited, Ibid.

75  Susan C. Bourque and Kay B. Warren. 'Democracy without Peace: The Cultural Politics of Terror in Peru,' *Latin American Research Review*, 24:1, 1989, pp. 7-34.

association with terrorism by headlines such as: 'It is barbarity, not protest. Was there terrorist infiltration?'[76] While there was some violence, independent press reports suggested that this was the result of a government decision to withdraw security from downtown Lima. Some military officers expressed their dismay at being ordered to refrain from acting, resulting in a security breakdown.[77] Similar strategies were deployed in the 28 July 2000 March of the Four Suyos, convoked by opposition candidate Alejandro Toledo, on the day of Fujimori's contested inauguration, to highlight the illegitimacy of his third term. Initially met by police repression, the protest later advanced to downtown Lima as security forces withdrew. The march remained largely peaceful, but a fire at the National Bank took the life of four bank guards. The regime immediately blamed the protesters for setting the fire, thus trying to link them in the public mind with the violent strategies of terrorist groups like Sendero. The opposition accused the regime of infiltrating the protest and setting the fire itself in order to discredit the opposition—a charge that was later borne out to be true.[78] Such media campaigns played deliberately and systematically with existing fears and memories of terrorist violence.

*Peruvian democracy the ultimate loser*

The Fujimori regime can be credited with overseeing a counterinsurgency policy that made strategic shifts that helped it defeat two insurgent movements by emphasising intelligence-gathering in order to decapitate their organisational structures, and by largely avoiding scorched-earth policies that in the past had deeply alienated peasants from the armed forces and the state itself. The shifts in counterinsurgency strategy paid off: by late 1992, the top leaders of the MRTA and Sendero Luminoso had been captured, their principal organisational structures dismantled, and their followers dispersed.

76 *Expreso*, Oct. 1, 1998.
77 Reported by Rospigliosi, Ibid.
78 CVR, Ibid.

This was a significant crossroads for political developments in Peru. After a dozen years of internal conflict, including Sendero's brutal attacks against government authorities and civil society and systematic human rights violations committed by government forces in the course of the counterinsurgency war, the country had an opportunity to consolidate its victory against terror and violence by seeking ways to incorporate insurgents who remained at large; demobilise armed militias; and seek to address the structures of poverty, inequality and exclusion that fed insurgent movements in the first instance. Instead, Fujimori and his allies sought to use their political victories against subversion to justify a long-term authoritarian neoliberal project, guarantee impunity for the armed forces, and conceal massive networks of corruption and cronyism.

Rather than capitalise upon its counterinsurgency successes to bring a definitive end to Peru's internal conflict, promote national reconciliation to establish the basis for national unity and citizenship, and rebuild democratic governance, the Fujimori regime politicised the terrorist threat in its effort to consolidate an authoritarian political project and maintain its hold on power. The regime thus lost an opportunity to move past the period of intense political conflict and instead sought to perpetuate the climate of fear, intimidation and polarisation that prevailed in the 1980s and early 1990s to perpetuate its power, preserve immunity from prosecution for members of the security forces, and conceal massive corruption. Playing politics with terror in Peru destroyed the basis of democratic politics, for it allowed the continual denial of civil and political liberties in the context of an all-out war against terrorism, even when the terrorist threat had largely disappeared. By providing justification for authoritarian political practices, it also provided cover for an extensive network of corruption that was revealed only as the regime itself began to unravel, evidencing the extent of government control over the media and the extensive collusion of the media and key elite sectors with the regime.

99

By playing politics with terror, the Fujimori regime also bartered away a critical opportunity to bring a definitive end to the insurgent movements, particularly the deadly Sendero Luminoso. Since his arrest, Guzmán has sought ways to prevent his organisation from being completely obliterated. The Fujimori government's political manipulation of Guzmán's proposal for peace talks gave the organisation an opportunity to direct its forces to retreat from the armed struggle and return to low-key political activities, much like its strategy in the 1970s prior to launching its revolutionary war in 1980. While there is no indication that Sendero could present a danger to the Peruvian state even in the medium term, the fact that the organisation has been able to rebuild itself, has developed a clearly defined political strategy, and is operative in universities, slums and remote rural areas throughout the country, is alarming in and of itself. Sendero may not again achieve the national power it once had, but it could conceivably become entrenched in some of these areas and contribute to the further balkanisation of Peruvian society and politics. Also worrisome is that its continued existence prevents the country from dealing with its past fully—despite the excellent work of the Truth and Reconciliation Commission, which presented its final report in 2003—and allows government elites to continue to play politics with terror when faced with legitimate social protest.

5

# THE USE AND ABUSE OF TERROR: THE CONSTRUCTION OF A FALSE NARRATIVE ON THE DOMESTIC TERROR THREAT

*Peter Oborne*

The first time I ever spoke to Tony Blair was by telephone at about 8.30a.m. on 10 March 1993. I was then a junior political reporter on the *Evening Standard*, while Blair was shadow Home Secretary. He rang me up in an anxious frame of mind. Labour as preparing to announce that it was keeping up its opposition to the renewal of the Prevention of Terrorism Act (PTA). Tony Blair told me that the Labour Party was committed to fighting terrorism. 'We are suggesting nothing,' he said, 'that in any way inhibits the police and security services from doing their job.' The youngish ex-barrister, who in those days still lived in Islington, told me that it would be disgraceful to accuse the Labour Party of being soft on terrorism simply because it opposed the PTA. He suggested that, on the contrary, Labour was courageously holding out against knee-jerk politics. I can remember an implication in our conversation of how easy it would be to pander to the right-wing press, yet how wrong to do so. He was adamant that there was no contradiction between respect for civil liberties and security against terrorism. He said that Labour was adamantly opposed to the 'exclusion orders' imposed by the Conservative gov-

* This essay first appeared as a pamphlet by the Centre For Policy Studies (CPS) in February 2006.

ernment, giving powers to restrict rights to travel. He expressed his concern about the PTA provisions that allowed suspects to be held for one week without a reason being given. 'If you are a terrorist you should be under lock and key,' the future prime minister told me. 'If you are not, you shouldn't. If you are suspected of being one, you should be under surveillance.'

Looking back at the copy I filed that day I can see that the *Evening Standard*, though then a Conservative supporting newspaper, gave Tony Blair a fair crack of the whip. This is what I wrote:

On the day of the discovery of an enormous cache of explosives in London, Labour is aware its stance will appear to some as if it is supporting civil rights for terrorists. But shadow Home Secretary Tony Blair is determined Labour will carry on with its long-standing opposition to the Act on the grounds that it makes unacceptable inroads into civil liberties.

The purpose of this essay is partly to examine why the prime minister no longer seems to believe that civil liberties and security are compatible. It will try and explain why, instead of holding out bravely against the tabloid press, he now appeases it. This essay will argue that the government is fighting terror in the wrong way. It will show that some legislation is less designed to fight terrorism than to fight a publicity campaign. Too much of its activity is aimed at generating newspaper headlines. Too often Tony Blair's key target is less Osama Bin Laden than the editor of the *Sun*. The prime minister prefers the short-term gratification that comes for being praised for being 'tough on terror' to the long-term slog of finding a solution. This false perspective has led to a series of serious mistakes. This essay will show how the prime minister does not tell the truth about terror. Rather than look the threat steadfastly in the face, the British public has been fed half-truths, falsehoods and lies. It will also demonstrate that New Labour has set out to politicise terror, to use it for narrow party advantage. Both major opposition parties have repeatedly offered to join with the government to confront the major terrorist threat that Britain undoubtedly faces. They were right to do so. Yet again and again, their offers have been spurned. Meanwhile those who stood up for civil liberties—as Tony Blair did in 1993—are now accused of giving succour to the terrorists.

The prime minister has promoted a false narrative on terror. He claims that only New Labour is ready and willing to face up to the terror threat. One way New Labour illustrates this point is through misleading statements and public scares, which in many cases turn out to be unfounded. At times, ministers have been so keen to make political use of the terror threat that their public statements have risked prejudicing impending criminal trials. It should be stressed that the government is by no means solely responsible for this distorted public discourse on terror. The police and, to an even larger extent, the British media organisations have had a reckless attitude. Two key case histories—the 'ricin plot' and the alleged terrorist conspiracy to blow up Old Trafford football ground—demonstrate the unreliability of both official statements and media reporting about terrorism. A significant amount of press coverage in the two cases mentioned above was fabrication. But it should be stressed that this level of fantasy and invention was only possible in the first place, and sustainable over time, thanks to official prompting and collusion. Just as it suited government policy that the 'forty-five minute threat' should gain currency ahead of the invasion of Iraq, so was it helpful to ministers that the British public should believe that ricin had been found in a north London flat. The experience of the past few years teaches us that what the prime minister, his ministers, or the police say on the subject of terror must be treated with great scepticism. This is damaging: only a government which possesses the trust of the British people is in a position to ask us to surrender our civil liberties. That trust has been forfeited.

## The Politicisation of Terror

There are occasional great crises in our national life when party distinction gets set aside. One is bereavement or tragedy. Politicians come together to mourn in the wake of a national disaster or the death of the sovereign. Another might be a profound economic disaster of the kind that led to the formation of the National Government in 1931. A third comes when the nation is confronted with some terrible external threat. Open party animosity was set aside during World Wars I and II. The threat from Islamic terrorism is of the same nature. It has already claimed scores of British lives and may well claim many more. It is reasonable to expect that our politicians should rise above party politics when terrorism comes onto the agenda. They have not done so. On the contrary, fighting terror has become a partisan issue. This is a betrayal of those who have already died, and those who may yet die, at the hands of the terrorists. In Britain, the war on terror is now being fought along party political lines.

## *The Prevention of Terrorism Act 2005*

An indication that New Labour was set on addressing the domestic terror threat from a narrow and mainly partisan perspective came with the controversy over the Prevention of Terrorism Bill of spring 2005. The crisis was prompted when New Labour's earlier piece of anti-terrorism legislation—the Anti-Terrorism Crime and Security Act of 2001—came unstuck in the House of Lords. The law lords ruled that section 23 of the 2001 Act contradicted the European Convention on Human Rights (ECHR). Section 23 allowed for the detention without trial of foreign nationals suspected of terrorist links, in particular those who could not be deported to their country of origin because they might be subject to torture there. It had always been likely that this section of the 2001 Act, which had been rushed through Parliament in response to September 11, was incompatible with the ECHR. The government had been warned of this difficulty many times, but appeared to be taken wholly by surprise by the Lords ruling. Casting around for a replacement, ministers came up with the idea of control orders. These included restrictions such as house arrest for suspects who had not been charged with any crime. The Prevention of Terrorism Act now gave the home secretary the power to apply to the courts to impose these 'control orders' on anyone who in his opinion 'is or has been involved in terrorism related activity'.

The government needed to rush these proposals through parliament as the detention of these men in Belmarsh under section 23 of the 2001 Act was about to become illegal. The opposition parties—and this was surely their proper function—wanted to debate these new and severe restrictions on the traditional liberties of the British subject. The issue was made graver and more urgent by the need for a solution in time for the imminent general election. So urgent was the problem that Parliament was required to debate the measure even before the government had worked out the details. In an interview for the programme, the former law lord, Lord Lloyd, described the situation as follows:[1]

The Home Secretary said that he wasn't in a position yet to say what was going to be in the Bill itself. He was going to introduce amendments at the very last moment, so that when the House of Commons had its committee stage, where they're supposed to examine the Bill clause by clause, they had nothing to examine. There wasn't a Bill.

In these exceptional circumstances, the Conservative Party offered a compromise proposal—a 'sunset clause', so that the act would lapse after twelve months. The government dismissed this proposal and steamrollered the PTA through Parliament, while attacking both the Conservatives and Liberal Democrats for being soft on terror.[2] Tony Blair warned the House of Commons that if the legislation was not passed:[3]

The shame will lie with the Conservatives who, faced with legislation to prevent terrorism—faced with legislation on which we were advised by the

---

1  On 30 July 2002 the Special Immigration Appeals Commission (a superior court of record) ruled that indefinite detention under the Part 4 Powers was incompatible with the ECHR. Though this was then overturned by the Court of Appeal, it was ultimately affirmed by the Law Lords in December 2004. For the 2002 SIAC ruling, see: www.statewatch.org/news/2002/jul/SIAC.pdf. See also Richard Norton-Taylor, 'Right Ruling, Wrong Reason', *Guardian*, 1 August 2002.

2  The government did eventually agree to a 'review' of the Act after 12 months.

3  Hansard, 9 March 2005.

police and security services—are going to vote against it. If they want to vote against it, let them: we will be content ultimately to have the verdict of the country on it.

This charge that the 'shame' lay with the Conservative Party was strong. All the Conservatives had wanted to do was impose a twelve month sunset clause so that a piece of legislation, which had profound implications for the liberty of the British subject and which was said by experts to be poorly drafted, could be properly re-examined at the end of a year. Peter Hain, leader of the commons, had already gone further than the prime minister. He told BBC viewers that:[4]

If we are tough on crime and terrorism, as Labour is, then I think Britain will be safer under Labour… we have to create a safer, more secure country and it is our Labour Party that is achieving that. It's our assertion that we are providing more security for this country and its citizens than alternative policies… the risk would be lower under Labour.

Labour's strategy was clear enough. It was determined to take the strongest, most populist line on terror; and then to brand its political opponents as weak or soft. There is strong evidence that this strategy worked.

## The London bombings and the smashing of consensus

In the immediate aftermath of the 7 July outrages, British politicians for the most part behaved perfectly. They came together to condemn the terrorists. As he so often does at a moment of crisis, Tony Blair found the correct words to articulate the national mood. He stressed the need not to panic, and advocated a steady and measured response. Opposition leaders Michael Howard and Charles Kennedy agreed that they would set aside party differences and do everything in their means to help the government. So on 11 July, Michael Howard assured Tony Blair that:[5]

---

4   *BBC Breakfast*, 24 November 2004. Quotation taken from the BBC website.

5   Hansard, 11 July 2005.

We wish to play our part by making constructive measures that we hope will help establish a durable consensus on the best measures to safeguard us all.

Tony Blair replied in similar vein:[6]

It is important if we possibly can, that when we come to look at any future legislation, we try to establish it on the basis of a consensus. If it is possible to do that, we should, and I assure him that I will work to see that that is done.

Meanwhile Home Secretary Charles Clarke was swift to make contact with his opposite numbers Tory shadow home secretary David Davis and Liberal Democrats home affairs spokesman Mark Oaten. Parallel lines of communication were developed between their staff members, and cemented by a regular exchange of letters and e-mails. The three offices swiftly agreed on three new laws that would help prevent a repetition of the London bombings: creating offences of acts preparatory to terrorism, indirect incitement to terrorism, and attending a terrorist training camp. There seemed to be a real chance that some good could come out of the calamity of the London bombings: politicians of all parties coming together to fight a ruthless common enemy.[7] This co-operation brought risks for the opposition parties, in particular perhaps for the Liberal Democrats where the libertarian tradition was strongest. But in due course the consensus was confirmed at a meeting of the three party leaders. By the start of August, there was a general agreement that everything was on course for announcements at the party conference season and the passing of an anti-terrorism act, with cross-party support, by Christmas. Charles Clarke, David Davis and Mark Oaten each set off on holiday (Clarke to the United States, Oaten to France and Davis to campaign for the Tory leadership). They had taken the precaution of sharing contact numbers in case of an emergency.

---

6   Ibid.

7   The following account is based on interviews with many of those most intimately involved, including the Home Secretary, Charles Clarke, Conservative Shadow Home Secretary, David Davis, and Liberal Democrats Home Affairs spokesman Mark Oaten.

On the afternoon of 4 August, both Oaten and Davis were surprised to receive a call from the Home Office minister Hazel Blears. Oaten was in St Tropez when he took his, while Davis was in the north of England. According to both Oaten and Davis, Blears gave the impression that the call was little more than a formality. She told them that there would be an announcement on terrorism by the prime minister the following day, but that it would not go further than had already been agreed between the three parties. Oaten recalls:

The basis of the conversation led me to believe that what the prime minister was going to announce was of very little political significance, that this was not a big shift, and that the consensus that we had had would continue. I then called Charles Kennedy, my boss, that night and said, look, I'm in France, the prime minister is going to make a statement tomorrow. As far as I'm concerned there's nothing in that which should trouble us, or put the consensus at risk. I went to bed that night assuming that it was business as normal, that the prime minister would be using his last day before holiday to reiterate some of the issues on terrorism. I was badly wrong.

Davis remembers:

I was sitting in a restaurant in Ambleside, and I got a telephone call from Hazel Blears telling me the next day the prime minister was going to be making an announcement on their counter-terrorism proposals, and that there were going to be four things in it, and she told me four things.

The following day (5 August), in his monthly Downing Street press conference, the prime minister went far beyond anything agreed or even discussed with the opposition parties. He dramatically announced a 'twelve point plan' which put forward new measures which he surely knew that the opposition parties could not support.

This twelve point plan at once shattered the harmonious working relationship between the three main parties. It remains unclear whether Hazel Blears was deliberately deceiving Davis and Oaten in her telephone calls. It seems more likely that she was acting in good faith. This theory gains currency from several credible reports that Home Office officials were taken aback by the prime minister's twelve point plan on the day itself. The *Evening Standard* political correspondent Paul Waugh was told by Home Office officials that their 'jaws dropped' during the Prime Minister's speech. According to Martin Bright, political editor of the *New Statesman*:

It was my understanding that it took Charles Clarke and the Home Office by surprise. Now what was extraordinary was that over the previous months Charles Clarke had been quite carefully building a consensus, not only with other political parties, but he was making a gesture towards liberal Britain on these issues, and it was a deeply humiliating moment for him.

Charles Clarke, it must be said, rebuts any suggestion that he was put under pressure from Downing Street or kept out of loop, saying:

I was on holiday in America at that time, and I was on the phone to the prime minister a great deal during that time, right up to the statements that he actually made. I was fully involved, fully supported it, and thought it was the right thing to do.

Be that as it may, there are grounds for speculation that 10 Downing Street had seized control of the terrorism agenda from the Home Office. It is possible that Blears may have been kept in the dark even twenty-four hours before the prime minister's announcement (though Charles Clarke today insists that Blears gave Oaten and Davis 'a very full briefing').

The context is important: the prime minister had been confronted by a concerted campaign in the tabloid press for new anti-terror laws. He may well have concluded that the thoughtful, consensual strategy worked out with the two main opposition parties came at too great a political cost. He may have decided that it was more profitable to give an impression of acting tough. That was the impression gained by many MPs, including his own supporters. John Denham, a former Home Office minister and chairman of the Home Affairs Committee, described the proposals as 'half-baked'. He told me later:

There must be concern that the government agenda is sometimes driven by public and media pressure in this area, rather than a concern for what is most effective.

Tony Blair's terror initiative showed numerous signs of having been cobbled together in a hurry. Some of the measures proved ill-thought out and unworkable.[8] However, it may have achieved the result that the prime minister, who left the following day to the West Indies to stay at Cliff Richard's holiday home, wanted. For days before the plan was announced, he had been heavy pressure from a tabloid campaign, led by the *Sun*, claiming that holidaying politicians were not taking the terror threat seriously enough. On 3 August, the *Sun* raged against holidaying MPs: 'LET'S HOPE THE BOMBERS ARE ON HOLIDAY TOO'. On 5 August an open letter from Trevor Kavanagh, political editor of the *Sun*, was headlined: 'DEAR MPs SIX WEEKS HOLIDAY IS ENOUGH FOR ANYONE'. Then on 6 August, as Tony Blair flew to the West Indies with his family, the *Sun* headline was much more reassuring: 'VICTORY FOR SUN OVER NEW TERROR LAWS.'

## *The Consensus Smashed Again: the Ninety Days Fiasco*

To their credit both the Home Secretary Charles Clarke and opposition politicians remained determined to maintain a cross party alliance on the Terrorism Bill in spite of the set back of 5 August. When Mark Oaten expressed his concern to Charles Clarke about the breakdown over the twelve point plan, the Home Secretary gave a reassurance that it was still his aim to get a consensus on counter-terrorism measures. According to Mark Oaten:

I'm very clear in my mind that the Home Secretary would rather have seen a situation where political parties weren't having to issue statements saying that consensus had broken down, and I think that he regretted that that had happened, and was very keen, on his return from holiday, to get together with myself and David Davis, so that we could re-engage in the kind of spirit that we'd had before Tony Blair had made that statement.

Charles Clarke was as good as his word. The Home Office did indeed work together with the two other main parties on the Terrorism Bill as it entered Parliament in the autumn. The most contentious point, it swiftly emerged, was the proposal for ninety days

---

8    Appendix I analyses the subsequent failure of the twelve point plan.

detention without charge for terrorist suspects, a proposal which smashed through the British tradition of freedom from arbitrary arrest dating back centuries. It can be traced back at least to article 39 of the Magna Carta, which states that the King cannot lock up his subjects until he puts them through a process of law. The proposal to break with this ancient principle had first emerged from the police. Though it was greeted with scepticism from opposition parties and many Labour backbenchers, there were numerous indications from the Home Secretary that he was looking for a compromise solution that could carry the support of his political opponents.

On 15 September, Charles Clarke gave Oaten and Davis concrete reason to believe that he was prepared to compromise on the ninety day point. He wrote to them saying:

In particular, it may be that you are convinced by the case for some extension, but feel that three months is too great an extension. I would be interested in your views on this particular point.

In an earlier draft of this letter, inadvertently released to the public, Clarke had been even more open to discussion:[9]

I think the case for some extension is clear, though I believe there is room for debate as to whether we should go as far as three months andI am still in discussion with the police on this point.

The following month, when grilled by the House of Commons Home Affairs Committee, the Home Secretary was even clearer. Questioned about his commitment to the ninety days, he replied:[10]

I never say never in politics and I would not say I have an absolute fixation on anything actually but not on three months either. I have said to the opposition parties if they are interested to talk about this, and in the interests of getting agreement, I am interested to talk about it too.

Clarke continued to indicate that he was ready to compromise right up to the bitter end. Dominic Grieve, the shadow Attorney

---

9   See reports in the, for example, the *Daily Telegraph*, 16 September 2005.

10  Evidence to the Home Affairs Select Committee, 11 October 2005.

General who was deeply involved in these negotiations, describes a meeting between the opposition parties and Charles Clarke at the end of the committee stage of the Terrorism Bill's passage through Parliament, on the morning of 7 November:

We explained to him that we had grave reservations, and I said to him that I thought that twenty-eight days was really the outside limit of what was acceptable but I waited for his proposals. And having listened to what we had to say he told us that he was going to go away and think about that and was going to try and come up with some compromise formula to put to Parliament.

Mark Oaten says:

I made it very clear to the Home Secretary that if we could find a way forward on ninety days, if they would look at alternatives to ninety days, we may still be able to support them. I was led, right until the last point, to believe that the Home Secretary wanted to achieve that.

Charles Clarke gives a different perspective on these discussions, insisting that he gained the impression that neither of the opposition parties were ready to compromise and it was therefore not worthwhile trying to pursue negotiations. Charles Clarke described the Conservative position:

We went through a wide range of proposals on which there was broad agreement and then I came to an end and said, you know, was there any possibility that they would go beyond the 28 days in a process that would carry through. They said no...

Those present at the meeting waited to hear back from Clarke about what the compromise was going to be. But early that afternoon, Tony Blair appeared to take control of the process. Rather than negotiate a solution, as Clarke had hinted only in the morning, ninety days was turned into an issue of principle during the course of the day.

This became clear to Labour MPs when the Prime Minister addressed a meeting of the Parliamentary Labour Party in the House of Commons at the end of the day. It was a closed meeting, and it is impossible to obtain a verbatim report. According to accounts from those present, the Prime Minister made the same kind of brilliant, emotive speech that he delivered to the House of Commons on the eve of the Iraq invasion. Those present say that he did not try to make a reasoned and well-constructed case. Rather the Prime Minister concentrated on the political utility of voting for the bill. According to one present, the Labour MP Mark Fisher:

He didn't attempt to address the case or the facts. It was entirely an emotional appeal to us as Labour politicians to support him in the lobbies and many of us felt that we could have done better if we'd heard from him why he believed that ninety days was important. Instead, we heard a passionate and brilliantly delivered appeal for why we should support him. He gave no argument at all. [He said that] our opponents were politically dangerous and misguided and this was very important for the next election and the credibility of the government. They were all political points... you could see the impact it was having particularly on new and younger Labour MPs. They were pinned in their seats at the prospect that if there was a further atrocity they might be held responsible. And in the Prime Minister's words, they would be held to have abetted terrorism and their constituents.

Some of the government's argument for ninety days veered into the infantile and the insulting. In an attempt to put pressure on Labour MPs wavering about whether to vote in favour of the Bill by showing it enjoyed widespread national support, the government despatched a questionnaire to Labour members. The questions misrepresented the complexity of the argument. Two examples from the questionnaire, which was displayed on the Labour Party website, are quoted below:

Do you think police should have the time and opportunity to complete their investigations into suspected terrorists?

Yes/No/Not sure

Do you think the Government should make sure there are new safeguards to protect innocent people?

Yes/No/Not sure

The pattern of events leading up to the so-called twelve point plan, and in the days leading up to the Commons vote over ninety days was uncannily similar. In each case the Home Secretary gave the strongest possible impression, almost right up to the final moment, that he was minded to act consensually and find a compromise. In each case, the two major opposition parties believe they were badly misled. In each case, Downing Street appears to have suddenly taken over the management of affairs at the end. In each case, the government's tough line on terror was made into a political point.

## How the prime minister misled the nation

The prime minister, the British government and the police have consistently misled the British public about the nature and scope of the threat to the British people over terror. Three examples are set out below.

### CONTROL ORDERS

On 28 February 2005, with the Prevention of Terrorism Bill being discussed in Parliament, Tony Blair made the following comment to listeners to Women's Hour:[11]

What they [the security services] say is that you have got to give us powers in between mere surveillance of these people—there are several hundred of them in this country who we believe are engaged in plotting or trying to commit terrorist acts—you have got to give us power in between just surveying them and being sure enough to prosecute them beyond reasonable doubt. There are people out there who are determined to destroy our way of life and there is no point in us being naïve about it.

These remarks were terrifying. Anyone listening to the Prime Minister's remarks must have felt that, within days of the Prevention of Terrorism Act being passed, the 'several hundred' individuals plotting to wreak devastation through Britain would have been under lock and key. And yet that is not the case at all.

---

11 This analysis follows that made by Dr David Morrison in his lucid paper 'What Became of Blair's 'several hundred' terrorists?', *Labour and Trade Union Review*, May 2005. www.david-morrison.org.uk/counter-terrorism/several-hundred-terrorists.htm

Nearly a year has gone by, and yet no more than seventeen individuals have been made subject to control orders. At least half of them seem to have been foreign nationals, who had already been detained under Section 23 of the Anti-terrorism, Crime and Security Act 2001. The Prime Minister's suggestion that the Security Services were demanding new powers in order to deal with a new category of terrorist suspect turns out to have been nonsense. His figure of 'several hundred' terrorists plotting mayhem was contradicted almost at once by Downing Street and what seems to have been a Home Office briefing.[12] It seems to have been plucked out of thin air.

## 'NO LINK WITH IRAQ'

In the immediate aftermath of the London bombings, the British Government went out of its way to deny any suggestion that there was any connection between the 7 July atrocity and the invasion of Iraq two years before. On 11 July, the prime minister told the House of Commons that there was no link between the two. Replying to a question from Scottish National Party leader Alex Salmond, he declared that:[13]

The one thing that is obvious from the long list of countries that have been victims of this type of terrorism is that it does not discriminate greatly between individual items of policy. I am afraid I must tell the Hon. Gentleman that it is a form of terrorism aimed at our way of life, not at any particular government or policy.

The Prime Minister could not have been more explicit: there was no connection between Iraq and the London atrocity. Senior ministers took the same line. Foreign Secretary Jack Straw added further substance to the denial on BBC News 24 on 18 July:

The terrorists have struck across the world in countries allied with the United States, backing the war in Iraq, and in countries which had nothing

---

12  See for example the *Daily Express*, 2 March 2005, "MI5 Protest that Blair 'sexed up' Terrorist Claims". See also the sharp downplaying of the prime minister's remarks in Downing Street official briefing, 11 a.m. 28 February 2005.

13  Hansard, 11 July 2005.

whatever to do with the war in Iraq. They struck in Kenya, in Tanzania, in Indonesia. They have struck this weekend in Turkey, which was not supporting our action in Iraq.

This was a disingenuous formulation. Far from being random attacks on Kenya and Tanzania, as Straw suggested, the targets in both countries were the United States embassy. In Indonesia, the targets had been foreign nationals from Australia, a leading member of the pro-war coalition. As for Turkey, the Foreign Secretary ought to have been aware that the attack there came from a Kurdish separatist organisation, and not al-Qaeda. There were similar protestations from the Prime Minister and the Foreign Secretary in the days after the bombings. They were dishonest. Both men had been advised many times that the Iraq War would increase the chances of a terrorist outrage in Britain. Some of the warnings have found their way into the public domain. For example, a month before the March 2003 invasion the Joint Intelligence Committee had warned that:[14]

The terrorist threat to Western interests... would be heightened by military action against Iraq.

In June 2005, some three weeks before the London bombings, Britain's Joint Terrorism Analysis Centre judged that:[15]

Events in Iraq are continuing to act as motivation and a focus of a range of terrorist related activity in the UK.

On 18 July 2005, the Royal Institute of International Affairs (also known as Chatham House) published a briefing on terrorism and national security which declared:[16]

There is no doubt that the situation over Iraq has imposed particular difficulties for the UK, and for the wider coalition against terrorism. It gave a

---

14  See the Intelligence and Security Committee Report, *Iraq Weapons of Mass Destruction—Intelligence and Assessments*, 11 September 2003.

15  Taken from a leaked document published in the *New York Times*, 19 July 2005.

16  RIIA, *Security, Terrorism and the UK*, July 2005.

boost to the al-Qaeda network's propaganda, recruitment and fundraising, caused a major split in the coalition, provided an ideal targeting and training area for al-Qaeda linked terrorists.

This document provided a reasoned and authoritative rebuttal of the denials emerging from Downing Street and the Foreign Office. Jack Straw responded:

I'm astonished if Chatham House is now saying that we should not have stood shoulder to shoulder with our long-standing allies in the United States.

Once again, the Foreign Secretary was guilty of distortion and misrepresentation. Chatham House had not questioned for a single second whether Britain should have stood 'shoulder to shoulder' with the US. All it had done was to reach the dispassionate conclusion that the invasion of Iraq had increased the terror risk to Britain. This judgement was shared by the intelligence services, as Straw must have known at the time he was speaking. In the wake of the Chatham House pronouncement, the Government was obliged to change its line that there was no link between the Iraq invasion and the London bombings. Tony Blair even went to the extraordinary lengths of reinventing reality by claiming never to have denied the link in the first place. This is what he said at his Downing Street press conference on 26 July:

I read occasionally that I am supposed to have said it [the London bombings] is nothing to do with Iraq, in inverted commas. Actually I haven't said that.

The Prime Minister was being disingenuous. From 7 July, until 18 July, he and his ministers had gone out of their way to give the strongest impression that there was no connection between the attack on London and the Iraq invasion.

### 'ARRESTING' THE TERRORISTS

At Prime Minister's Questions on 9 November 2005, Tony Blair claimed that 'just this last weekend, we arrested people on a terrorist operation.' He had made a similar claim on Channel Four television on 8 November, and at a press conference on 7 November. In fact there had been no arrests over the weekend. Some suspected terrorists had been charged, a crucial distinction since the debate raging at the time concerned the length of time that should elapse between arrest and charge. When Michael Howard wrote to the prime minister to ask for a correction, Tony Blair replied unapologetically:[17]

The point I was making remains entirely valid. The point was not about the difference between arrest and charge but rather that we face a continuing threat, and whether arrested on 21 October or 4 November makes no difference to this essential point.

This is a relatively trivial example. But it illustrates the British Government's habitual casualness about factual accuracy in terrorism cases.

## Ricin

In early 2003, just as the British government was seeking to persuade the British people to wage war against Saddam Hussein in order to prevent him distributing weapons of mass destruction to terrorists, the police made a significant announcement. They had, they said, foiled a terrorist ring in its attempt to launch a chemical attack in Britain using the deadly poison ricin. According to a press release from Scotland Yard issued in the names of Deputy Chief Medical Officer Dr Pat Troop and Metropolitan Police Assistant Commissioner David Veness,[18] ricin poison had been found in a flat in Wood Green, North London.

The Government latched onto the news. On 7 January, the Metropolitan Police and the Deputy Chief Medical Officer at the Department of Health issued a joint statement stating that 'traces of ricin' had been found. 'ricin is a toxic material which if ingested or inhaled can be fatal,' they announced. 'Our primary concern is the safety of the public.'[19] The Prime Minister joined in by warning

---

17 Letter from Tony Blair to Michael Howard, placed in the House of Commons Library, 11 November 2005.

18 See Appendix II for the full text of the Metropolitan Police Press Release issued on 6 January 2003.

19 Quoted in Severin Carrell and Raymond Whitaker, *Independent on Sunday*,

that the discovery highlighted the dangers from weapons of mass destruction, adding: 'The arrests which were made show this danger is present and real and with us now. Its potential is huge.'[20]

Within weeks the ricin case was being cited around the world as further justification for the war in Iraq. US Secretary of State Colin Powell told the UN Security Council of a direct link between the British 'ricin plot' and an alleged al-Qaeda 'poisons camp' in Iraq.[21] The following day Tony Blair endorsed these remarks, saying in a Newsnight interview that 'what Colin Powell was talking about yesterday is correct', adding that 'it would not be correct to say there is no evidence linking al-Qaeda and Iraq.'[22] In late March 2003, US commanders in Iraq claimed to have destroyed a 'poison factory', though no chemicals or laboratories were found. The US commander in chief, General Richard Myers, claimed:[23]

And then just recently we attacked and now have gone in on the ground into a site in north-eastern Iraq where the Ansar al-Islam and al-Qaeda had been working on poisons. And it's from this site where people were trained and poisons were developed that migrated into Europe. We think that's probably where the ricin found in London came from.

It is unusual, and potentially prejudicial, for ministers to comment on upcoming court cases. Nevertheless, as the ricin case moved towards trial, ministers continued to regard the ricin trial as an important publicity resource. In due course, the trial judge

---

17 April 2005.

20 From a speech to diplomats on UK foreign policy, in London on 7 January 2003. See www.news.bbc.co.uk/1/hi/uk_politics/2635807.stm

21 For a transcript of Powell's statement to the UN Security Council in New York on 5 February 2003, see www.un.int/usa/03clp0205.htm

22 Comments made in an interview with Jeremy Paxman for a Newsnight Special, 6 February 2003. For a transcript, see www.news.bbc.co.uk/1/hi/programmes/newsnight/2732979.stm

23 General Myers made this claim on CNN's 'Late Edition With Wolf Blitzer', on 30 March 2003. For a transcript, see www.edition.cnn.com/TRANSCRIPTS/0303/30/le.00.html

was provoked into warning the Home Secretary to curb his public remarks for fear of prejudicing the case.

No ricin was ever found in the Wood Green flat—just a small number of ingredients for the manufacture of ricin. The announcement from David Veness and Pat Troop that 'a small amount of the material recovered from the Wood Green premises has tested positive for the presence of ricin poison' was misleading: the tests were only capable of indicating that ricin *might* be present.

But they did not establish its presence. The press release also said that: 'Tests were carried out on the material and it was confirmed this morning that toxic material was present'. This latter statement was utterly wrong. No confirmatory tests had yet been carried out. All that had taken place by the time they issued their joint release was a preliminary test. When a definitive test was done, it confirmed that there was no ricin at all.[24] At that time, Veness and Troop had no way of knowing whether or not ricin had been found.

On 7 January, chemical weapons experts at the government research facility at Porton Down carried out more accurate tests into the presence of ricin. These tests established that there was no ricin.

Curiously, Porton Down apparently did not pass on this information to the British Government until late March. And apparently the government never asked for the results of this definitive test.[25] Yet, thanks to a series of events that at times defy belief, the existence of ricin continued to be proclaimed for over two years. By the time that Porton Down belatedly passed on its negative finding to the government, the matter was deemed *sub judice*, as by then charges had been laid against the accused. This decision infuriated the defence lawyers. One of them, Alastair Lyon, argues:

---

24 It is unusual for the Deputy Chief Medical Officer to countersign a Police Press Release. It is stranger still that she endorsed a statement that proved to be so inaccurate.

25 This time-lag was confirmed in the ricin trial in 2005.

Judges are reasonable human beings. Evidence that corrected a press campaign that was wrong and prejudicial surely could have been put into the public domain. If the argument behind the publicising of the find of ricin was that the public had a right to know, then telling the public the truth—the finding that there was no ricin—was surely even more in the public interest.

## THE BACKGROUND TO THE RICIN PLOT

On 18 September 2002, one alleged mastermind of the so-called ricin plot, an Algerian named Mohammed Meguerba, was arrested in north London and found to possess fake IDs. Bailed after suffering an epileptic fit, he absconded, turning up in Algeria on 16 December 2002, where he was arrested by security police after allegedly being smuggled in by Islamist militants. After being interrogated and possibly tortured for two days, he allegedly revealed a poisoning plot in north London, naming the Algerian Kamel Bourgass as ringleader and other Algerians as co-conspirators. Meguerba's information led police to a flat in Wood Green, where they arrested several men, though Bourgass was not there. The police did discover recipes for ricin, a mortar and pestle, and castor beans, from which it is possible to extract ricin. On 14 January 2003, while on the hunt for another terror suspect, the police raided a flat in Crumpsall, Manchester. By chance they found Bourgass and another alleged conspirator. After a violent struggle, Bourgass murdered DC Stephen Oake and wounded several other police officers.[26]

On 29 June 2004 Bourgass was sentenced to life imprisonment for the murder of DC Oake after an eleven week trial at the Old

---

26 Both Bourgass and Meguerba had been separately arrested for minor offences before. Both times, although being suspected of being in breach of immigration laws, they were freed without charge by the police. Both times, the immigration authorities were informed but appear not to have acted on the information. Had they done so, and had they deported Bourgass and Meguerba, the ricin plot would never have happened. It is this lack of co-ordination which failed to prevent the ricin plot, not the inadequate detention powers as the Police later claimed.

Bailey. The sentence was kept secret because of the impending trial for the ricin plot. On 13 September 2004 an Old Bailey case began against Bourgass, Mouloud Sihali, David Khalef, Sidali Feddag and Mustapha Taleb. Six months later, on 8 April 2005 the jury acquitted Sihali, Khalef, Feddag and Taleb. Four days later the jury acquitted Bourgass of the most serious charge—conspiracy to murder. It did find him guilty of 'conspiracy to commit a public nuisance by the use of poisons or explosives to cause disruption, fear or injury.' The judge sentenced him to seventeen years. The Director of Public Prosecutions Ken MacDonald abandoned the trial, due to start the following day, of another four men accused of the conspiracy. Meguerba has yet to stand trial in Algeria and remains in custody.

### HOW THE MYTH OF THE RICIN PLOT SURVIVED

The press has continued to report the ricin plot as if it was real, while the Government has never formally announced that there was never any ricin at the Wood Green flat. For example, on the very night of its collapse, Newsnight ran a long piece which implied that ricin had been found in the flat.[27] Later, Metropolitan Police Commissioner Ian Blair said on the 'Breakfast with Frost' programme on 17 April 2005 that the ricin case demonstrated the need for new laws. This was after the case had failed. In a report as recent as 5 October 2005, Metropolitan Police Assistant Commissioner Andy Hayman used the ricin plot as an argument in the police campaign for a ninety day period of detention without trial.[28] This report was sent to the Home Secretary and distributed to members of the Press at the prime Minister's press conference on 11 October. Hayman claimed that Meguerba could have been successfully convicted if the police had been able to hold onto him for longer than seven days. This suggestion was wrong: the police

---

27  See A Gilligan, 'Ricin Certainties', *Spectator*, 23 April 2005, for an account of *Newsnight*'s uncritical acceptance of the police and government line.

28  Anti-Terrorism Branch (SO13) report, 5 October 2005, 'Three Month Precharge Detention'.

did not use even the seven days they were allowed. Meguerba had been held only for three days.

## Old Trafford

On the evening of Monday 19 April 2004, the British people were alerted to an amazing coup. They learned how the police had seized a terrorist gang just as it prepared to launch an audacious bomb attack on Old Trafford stadium on match day, an attack which could have killed thousands of people. The story was billed by the *Sun* as an 'exclusive' but splashed in other papers too. It dominated ITN and Sky News for two days. It was a national sensation.

And yet there was not a shred of truth in the story. It was a complete fabrication. It caused needless alarm amongst millions of TV viewers and newspaper readers. It stirred up anti-Islamic prejudice. It ruined the lives of several of the suspects. They lost their homes, their jobs and their friends as a result. They have never received a personal apology, either from the police or from the press. Unlike in the ricin case, the British Government cannot be blamed. The police and, to an extent the media, are responsible for the invention.

### THE BACKGROUND

On the morning of Monday 19 April 2004, over 400 officers from four police forces, many of them armed, raided half a dozen houses, flats and businesses in and around Manchester. They arrested eight men, one woman and a sixteen-year-old boy. They were held for several days and intensively interrogated. According to Gill Crossley, a lawyer who represented one of the suspects, 'I was never told why it was that my client had been arrested, or any of the particulars relating to the offence that was under investigation.' She recalls that 'the questioning went on over days and days, but with no real substance to any of the questions.' In due course the suspects were released. No charges were ever laid.

### THE MEDIA COVERAGE

The newspapers, by contrast, had no doubt about what the story was. The front page of the *Sun* proclaimed: 'MAN U SUICIDE BOMB PLOT'. On pages four and five the paper claimed:'EXCLUSIVE: MAN UTD SUICIDE BLASTS FOILED'. Once the story had started to run, it was further fuelled by the Manchester police. Rather than issue a cool denial, they played it up by holding a press conference. The accompanying press release read: 'We are confident that the steps that we have taken to date have significantly reduced any potential threat in the Greater Manchester area.' With the weekend fixtures looming, it went on: 'Greater Manchester Police and Manchester United Football Club have put in place extra security measures to reassure the public about the safety of both matches.'

### HOW THE STORY WAS FABRICATED

The police and security services have, very properly, refused to discuss what intelligence led to the raids of 19 April being made. But the police interrogations of the suspects shed a ray of light. One of the suspects, a Kurd, suffered so badly from having his name linked to a terrorist plot that he wants to remain anonymous. He told me how Old Trafford had cropped up in his interrogation:

I was in the police station, and the interview stopped, like a rest, and somebody they bring in the coffee, and they ask me what you like? I say I like the football. Oh, who do you support? They ask me just like a friendly, who do you support? I say Manchester United. Oh, how long you support Manchester United? I said a long time I support Manchester United, when I was tiny, I was small, you know and all my family supported Manchester United… they asked me, have you been football ground? I said, of course I've been to the football ground. Two years ago, long time ago, I can't remember.

These questions were surely prompted by the discovery at the anonymous suspect's flat of Manchester United paraphernalia: a poster of Old Trafford, and ticket stubs the suspect had kept as souvenirs of his only visit to the ground, when he had gone with a friend to watch United play Arsenal the year before. The two friends had bought their tickets from touts, which meant that they sat at different parts of the ground. The *Sun* reported that the bombers planned to sit at different parts of the ground in order to cause maximum damage with their bombs. This claim can only have been based on the fact that the old ticket stubs found by the police were for seats in different parts of the stadium. This information had not been made public, so the *Sun* could only have obtained it from the police. The Kurds I spoke to had come to Britain in order to escape the brutality of Saddam Hussein's regime. Perhaps their most meaningful emotional connection with Britain was a love for Manchester United, which was why they kept the souvenirs in their flat. The Manchester police discovered nothing else suspicious. Indeed they found plenty of evidence that they could not possibly have been Islamic extremists, ranging from a fridge full of beer to a picture of a girlfriend to a collection of video cassettes. Nevertheless the police probably viewed the Manchester United souvenirs as potential evidence of a bomb plot.

This evidence was then prematurely leaked, through unofficial police sources, to the press. The Manchester police then encouraged the story to run by issuing public statements that, while falling a long way short of giving outright confirmation, could be read as corroborating the story. Disgracefully, the Greater Manchester police refused to launch an investigation into the numerous leaks. The reporting of this incident was inflammatory and misleading.

## Conclusion

What have been the consequences of these failures to discuss responsibly the threat of domestic terror?

### THE TWELVE POINT PLAN

The Prime Minister claimed on 5 August 2005 that his twelve point plan would 'set a comprehensive framework for action in dealing with the terrorist threat in Britain.' That claim was exaggerated and, in large part, false. Some of the measures, such as the Prime Minister's announcement that anyone with links to terrorism would be barred from claiming asylum, were not new. The prime minister failed to point out in his televised statement that terrorists are already ineligible for asylum under the terms of Geneva Convention. There appears to have been no progress in the Prime Minister's pledge to draw up a list of 'extremist' websites, bookshops and so forth, and deport anybody who 'actively engages' with them.

The Prime Minister pledged to set a maximum time limit on extradition cases involving terrorism. This pledge also appears to have been dropped. There has been no indication that it is being taken forward, and it is hard to see how the proposal might work in practice. Similarly, the proposal to close places of worship used for 'fomenting extremism' has been abandoned, though here the Prime Minister can claim to have kept his word because he did no more than pledge to 'consult' on the measure. He also promised to extend the use of control orders. Progress on this is unclear. The creation of a new offence of 'glorifying' terrorism has not been dropped, but it is in jeopardy. It is one of the most controversial parts of the Terrorism Bill, with important legal voices warning that it would be impossible to enforce. There is a possibility that the Government will be defeated on the measure. The Government already has been defeated on the proposal to extend the period that suspected terrorists could be imprisoned for without charge from fourteen to ninety days. To be fair to the Prime Minister he did not mention a specific time limit on 5 August, merely promising that the detention without trial period would be 'significantly extended'. Technically he can claim to have met this objective (as the period was eventually extended to twenty-eight days), but the defeat over ninety days was of course a humiliation and a severe defeat for Government policy. Some of the objectives in the twelve point plan are being carried out. Progress is indeed being made towards consultation on an extension of powers to strip individuals of British citizenship; point eight pledged an increase in the number of special judges hearing terrorism cases; the Bill does indeed widen the criteria for the proscription of terrorist organisations; work is afoot to review the competence in English needed to acquire British citizenship; the FCO has developed a database of those whose activities or views present a threat to the UK with a view to the exclusion of anybody who appears on that database.[29] The Home Office produced their own progress report on the twelve point plan on 15 December.[30] This report places a good gloss on the record. But the overall failure is striking. The headline announcement from the prime minister was his promise to deal with the 'preachers of hate' against whom tabloid newspapers campaigned hard in the wake of the London bombs. The Prime Minister, almost certainly in response to this pressure, promised that the 'rules were changing' so that these preachers could be expelled. Eight months have passed and none has been thrown out of Britain. By comparison, Germany has expelled some twenty imams, Italy and France around four. Just one prominent preacher has been banned from this country. Sheikh Omar Bakri Mohammed, leader of the al-Muhajiroun group, travelled to Beirut of his own free will and has since been prevented from returning.

The failure of the Prime Minister to deport foreign nationals is not surprising. The 'measure' to deport foreign nationals which Tony Blair announced on 5 August was actually far from new. Though spun as new by the Prime Minister, it was in fact thirty-four years old. The Immigration Act 1971 gave the Home Secretary powers to deport individuals from Britain on the grounds that their presence was 'not conducive to the public good'.

The Prime Minister created the illusion of fresh action by saying that the Home Secretary was being given 'new grounds for deportation and exclusion' which included 'fostering hatred, advocating violence to further a person's beliefs, or justifying or validating such violence'. Indeed, the accompanying press statement from the Home Office boasted that:[31]

---

29  The twelve point plan, and its progress, can be found in Appendix I.

30  See www.press.homeoffice.gov.uk/Speeches/15-12-05-st-ct-progressreport ?view=Standard

31  Home Office Press Release, 24 August 2005, 'Tackling Terrorism—Behaviours Unacceptable in the UK' www.press.homeoffice.gov.uk/press-

The Government's ongoing work to tackle terrorism and extremism took another step forward today as the Home Secretary, Charles Clarke, published a list of certain type of behaviours that will form the basis for excluding and deporting individuals from the UK.

This announcement, one can guess, was made primarily to appeal to tabloid newspapers that had been campaigning against the continued presence in Britain of a small number of outspoken Muslim clerics. In common with many New Labour anti-terrorism measures, it concerned perception as much as reality. The impression given that the twelve point plan would increase the chances of deporting the 'preachers of hate' was misleading. Even the 'notes to editors' at the bottom of the Home Secretary's press release relating to the Home Secretary's list of 'unacceptable behaviours' stated: 'the list published today does not give the Home Secretary new powers.'

The problem with deporting unwanted foreign nationals from the UK does not lie with the 1971 Immigration Act, which actually gives the Home Secretary wide discretion. The difficulty lies with the European Convention on Human Rights (ECHR), which makes it illegal to deport an individual to a country where he may be subject to torture. The Labour government had put the ECHR into British law in 1998. At the time of the 5 August announcement, the British government had no way of overcoming this difficulty. The government has since sought to engineer a solution by negotiating memoranda of understanding, which would give assurances about the treatment of deportees. In the last six months such memoranda have been negotiated with just three countries: Lebanon, Jordan and Libya. However, not one has yet led to a deportation. In addition, the courts have yet to test whether these 'assurances' are sufficient to overcome the obstacle of returning people to countries which permit torture. Scarcely any of the measures announced by the Prime Minister have yet become law. His claim that the twelve point plan 'set a comprehensive framework for action in dealing with the terrorist threat in Britain' is absurd. It can more accurately be described as a

releases/Tackling_ Terrorism-Behaviours_Un?version=1

fairly successful short term device for dealing with calls for action from tabloid newspaper editors.

## MUSLIM WORKING GROUPS

In the wake of the London bombings, the Prime Minister made a series of announcements aimed at averting another catastrophe. One of the most visible was the setting up of seven task forces to investigate Muslim extremism and to recommend initiatives for tackling it. This was a considerable enterprise by any standards, requiring deep learning and insight, and generous resources. But Tony Blair's task forces into the roots of Muslim extremism were given six weeks to do their business. They seem to have met just three times before reaching their conclusions. One of the Muslim leaders involved, the Liberal Democrat peeress Kishwer Falkner, told us:

When we agreed to be on the Working Groups, and we were told what the deadlines were, we were taken aback. We spoke to one another and queried whether we were just being set up as a tokenistic exercise, because it didn't seem to me, in the middle of August, when half the country's on holiday, that two or three meetings of a couple of hours each would set to right a host of intractable and difficult long-term problems to do with how we coexist, how we integrate with each other.

Falkner feels that the recommendation of her working parties were second guessed by the Prime Minister's twelve point plan, announced just two weeks after the working parties were set up. She says she was:

…completely dismayed within days of being set up to discover in the speech the Prime Minister made on 5 August, that he was proceeding full steam ahead with a raft of measures, without waiting for us to come up with our recommendations, or indeed, our analysis of the problems. And the raft of measures was completely counter to reducing alienation and extremism. In fact, if anything, it was going to increase alienation in terms of the Muslim community.

Her criticism was echoed by Haras Rafiq, co-founder of Bridges TV (UK), a Muslim television organisation which will start broadcasting later this year. He told us:

The brief was to find ways or find a solution to the problem of extremism and radicalisation within the Muslim community. Now let's just reflect on that. Find a solution for extremism and radicalisation in the Muslim community in the UK, that's a huge piece of work. It isn't something that can be tackled, you know, in the space of a month, two months. The whole process smacked to me a little bit of presentationalism, and to be seen to be doing something rather than actually producing an effective and constructive piece of work.

It is hard to regard these task forces as a great deal more than some shallow spin from the government. In the three years before the London bombings, the government had commissioned two major enquiries into the problems of Muslim segregation and extremism—Ted Cantle's report in the wake of the Bradford riots and a government report of 2004, *Young Muslims and Extremism*—and largely dismissed both. The idea that Tony Blair's hurriedly-formed and short-lived Muslim working groups could provide a better analysis than either of these two earlier studies was absurd.

## A FALSE ANALYSIS OF TERROR

The British government has persistently failed to tell the truth either to itself or to the British public about the terror threat in Britain. These failures of diagnosis have led to failures of response. An example is the Prime Minister's denial that there is a connection between the Iraq War and domestic terrorism. That denial is not merely false. It also inhibits the kind of deep understanding of the motives of Muslim terrorists which the Prime Minister presumably wants. It causes intelligence experts to ignore some obvious lines of inquiry, and to adopt others that are less fruitful. Before the invasion of Iraq British intelligence, under pressure from the Government, falsely identified something that was not present—weapons of mass destruction. There is now a danger that the Government's refusal to acknowledge the link between terror and Iraq will cause the intelligence services to steer away from something that palpably is present—namely burning Muslim anger about British policy in Iraq and the wider Middle East.

But there is a wider problem: that Government policy appears to be dictated by short-termism and an obsession with newspaper headlines. The prime minister's response to the terror threat has been unfortunate. Again and again he has rushed into poorly drafted legislation which severely curtails the liberty of British subjects, and which in due course turns out to be bad law. The long-term effect is the creation of anger, disillusion, distrust and the further alienation of the Muslim community. In the end it is unrealistic to expect that the problem of Muslim terrorism in Britain will be dealt with by meretricious legislation. On the contrary, only a profound and subtle response, requiring full engagement with the needs and aspirations of Muslim communities, will succeed. There is very little sign of this, as the superficiality of the Muslim working parties set up after the London bombings demonstrates. In the meantime, much of the government response to terror, while claiming to confront the problem, may actually be making things worse in the medium to long term. An example of this is the hurried and panicky proposals for ninety days detention without trial. As the intelligence expert Crispin Black said to us:[32]

Everything we do in response to terrorism should have two factors in mind. One is hearts and minds and the other is the flow of intelligence. ninety days is a very good example: would that improve our performance in securing or protecting of shoring up the hearts and minds of the small numbers in our Muslim communities that might be affected by this virus of terrorism? Yes or no? It seems to me no. It was an over the top measure. If you sitting, say, in a Muslim part of Yorkshire and you are looking at your telephone thinking those three young men that I saw last night outside the garage, maybe I should phone the police? And you've suddenly been presented with the fact that they can be detained for ninety days, does that make you more or less likely to produce that information to the authorities?

---

32  For an invaluable analysis of the fundamental flaws in our current approach to calibrating and understanding the terrorist threat, see C. Black, 7-7: The London Bombings: What Went Wrong? (London, 2006).

## CONSEQUENCES FOR PUBLIC TRUST

The defeat in the House of Commons of the Government's proposals for ninety days detention without trial for terrorist suspects was represented at the time as an indication of Tony Blair's political weakness. This analysis missed the point. That Commons defeat signalled a national crisis in public trust in politicians, the police and the security services.

Consider this: the Prime Minister of the day, fully backed by the police, had thrown his weight behind a measure he described as crucial for national security and the fight against terrorism. And yet it was comfortably rejected by MPs.

This collapse in trust has come about because few people now believe what the Prime Minister, the security services and the police tell us about security matters. Before the Iraq War, the state security services, encouraged by elected politicians, issued assurances about the existence of weapons of mass destruction in Iraq. These turned out to be false. There is now a comparable dissonance between public statements made by Government ministers and the truth about domestic terror. This dissonance is a massive problem. Britain today faces a threat from international and domestic terrorism which is far more dangerous and insidious than anything it has confronted before. We need to trust our politicians, our police, and the media. But that trust has been betrayed.

# APPENDIX I

## *The Twelve Point Plan*[33]

1 (a) *Take steps to deport suspected terrorists to countries which practise torture; amend the Human Rights Act if necessary.*

This seems to be happening. Three memoranda of understanding (MoU) have been signed, with Jordan, Lebanon and Libya; other MoU are pending. And the HRA could still be amended. However, legal advice from Amnesty and others suggests the courts are likely to reject these documents as guarantees against torture. In addition, the MoU signed so far do not provide cast iron guarantees against torture and execution and it is still unclear how compliance will be monitored.

1 (b) *Draw up a list of 'extremist' websites, bookshops etc and deport anyone who 'actively engages' with them.*

Nothing has been heard about this. There is no indication in the Home Secretary's progress report that this is being taken forward.

2 *A new offence of glorifying terrorism.*

This has been one of the most controversial parts of the Terrorism Bill and will be subject of a tight vote in the Commons when the Bill returns from Lords. There is a significant possibility that the Government will lose.

3 *Bar terrorists from claiming asylum.*

This was already law. Terrorists are already ineligible for asylum under the terms of the Geneva Convention. The government is however seeking to extend the circumstances in which the bar applies in the Immigration, Asylum and Nationality Bill (currently in the Lords).

---

33 This Appendix has been prepared by Waleed Ghani and is in part based on Charles Clarke's progress report (www.press.homeoffice.gov.uk/Speeches/15-12-05-st-ct-progressreport? view=Standard). I am also grateful to Matthew Grimshaw for his analysis.

4 *Consult on extending powers to strip individuals of their British citizenship.*

No formal consultation has taken place, although an extension to the Home Secretary's powers to strip individuals of their citizenship has been included in the Immigration, Asylum and Nationality Bill.

5 *Consult on setting a maximum time limit on extradition cases involving terrorism.*

Nothing has been heard about this. There is no indication in the Home Secretary's progress report that this is being taken forward. It is also very hard to see how such a limit could work in practice. If the limit is reached, does the extradition attempt fail? If so, this would provide an incentive for the defence to delay proceedings. Extradition could not legally go ahead without judicial authorisation.

6 *Significant extension to pre-charge detention of terrorist suspects.*

This measure was defeated in the House of Commons with the Government's proposed ninety day extension reduced to twenty-eight days.

7 *Extend the use of control orders.*

This seems to have been dropped. The Prime Minister did not make it clear whether he intended to make changes to the control order system. There was no mention of control orders in the Terrorism Bill. However, further terrorism legislation expected later in the spring; and the number of control orders in force has increased to eight.

8 *Increase the number of special judges hearing terrorism cases.*

This is happening. The Department for Constitutional Affairs is reviewing the capacity of the courts, specialist tribunals and the judiciary to deal with existing and anticipated caseloads relating to terrorism, with a view to meeting the demands of counterterrorism. The judiciary has put in hand new procedures for the allocation, handling and case management of such trials. The court service is making an additional suitable courtroom available.

9  *Proscribe Hizb-ut-Tahrir and Al Mujahiroun.*

This is happening. The Terrorism Bill widens the criteria for proscription and the list of proscribed organisations will be reviewed on the basis of the new Bill.

10 (a) *Review the threshold of competence in English needed to acquire British citizenship.*

This is happening. Measures contained in the Immigration, Asylum and Nationality Bill address this point.

10 (b) *Set up a Commission on Integration with Muslim groups.*

Muslim Working Groups were set up in the summer of 2005, but not very satisfactorily (see Chapter 6).

11 *Consult on new powers to close places of worship used for omenting extremism.*

This was dropped by the Home Office in December.

12 (a) *FCO to develop a database of individuals whose activities or views present a threat to UK security.*

This has been achieved.

12 (b) *Exclude anyone who appears on this database and only allow them to appeal the decision from outside the UK.*

This is happening. Some individuals have been deported; changes to the rules to allow 'non-suspensive' appeals (i.e. post deportation) are contained in the Immigration, Asylum and Nationality Bill. Tighter security at ports, biometric tests, etc are also proposed.

# APPENDIX II

*The Metropolitan Police Press Statement of 6 January 2003*

Joint statement from MPS Assistant Commissioner David Veness and the Deputy Chief Medical Officer Dr Pat Troop:

In the early hours of Sunday, 5 January 2003, six men and one woman were arrested under the Terrorism Act 2000 at premises in North and East London by officers from the Metropolitan Police Anti-Terrorist Branch. The six men, aged in their late teens, 20s and 30s, remain in custody and are being interviewed by Anti Terrorist Branch Officers. The woman has been released. This successful joint operation between the Anti-Terrorist Branch, MPS Special Branch and the Security Service follows receipt of intelligence. A quantity of material and items of equipment were found at a residential premises in Wood Green, north London, where one of the men was arrested. This material has been analysed at the Defence Science and Technology Laboratories at Porton Down. A small amount of the material recovered from the Wood Green premises has tested positive for the presence of ricin poison. Ricin is a toxic material which if ingested or inhaled can be fatal. Our primary concern is the safety of the public and the police have worked closely with the Department of Health throughout.

Tests were carried out on the material and it was confirmed this morning that toxic material was present. The Department is now alerting the health service, including primary care, about these developments. It is also ensuring that the Health Service is able to provide advice to the public, including through NHS Direct. If any new developments have implications for public safety we will ensure that the public is informed immediately. Intensive police investigations are continuing and forensic analysis of the premises in Wood Green will take some time to complete. We have previously said that London and indeed the rest of the UK continues to face a range of terrorist threats from a number of different groups. And while our message is still 'alert not alarm we would reiterate our earlier appeals for the public to remain vigilant and aware and report anything suspicious to police. We are asking people to be vigilant about their surroundings, particularly in public places and if they see anything suspicious to dial 999 immediately. We are also encouraging the public to call the free confidential Anti-Terrorist Hotline 0800 789 321 if they have any information about people or activities that could be linked to terrorism. The Metropolitan Police is doing everything possible to combat the threat of terrorism but it is only with the help and support of the public that we can reduce the harm which it causes.

## NOTES TO EDITORS

1. Ricin is a protein toxin that is derived from castor oil seeds. It inhibits protein synthesis and has widespread toxic effects on the body. These include damage to most organ systems and a combination of pulmonary, liver, renal and immunological failure may lead to death. No antidote is known: treatment can only be supportive.

2. Clinical features of ricin: The early symptoms depend on the route of exposure. Fever, gastrointestinal upset, coughing may be amongst the first effects noted. Absorption via the lung as a result of exposure to aerosolized toxin leads to particularly serious lung damage including pulmonary oedema and adult respiratory distress syndrome. Ingestion of ricin causes irritation of the gut: gastroenteritis, bloody diarrhoea and vomiting. Effects on the central nervous system have been reported including seizures and CNS depression. The effects of exposure to ricin may be delayed for some hours after exposure and patients who develop a fever may consult their own doctors.

3. We placed a full range of guidance on ricin and other chemical and biological agents on the PHLS website. In September 2002, we drew this to the attention of PCTs. We have kept the specialist poisons service alert to concerns.

# CHRONOLOGY[34]

7 DECEMBER 2000 Terrorism Act 2000 passed.

11 SEPTEMBER 2001 Al-Qaeda attacks on the World Trade Center and Pentagon.

21 DECEMBER 2001 Anti-terrorism, Crime and Security Act 2001 passed in direct response to the World Trade Center and Pentagon attacks.

5 JANUARY 2003 Six men are arrested after a flat is raided in Wood Green, London. Police find recipes for ricin, and ingredients and equipment for extracting ricin in the flat.

6 JANUARY 2003 Scotland Yard issue a press release in the names of Deputy Chief Medical Officer Dr Pat Troop and Metropolitan Police Assistant Commissioner David Veness. This press release claims that 'a small amount of the material recovered from the Wood Green premises has tested positive for the presence of ricin poison.'

7 JANUARY 2003 Home Secretary David Blunkett and Health Secretary John Reid issue a joint statement stating that 'traces of ricin' have been found at the Wood Green flat. On the same day, chemical weapons experts at the government research facility at Porton Down carry out further and more accurate tests into the presence of ricin. These tests establish that there was no ricin at the Wood Green flat. This information was, apparently, not passed on to the British government until late March.

14 JANUARY 2003 Police raid a flat in Crumpsall, Manchester. They find Bourgass and another alleged conspirator. After a violent struggle, Bourgass murders DC Stephen Oake.

5 FEBRUARY 2003 In a speech to the UN Security Council on the need to launch a pre-emptive war against Iraq, US Secretary of State Colin Powell cites the British ricin case as an example of Iraq's malignantinfluence throughout the world.

---

34 This Appendix has been prepared by Waleed Ghani.

# 6

# BRITAIN AND THE IRA:
# LEGACIES OF RESTRAINT

## *Jonathan Stevenson*

The United Kingdom's experience with Irish republican terrorists demonstrates that a democratic state can effectively counter terrorism by bestowing the fruits of democracy on the popular base of terrorist support. The institutions of democracy itself—in particular, access to electoral politics and due process of law—promote pluralism, transparency and equity. These features constitute a kind of 'soft power' through which democracies can tame destabilising indigenous forces. By the same token, the long British encounter with the IRA demonstrates that overstating or mischaracterising the terrorist threat for political advantage in the end usually redounds to the insurgency's advantage. The UK's relative success in containing and ultimately reducing Provisional Irish Republican Army (IRA) violence reflects the government's evolved understanding that attempts to leverage the despicability of terrorism to impose hard security measures for political as well as operational gain don't usually work. Doing just that, though, is often a temptation that is difficult to overcome. The fundamental reason is simple: the threat of terrorist violence is a power multiplier in a democracy, so it enables whatever group wields it to punch exasperatingly more than its electoral weight.

For a government stunned by terrorism or insurgency, the frequent—and usually errant—impulse is to try to defeat this phenomenon mainly with stentorian opprobrium and extraordinary exceptions to civil standards. For example, in the late 1980s, British security

forces appeared sporadically to apply a tacit 'shoot to kill' policy. Special Air Service (SAS) commandos in 1987 ambushed eight armed
IRA men who were trying to blow up a police station and shot them
all dead in Loughgall, and in 1988 killed three unarmed IRA operatives in Gibraltar as they attempted to escape capture while conducting reconnaissance for a bombing against British military assets and
personnel. The political fallout of these enforcement actions arguably
outweighed their operational effect. Republican lawyers succeeded in
getting a special inquest into the first incident, and won a judgment
in the European Court of Human Rights that the second incident
involved the illegal use of excessive force.

## The erratic British learning curve

The IRA's ceasefire materialised in 1994 mainly because modern
British democracy had substantially redressed most of the IRA's
ground-level grievances. Between the partition of Ireland in 1921
that ended the Anglo-Irish War and the inception of British direct
rule in 1972, Northern Ireland's Protestant unionist majority dominated the devolved parliamentary assembly, which the 1922 Anglo-
Irish Treaty partitioning Ireland had validated. Informally known as
'Stormont' after the grand neo-classical building in which it met, the
parliament's political and social marginalisation of Catholics (then
a 35 per cent minority in the province), was decidedly unfair, even
though there was relative stability during Stormont's fifty-year tenure.[1] From partition, however, Irish republicans had opposed the political principle—known as the 'consent principle' to unionists, and
the 'unionist veto' to nationalists—that any change in the province's

---

1   In Northern Ireland, Protestants now constitute about 58 per cent of
    the population, Catholics about 42 per cent. Virtually all Protestants are
    'unionists,' which means they support the union with Britain; the vast
    majority of Catholics are 'nationalists', meaning they wish the Republic of
    Ireland and Northern Ireland to unite and become one nation. Unionists
    who have practised or endorsed terrorist violence in order to preserve the
    union are generally called 'loyalists'. Nationalists who have used or supported
    terrorism to try to effect Irish unification are known as 'republicans'.

constitutional status had to be approved by a majority of its electorate. When civil rights protests in the late 1960s provoked a violent loyalist backlash, the IRA acquired the popular momentum to build its membership and reassert its rejection of the consent principle. The IRA developed the position that Catholics could be protected only if Ireland were united and the British ejected—by terrorist violence if necessary. Loyalist paramilitaries insisted that Northern Ireland retain British sovereignty and were also willing to engage in terrorism. Thus in 1969, the conflict quaintly known as 'the troubles' began.

In 1972, political violence in Northern Ireland peaked at 476 deaths in one year. Westminster deemed Stormont to have lost the confidence of the populace and unable to contain the deteriorating security situation, prorogued the devolved parliament and assumed direct rule. For nearly twenty five years, the 'constitutional question' of whether Northern Ireland should remain part of the United Kingdom or unite with the Republic of Ireland was the only major issue in Northern Irish politics. Given the stark polarity of this question, little lasting progress was made toward resolving the conflict.

Before London took over the governance of Northern Ireland, it committed serious excesses as a sovereign power. These included the British army's internment of over 300 republican (and a few loyalist) terrorist suspects beginning in 1971. Internment, though premised on civil emergency, involved the detention of large numbers of people for lengthy periods on the basis of stale intelligence. Many of those interned were, in fact, harmless older men, seized by virtue involvement in past—and generally feckless—campaigns waged by the Provisional IRA's weaker predecessors. Thus, although the British government hoped to gain the political backing of the wider Catholic community in arraying apparent bad actors en masse, the thinness of the link between those interned and actual threats, coupled with the deprivation of due process implicit in internment, won the IRA recruits. One of the men taken into custody was the father of Gerry Adams, whose resistance to British rule was thereby galvanised. Adams became the commander of the IRA's Belfast

Brigade and later, of course, the republican movement's most durable and important political leader. To make matters worse, several internees were subjected to abusive interrogation techniques and later won lawsuits against the Crown. Internment also fuelled public protests, which the Northern Irish government made illegal. As protest marches proliferated nonetheless, the British government again sought to demonise the wider Catholic community for supporting them. On January 29, 1972, the Royal Ulster Constabulary and the British army issued a joint statement that read, in pertinent part, as follows:

Experience this year has already shown that attempted marches often end in violence and [sic] must have been foreseen by the organisers. Clearly, the responsibility for this violence and the consequences of it must rest fairly and squarely on the shoulders of those who encourage people to break the law. The security forces have a duty to take action against those who set out to break the law.

The next day, during a march in Londonderry, British soldiers shot dead thirteen unarmed Catholic civilians and one IRA man. The incident came to be known as 'Bloody Sunday' and has stoked Catholic grievances and republican armed action and political protest for almost thirty five years.

In the early 1970s, then, politically-motivated hard counter-terrorism measures backfired on the British government. In effectively imputing a real security threat to the entire Catholic community, and justifying harsh measures with the imperative of public safety, it had in fact increased the support of that community for the terrorists. But the British learned. Internment was ended in 1975. In 1976, the British government instituted a programme of 'criminalisation' and 'normalisation' of counter-terrorism. The idea was to ignore IRA protestations of its political ends and focus on its violent means. Since the latter were illegal, IRA volunteers would be treated as criminals, dealt with mainly by the police rather than the army, duly tried for their acts in criminal courts, and if convicted sent to prison. Meanwhile, the larger law-abiding Catholic community would be treated with respect. The inequities it had suffered in terms of civil rights, housing, and employment under Stormont were substantially ameliorated through Westminster legislation. Under direct rule, while there were occasional excesses and isolated instances of collusion with loyalist paramilitaries by the security forces, local support for the IRA waned and political backing for a non-violent nationalist party—the Social Democratic and Labour Party (SDLP)—grew.

By 1980, the IRA was weak: penetrated by the security forces, lacking in seasoned recruits, losing community backing and much of the sympathy in the wider world that it had garnered. Indeed, in that year, Amnesty International—which had criticised the British government for internment and rough interrogation techniques—now condemned IRA assassinations of prison officers, declared that imprisoned IRA members were not 'prisoners of conscience', and refused to support their attempts (generally, refusals to wear state prison clothing) to secure political status. A precipitous error of judgment on the part of Prime Minister Margaret Thatcher's government, however, revived the IRA's prospects. In 1981, over the course of seven months, ten republican hunger-strikers died in defiance of Thatcher's refusal, essentially, to let republican prisoners wear their own clothes. She felt that the IRA had to be deprived of the trappings of political status both on principle and to limit its popular trajectory. In the event, the hunger-strikes so moved local and global observers that they revived the IRA's political prospects and compelled Thatcher largely to accede to a demand which, at least in retrospect, was rather modest. The Iranians named a street in Tehran after Bobby Sands, the first IRA martyr. American donations to the Irish Northern Aid Committee (Noraid) skyrocketed. Thatcher later provided the IRA with a less dramatic source of public sympathy in banning the broadcast of all republican spokespeople—a measure that made London seem both harsh in suppressing political speech and ridiculous in spawning a cottage industry of Gerry Adams impersonators.

Eventually, however, the British government regained its acumen. The most rigorous fair employment laws in Europe, verging on affirmative action, came into effect in Northern Ireland.[2] Workers are entitled to damages even if they have been only indirectly and unintentionally discriminated against. Such provisions, though often resented by the Protestant majority, have helped close the Catholic/Protestant employment gap in Northern Ireland (and have almost certainly kept some young Catholics from joining the IRA). Sinn Fein, the IRA's political wing, had been made legal in 1974 and was continually encouraged to participate in the democratic process. Of course, neither the IRA nor the far more numerous contingent of non-violent Irish nationalists abandoned the goal of a united Ireland. Violence continued apace for over twenty five years. Ritual cross-community murder, as well as intra-community 'self-policing' in the form of punishment beatings, kneecappings, and executions, claimed roughly a hundred deaths per year. In all, political violence claimed the lives of about 3,500 people—mostly innocent civilians.[3] Nevertheless, the combination of effective counterterrorism and enlightened direct rule—reflecting Britain's general resistance to playing politics with terrorism—weakened the IRA's argument for 'physical force' as a means to a united Ireland. Persistent British and unionist resistance to IRA terrorism, in turn, convinced even hard-line IRA men that they could not win a strictly military struggle: Northern Ireland would not become Britain's Algeria.

This reality had a calming effect on the IRA. In 1986 the republican movement adopted the so-called 'Armalite and ballot-box' approach.

---

2  Known as 'positive discrimination' in Europe, affirmative action is technically illegal in the UK. But because Northern Irish Catholics avail themselves so readily of the thoroughgoing fair employment laws, and the Fair Employment Commission there is so attuned to the political sensitivities of the workplace, the fair employment laws have had the effect of an affirmative action policy. Note that those laws were enacted specifically with an eye towards improving ground-level conditions for Catholics in order to defuse the political conflict—and diminish terrorism—in Northern Ireland.

3  See, e.g., Malcolm Sutton, *An Index of Deaths from the Conflict in Ireland, 1969-1993* (Belfast, 1994), p. 206.

More selective terrorism was supplemented with straightforward politicking, which to many made Sinn Fein the IRA's acceptable public identity and its president, Gerry Adams, the movement's more agreeable face.[4] The constitutional question became more emotional and nationalistic than substantive. Nationalist opinion became more moderate, the IRA more politically sophisticated, and Sinn Fein a stronger political force. In parallel, the low-intensity military conflict between the IRA and British troops settled into an indefinite stalemate. Furthermore, as the Cold War drew to a close, the United Kingdom disavowed the province's strategic and economic value. In the Downing Street Declaration of December 1993, the British and Irish prime ministers publicly relaxed their countries' claims on Northern Ireland and left its constitutional future wholly to the electoral will of the province's population. The Clinton administration took a special interest in Northern Ireland, arranging a visa long denied to Adams.[5] In apparent acknowledgement of these developments, the IRA declared a unilateral ceasefire on 31 August 1994.[6] Six weeks later, on October 13, the two primary loyalist terrorist

---

4   There is another key reason. Gerry Adams evolved from a West Belfast bartender and IRA leader into an ambitious political figure, singularly articulate and charismatic among republicans. He was no longer satisfied to be a pariah, and sought worldly power. Implicit American guarantees of support enabled Adams to convince the larger republican movement that a unilateral ceasefire would yield political dividends that continued terrorism could not.

5   The US contribution to the peace process tends to be overvalued, particularly by Anglo-Irish and Irish-American commentators. For a particularly grandiose account, see Conor O'Clery, *The Greening of the White House* (Dublin, 1997). Third parties, whether the United States or other external actors, are limited as to how much they can do to broker peace when a terrorist insurgency is involved, and even more limited as to what they can do to sustain peace in the long term. See Jonathan Stevenson, 'Northern Ireland: Treating Terrorists as Statesmen,' *Foreign Policy*, no. 105, Winter 1996-97, pp. 125-40.

6   See Michael Cox, 'Bringing in the "International": The IRA Ceasefire and the End of the Cold War', *International Affairs*, vol. 73, no. 4, October 1997, pp. 671-93; Jonathan Stevenson, 'Peace in Northern Ireland: Why Now?,' *Foreign Policy*, no. 112, Fall 1998, pp. 41-54.

groups, the Ulster Freedom Fighters/Ulster Defence Association (UFF/UDA) and the Ulster Volunteer Force (UVF), announced their ceasefires. A fraught, drawn-out peace process ensued, but in April 1998, it resulted, quite improbably, in the Belfast Agreement (also known as the Good Friday Agreement), which provides for a devolved power-sharing government in Northern Ireland and sub-sovereign cross-border agencies jointly run by the Northern Ireland assembly and the Irish parliament. The agreement was approved on May 22 in simultaneous referendums in Northern Ireland (by 71 per cent) and the Irish Republic (by 94 per cent).[7]

## *The Belfast Agreement and 'constructive' ambiguity*

On account of the British government's implicit understanding of the constraints that hardliners impose on the IRA and Sinn Fein, so-called constructive ambiguity on disarmament was built into the Good Friday Agreement. Whether this aspect of playing politics with terrorism has in fact been 'constructive' is debatable. By its terms, the Belfast Agreement does not strictly require IRA decommissioning, but merely establishes it as an objective of the peace process 'in the context of the implementation of the overall settlement'. In the run-up to the Agreement, however, David Trimble—leader of the Ulster Unionist Party (UUP), which was then the province's largest—needed London's affirmation that Sinn Fein would not be allowed to participate in the executive unless the IRA had first substantially disarmed. On Good Friday, April 10, 1998, the day before the Agreement was signed, Trimble received a letter from Tony Blair in which he stated that 'the effect of the decommissioning section of the agreement, with decommissioning schemes coming into effect in June [1998], is that the process of decommissioning should begin straight away,' and clearly implied that meaningful decommissioning after six months, the British government would 'support changes' to provisions of the Bel-

---

7   For a historical précis of the Northern Irish conflict, see, for example, Jonathan Stevenson, *'We Wrecked the Place:' Contemplating an End to the Northern Irish Troubles* (New York, 1996), pp. 7–30.

fast Agreement 'preventing' uncooperative parties from holding office in the devolved assembly's governing executive.

The letter finessed the timing issue, but its obvious intent was to reassure Trimble that the British government would honour his wish to deny Sinn Fein executive participation in the absence of decommissioning. Unionists argued that insofar as such reassurance was an integral part of the quid pro quo, it was effectively part of the Agreement. Thus, they contended, the UUP council's allowing Sinn Fein into government prior to IRA disarmament in December 1999 signified the re-negotiation of the 'no guns, no government' condition and justified the imposition of a shorter deadline set by the UUP. When the IRA missed that deadline and Westminster suspended the devolved assembly in February 2000 as a consequence, Sinn Fein countered that the Agreement also specified that decommissioning must begin only 'in the context of . . . overall implementation'. This 'context' was republican code for loyalist disarmament, the literal or de facto disbandment of the then-88 per cent Protestant police force (formerly known as the Royal Ulster Constabulary, but in 2001 renamed the Police Service of Northern Ireland as a concession to nationalists), and a comprehensive British military withdrawal.

When the peace process began in 1994, the republicans' public stance was that because the IRA was not defeated militarily it was not obliged to relinquish any arms. As it became clear that unionists and the British government would insist on some form of decommissioning, Sinn Fein changed its position, maintaining that the Belfast Agreement requires only that the party use its influence to attain IRA decommissioning. When the assembly was suspended in February 2000 after less than three months over the IRA's refusal to decommission, Sinn Fein argued that with devolution delayed by the decommissioning impasse, republicans had not had enough time to establish the 'trust' in devolved institutions that the agreement's original timetable would have allowed.[8]

---

8   Unionists consider the original deadline to be 22 May 2000. Although that date occurs nowhere in the text of the Belfast Agreement, the referendums

Thus, ambiguity—without which an agreement admittedly might have been impossible—permitted unionists and republicans alike to construe the agreement as they wished. Yet the IRA's unwillingness to decommission and unionists' insistence that it do so continually plunged the assembly into crisis. The IRA's agreement in May 2000 to allow international arms inspectors (former African National Congress secretary-general Cyril Ramaphosa and former President of Finland Martti Ahtisaari) did not satisfy unionists, but did, in effect, allow the IRA to retain control of the inspection process. All the while, security forces were under tacit but unmistakable pressure to relax anti-terrorist enforcement efforts. In the event, the IRA allowed only three inspections. Nevertheless, Sinn Fein governed with unionists for thirteen months until Trimble's July 2001 resignation.

In political terms, unionists' insistence on decommissioning has not served them well. It has decreased their leverage over other issues of serious concern (in particular, police reform) and has afforded Sinn Fein a greater degree of control over the agenda than it might otherwise have had. But the unionist community is the operative majority in Northern Ireland. For better or worse, it entrenched IRA decommissioning as a moral imperative. Sinn Fein, for its part, has consistently argued that the key ingredient of the peace process is not a formal handover of weapons but rather the integrity of the IRA ceasefire.[9] At the same time, it has cleverly exploited the unionists' immovable preoccupation with decommissioning to control the political process, understanding that because

---

approving the Agreement were held on 22 May 1998 and thus, under the Agreement's specification of 'two years following the... referendums,' established the later date as the target for decommissioning.

9   The IRA cessation lasted from September 1994 to February 1996 when the Canary Wharf bombing ended it, was reinstated in July 1997, and since then has largely held up. Although the ceasefire declared by the two main loyalist groups in October 1994 started deteriorating in 2000, it substantially endured for over five years and loyalist violence still has not resumed full force.

the IRA possesses the weapons it can dictate unionist behaviour through flexibility or rigidity.

## Asymmetries of enlightenment

In Northern Ireland itself, overall British judiciousness has afforded republicans some further significant political advantages. Super-majority and consensus requirements in the devolved assembly effectively accord disproportionate power to nationalists, and the allocation to nationalists of seats on the assembly's ruling executive exceeds their share of the general population. These exceptional features of the political arrangements in Northern Ireland distort pure democracy, but such power-sharing artifacts may be necessary for stability in a historically divided society. (They are modest compared, for example, to the dispensation that Turkish Cypriots are seeking in Cyprus.) It is also worth observing that the IRA's willingness to participate in a devolved government under British sovereignty—and thus tacitly concede the current legitimacy of the British state in Northern Ireland—did represent a radical departure from its historical position and was no doubt ideologically painful. At the same time, it is plain that the IRA coldly calculated the benefits that would flow from that concession. Chief among these were leverage over the Labour Party in Britain; a freer hand to rally financial and diplomatic support in the United States; and a higher political trajectory in Irish politics. Indeed, whereas Sinn Fein's popular support had peaked at 10–12 per cent before 1994, by the time the Belfast Agreement was signed it stood at about 18 per cent. This rise had improved conditions for agreement in several ways—in particular, by engendering greater confidence among the non-violent parties—unionists, the British government and the Irish government, as well as the United States as 'honest broker'—that the republican conversion was worthwhile to the movement and therefore sustainable.[10]

---

10 Several pre-existing realities reinforced the parties' confidence: a military stalemate; Sinn Féin's tentative political success in Northern Ireland; good

More broadly, the IRA's adherence to a non-violent agenda was and remains contingent on political conditions it deems favourable. Among those is the heightened intolerance for political violence engendered by the 9/11 attacks.[11] A number of developments could change the IRA's assessment, and send it back to terrorism. The Belfast Agreement requires that a majority of Northern Irish voters approve unification. In effect, any such approval would require a Catholic majority in Northern Ireland. The 'demographic time bomb' on which republicans are relying for ultimate victory could fizzle out. While the Catholic share of Northern Ireland's population has been increasing, Catholic and Protestant birthrates may be converging. Moreover, there is firm evidence that up to 20 per cent of Catholics candidly favour the union with Britain; some analyses put that figure as high as one-third. Thus, despite its nods towards peace, the IRA remained on a war footing for years after the Belfast Agreement was signed. On St Patrick's Day 2002, the Police Service of Northern Ireland's Special Branch headquarters in East Belfast was broken into, and sensitive intelligence files were stolen, including those concerning informants against the IRA. The Provisional IRA may have been involved. Then, in April, police uncovered a 'hit list' of senior British and Northern Irish officials in West Belfast. Also in April, Russian security services informed British military intelligence that the Provisionals had purchased at least 20 sophisticated AN-94 armour-piercing assault rifles from Russian sources in fall 2001. This demonstrated the intentional and cynical operational emptiness of the decommissioning gestures early in the decade: as the IRA put old weapons 'beyond use', they were simply replaced with newer and more effective ones.

---

bilateral relations between the two 'mother countries'; and, not least, the well-entrenched observance of the rule of law in each of those countries (particularly the United Kingdom, whose sovereignty Northern Ireland retained).

11 See Jonathan Stevenson, 'The Two Terrorisms,' *New York Times*, 2 December 2003, p. A31.

There is also some evidence that British and Irish forbearance emboldened the IRA to undertake provocations elsewhere. In April 2002, a report to Congress by the US State Department's Office of Counterterrorism substantiated suspicions that, in direct contravention of American security interests, up to fifteen Provisional IRA men had joined Iranian, Cuban and possibly Basque terrorists in Colombia between 1998 and 2001, and trained the anti-American Revolutionary Armed Forces of Colombia (FARC) in urban terror techniques, including the use of secondary explosives and homemade mortars—both IRA innovations. Palestinian pipe bombs found in the West Bank appeared to be of IRA design, and Palestinian snipers were suspected of having been trained by the IRA. But after the arrests in Colombia of the three IRA men for training the FARC in August 2001 and then the September 11 attacks, any American tolerance for terrorism in general and IRA coyness on decommissioning in particular evaporated.

Although Washington's diplomatic support for Sinn Fein dampened, the IRA and Sinn Fein continued to receive public credit for walking the walk and talking the talk of peaceful politics. During the three years following the signing of the Belfast Agreement, Sinn Fein's backing in Northern Ireland increased to roughly 24 per cent of the electorate, overtaking the SDLP's share of the vote. Perversely, this made it more difficult for London to exert political pressure on the group. Yet unionists increasingly clamoured for the IRA's disarmament. Republicans, for their part, refused to disarm or even to forswear a return to the armed struggle. In the calculations of republican leaders, there was no need to do so: erstwhile IRA targets would remain relieved that they were not being bombed or shot at regardless of any declaration that the war was over. Moreover, republicans believed, preserving the salience of the threat of retrogression to terrorism might move some of those targets to accord republicans advantages that were vastly disproportionate to their electoral power. Sinn Fein is only the second-largest party in a discrete part of the United Kingdom that contains less than 3 per cent of the country's total population. As of May 2005, only five members of Parliament (out of 659 in total) were from Sinn Fein, and they did not participate in national government. Yet, as one journalist has noted, the IRA's threat of violence 'makes the British government dance'.[12]

If the British Governments's civil restraint in the face of terrorism, and its corollary acceptance of Sinn Fein as a legitimate political force, promoted the completion of a formal negotiated agreement, that restraint may have also encouraged the corruption of that agreement's implementation. Downing Street tried to get republicans to disarm with concessions on police reform and demilitarisation that were highly problematic for unionists, and politically futile. Blair never took a harder line, even though there was one readily available. For example, he could have levied threats that police reforms would be held in abeyance unless weapons were handed over. Instead, from unionist standpoints, Blair repeatedly cut Sinn Fein extra slack. Though the Belfast Agreement could be construed as pledging its signatories to complete paramilitary disarmament by May 2000, when that deadline arrived the goalpost was simply moved to May 2001; the deadline was then put off through legislation until 2007.

Unionists worried that he would never keep his pre-agreement pledge to enforce decommissioning. The June 2001 unionist electoral choices—favouring anti-agreement over pro-agreement candidates—can be interpreted as a protest vote over a government policy that seemed to have internalised the IRA threat. Instability in the loyalist ceasefire and heightened dissident loyalist violence appeared to be similarly motivated.[13] Continued stasis on the decommissioning issue led the British government to suspend the Northern Ireland assembly several times, and it remained inoperative from October 2002 until March 2007. Blair might have refrained too much from playing politics with terrorism. In the event, it was primarily local

---

12 Lionel Shriver, 'The Ian and Gerry Show,' *Wall Street Journal Europe*, 14 June 2001, p. 8.

13 See, e.g., Toby Harnden, 'IRA Acted After Bush Warning on Terrorism,' *Daily Telegraph*, 25 October 2001, p. 9.

Catholic community pressure resulting from the murder of a Belfast Catholic (Robert McCartney) by several IRA men in January 2005 and growing national disgust towards terrorists in Britain emanating from the 7 July London bombings that produced the IRA's offer in late July 2005 to disarm completely provided Sinn Fein could resume participation in a functioning devolved government.

## The Troubles as political history

Since the beginning of the troubles in the late 1960s, the IRA has used violence with restraint to preserve a place at the bargaining table, where it would argue for what it and a fairly large contingent of sympathisers considered a realistic if revolutionary political outcome: the unification of Northern Ireland and the Irish Republic. These two characteristics—operational restraint and political feasibility—made the IRA the archetypal 'old' terrorist group, as distinct from operationally and politically maximalist 'new' terrorist outfits of al-Qaeda's stripe.[14] As such, the IRA was always to some degree susceptible to political compromise.[15]

Even so, from a practical unionist perspective, the IRA's manipulative foot-dragging on the inspections, burgeoning evidence of its conditional intent to take up arms again, and the continuation of brutal self-policing necessitated disarmament.[16] Yet decommission-

---

14 See, e.g., Steven Simon and Daniel Benjamin, 'America and the New Terrorism,' *Survival*, vol. 42, no. 1, Spring 2000, pp. 59-75; 'The Terror', *Survival*, vol. 43, no. 4, Winter 2001, pp. 5-17.

15 Gerry Adams, for instance, first engaged in political negotiations with the British government not in 1994 but in 1972, when hostilities reached their peak.

16 In June 2000, a Florida court convicted four IRA gunrunners of illegally attempting to ship weapons to Ireland in 1999—apparently with high-level IRA approval. Security forces also have solid evidence that the IRA has been actively purchasing weapons from the United States and Eastern Europe, and it has killed a suspected member of the dissident Real IRA. The rate at which the IRA and loyalist groups have executed drug-dealers and administered kneecappings and punishment beatings to 'anti-social' elements of their respective communities actually increased by 40 per cent

ing is merely a political necessity rather than an operational security requirement: most unionists understand that the IRA is sufficiently resourceful to repurchase weapons and compose bombs out of fertiliser. The IRA, however, appears to understand that 7 July made it politically mandatory for Blair to be tough on terrorists of any variety. The IRA's permanent renunciation in July 2005 of armed force of all kinds (i.e., 'self-policing' as well as political violence) and pledge to render all of its weapons unusable, and subsequent confirmation that it was making good on these representations, appears to amount to substantial disarmament. It thus comes close to providing what most unionists require.

In a time when terrorism of any kind is seen as an existential threat, the Belfast Agreement without substantial disarmament would have functioned as especially bad precedent. For several years, it did indeed function as precisely that. On the strength of the Agreement, the Basque separatists of Euskadi ta Askatasuna (ETA) overtly modeled its 1998-99 flirtation with a ceasefire and peace process on the IRA's strategy.[17] ETA hoped to get mass prisoner release without disarmament. Yet then-Prime Minister José María Aznar's government would not consider prematurely setting ETA prisoners free or foregoing disarmament. ETA's unrealistic expectations, based on a decommissioning-free version of the Belfast Agreement, stopped negotiations in Spain at the door and sent ETA back to terror. More broadly, negotiated resolutions of the Israeli-Palestinian and Kashmir conflicts that do not involve the arrest and disarmament of terrorists are scarcely imaginable.

---

from 2000 to 2001. See Dick Hogan and Jim Cusack, 'Four Arrested as Guns are Found in Car,' *Irish Times*, 31 January 2001, p. 6; David Sharrock, 'Silence Over Street Execution of a Terrorist,' *Daily Telegraph*, 28 October 2000, p. 14; Christopher Walker, 'Ulster Punishment Beatings Soar,' *Times of London*, 22 January, 2001, p. 2.

17  See, e.g., Paddy Woodworth, 'Why Do They Kill? The Basque Conflict in Spain,' *World Policy Journal*, vol. XVIII, no. 1, Spring 2001, p. 9.

Even with disarmament, arguably it remains counter-productive that the Belfast Agreement has established the precedent that politically motivated terrorists (i.e., most of them) can get out of jail free when their friends end violence. This dispensation increases the incentives of all political malcontents to kill for political advantage. Other requirements of the agreement punitive police reform, super-majorities, and the institutional entrenchment of sectarian polarities, to name three—may also provide political ammunition to minority-backed insurgencies. Thus, many of the Belfast Agreement's features could encourage governments and terrorists alike to play politics with terrorism. Nevertheless, prisoner release and over a decade of comparative calm have also made more IRA men reluctant to risk jail and the security forces less inclined to alienate the nationalist community. Even if the IRA were to return to violence, it would find world opinion less susceptible to manipulation than it has been in the last decade. Post-September 11, the IRA would garner less financial and moral support from Irish America, its traditional source of strength. By the same token, the prospect of outright Irish-American condemnation would make the IRA think twice about turning to al-Qaeda for help, just as it balked at accepting aid from the Soviet Union during the Cold War.

The salient reality, of course, is that Northern Ireland is now a more peaceful place and its politicians consequently better equipped for self-government. The most immediate achievement of the Northern Irish peace process was the creation of a non-violent political environment that gave each side credible hope that it could fulfill its political agenda even though the ultimate harmonisation of those agendas—remaining under British sovereignty for unionists, uniting with the Irish republic for nationalists—is impossible. Yet the peace process is still subject to enduring risks. The IRA's July 2005 announcement may have symbolised surrender to many hardline Irish republicans and could produce some defections from the Provisional IRA to the Real IRA, which opposes the peace process, at least if unionists continue to resist Sinn Fein's full participation in devolved government. Loyalist terrorists also continue to pose a threat to political stability. Unlike Sinn Fein and the IRA, loyalists have no real political power to lose from intransigence, and therefore little incentive to relinquish their primary source of influence: weapons. Gerry Adams has said that Sinn Fein will not press for loyalist decommissioning but requires only an intact loyalist ceasefire. Still, loyalist criminality is on the rise. Unionist concessions and Catholic social ascendancy may fuel loyalist violence, which could in turn produce community pressure on the Provisional IRA as well as the Real IRA to take provocative action in the name of community protection. But these are residual hazards. The troubles have provisionally been consigned to history. The dominant reason for that has been both the British Government's and the republicans' political savvy—and the mutual recognition by each of the others' political limits. Both sides played politics with terrorism, but predominantly with an eye towards its termination.

# 7

# A NESTED GAME: PLAYING POLITICS WITH TERRORISM IN THE UNITED STATES

*Leonard Weinberg and William Eubank*

The claim that some individuals or groups are 'playing politics' with terrorism is to suggest they are participating in a game, a competition between players '… involving opposing interests given specific information and allowed a choice of moves with the object of maximising their wins and minimising their loses.'[1] The wins and loses in this situation are 'political' in that they have to do with gaining or losing power and influence in government and related arenas. In this essay we seek to understand how different players, really different teams, responded to the 9/11 attacks in the United States and determine who gained and who lost.

Are we dealing with one game or multiple games? We intend to discuss the post-9/11 game(s) played out in three arenas or domains. First, we review the game of the intellectuals; the debate among academics, journalists, media specialists, writers and others who normally make public comments about a wide range of public issues. Next, we examine the 'inside the beltway' game. This is the domain of domestic and foreign policy-making, a place where binding decisions are made anew or modified to accommodate new circumstances. It is also an arena in which a competition takes place

---

1  *Webster's Seventh New Collegiate Dictionary* (Springfield, MA, 1967), p. 343.

involving significant players within the Washington establishment. In this case, the 'inside the beltway' game involves the 9/11 Commission and other investigatory bodies' recommendations for the reform of the country's domestic and national security apparatus. Third, we scrutinise the impact of the 9/11 attacks on the 2004 Presidential election campaign and the success of President George Bush in winning a second term by defeating his Democratic opponent Senator John Kerry.

At first glance, these three competitions may appear to be separate games involving different players playing for different stakes or seeking different payoffs. In fact, we would argue, the three competitions may not be identical to but certainly approximate what exponents of 'game theory' mean when they refer to a 'nested game'.[2] A nested game is a complex competition played out in different arenas between the same or similar players where winning and losing may vary from one venue to another.

## The game of the intellectuals

Not all that many decades ago intellectual life in the United States was dominated overwhelmingly by the left. Since the Vietnam era however other ways of thinking have come to the fore. A conservative movement, perhaps not one completely recognisable to members of the historic European right, linked to the ascendancy of Ronald Reagan, has become a major force in public policy debates in regard to both domestic and foreign policy. Support for free enterprise, opposition to the welfare state, anti-communism and a defence of 'traditional values' were, and to a considerable extent still are, major themes in conservative discourse. For mainstream or traditional conservatives the collapse of communist regimes around the world of course was a source of vast satisfaction. The fact that a number of left-wing writers (e.g. Paul Kennedy, *The Rise and Fall*

---

2  For a discussion see, for example, George Tsebelis, *Nested Games: Rational Choice in Comparative Politics* (Berkeley, CA, 1990), pp. 1-11.

*of the Great Powers*) had forecast a decline in American power did not go unnoticed. [3]

With the disappearance of the Soviet Union and the communist enterprise more generally, the Cold War-based enthusiasm conservative intellectuals had expressed for foreign political adventures began to wane. Struggles with the Soviet Union for power and influence in the Third World was one thing; the post-1989 promotion of 'nation-building', particularly if it was expensive and involved the use of military force, something else.

In addition to the liberal left and the traditional conservatives, the third group of players among American intellectuals to participate in the post-9/11 game are the neo-conservatives or 'neo-cons'. Led originally by such social scientists and journalists as Irving Kristol, Daniel Bell, Nathan Glazer and Norman Podhoretz, the neo-conservatives were originally a group of liberals who came to believe during the Vietnam War years that the cultural and political contempt expressed by the 'New Left' for America was itself contemptible. [4]

The 'neo-cons', apostates for many on the left, supported a vigorous American foreign policy both during and after the Cold War. At home, they defended the welfare state (though not Lyndon Johnson's version of it) but opposed various forms of social engineering, 'affirmative action' most especially. Culturally the neo-conservatives continued to wage a war of words against the 'hippie' subculture long after the 1960s-era hippies themselves had entered middle age or, in some cases, retirement homes.

How have these three groups of intellectuals reacted to 9/11 and to the reactions to 9/11 undertaken by the Bush administration? The way we have framed this question leads inevitably to over-generalisations; certainly there were differences of opinion within each group,

---

3   See, for example, Owen Harries, 'Suffer the Intellectuals' in *The American Interest* 1:1 (Autumn 2005) pp. 80-84.

4   On the history of the neo-conservatives see Peter Steinfels, *The Neo-Conservatives* (New York, 1980), pp. 25-48.

but it is still fair to identify central tendencies about how each group played politics.

If there was a central and immediate response on the part of America's left-wing intellectuals to the attacks on the World Trade Center and the Pentagon, it was to place the blame on a heterogeneous collection of sources with the exception of those nineteen individuals, and the group to which they belonged, actually responsible for perpetrating the attacks.[5] One or two observers applied aesthetic criteria. The Twin Towers deserved to be destroyed because they were architecturally unappealing. In this vein, some followed the German composer Karlheinz Stockhausen in referring to the event as 'the greatest work of art in the history of the cosmos.'[6] Others, like Stanley Aronowitz, Claudia Koonz, Michael Parenti, Howard Zinn and Gore Vidal mentioned the World Trade Center as a symbol of capitalism.[7] The Pentagon deserved what it got because it was, after all, a symbol of modern warfare. More commonly however, left-wing reactions to the 9/11 attacks, such as those of Noam Chomsky, involved a search for the 'conditions' that brought them about. Among the most commonly cited of these conditions were the political and economic circumstances prevailing in those Middle Eastern countries from which the perpetrators had come. By virtue of its wrong-headedness, American foreign policy was assigned considerable blame. American support for repressive regimes in Egypt and Saudi Arabia was identified as a root cause; another root cause for the attacks was America's uncritical support for Israeli repression of the Palestinians. In other words, according to left-wing voices, the United States itself was largely responsible for the events of 9/11.

---

5   For a summary of reactions see, Jonathan Raban, 'September 11: the View from the West' *The New York Review of Books*, 22 September 2005, pp. 4-8; Anthony Lewis, 'Un-American Activities' *The New York Review of Books*, 23 October 2003, pp. 16-19.

6   Quoted in Mark Danner, 'Taking Stock of the Forever War' *The New York Times Magazine* 11 September 2005 p. 46.

7   For a discussion see, Jean Bethke Elshtain, 'Intellectual Dissent and the War on Terror,' *The Public Interest* (Spring 2003) pp. 86-95.

Given the atmosphere in the country in the weeks following 9/11, it is hardly surprising that the interpretation offered by the left did not achieve much popular support. In fact in a few instances there were popular demands to fire instructors at some state universities (e.g. the University of Colorado) who expressed such sentiments. If the left was 'playing politics', it did not seem there was much for the left to gain, at least in the short term, from asserting these views. If we assume rationality, gaining power and influence, was the left then acting irrationally? The answer has to do with the solipsistic nature of contemporary left-wing discourse. Much of it appears directed at the self or small groups of like-minded intellectuals, the purpose of which is the cultivation of an elevated sense of self-righteousness. In fact we might argue that a sense of self-righteousness is the real 'opium of the intellectuals' about which Raymond Aron wrote so many years ago now.

As it turns out, the cultivation of this sense of self-righteousness did have a tangible payoff: in the month following 9/11 the Bush administration pushed Congress to enact the Patriot Act, legislation that extended broad new powers to federal law enforcement agencies in the areas of personal privacy, i.e. surveillance, intelligence gathering, search and seizure. The Patriot Act became a lightning rod for attacks by civil libertarians' on the Bush administration's 'war on terror'. The same may be said, only more so, about the establishment of a detention centre at the American base at Guantanamo Bay in Cuba to house 'enemy combatants' for indefinite periods with virtually no legal protections. The role of torture became an issue not only in connection with suspected al-Qaeda militants captured in Afghanistan in the fall of 2001, but also in connection with other venues as well. The practice of 'rendition' came under attack. Foreign nationals suspected of terrorist activities and captured by American agents might be turned over to foreign governments, e.g. Egypt, whose investigatory tools included humiliation and torture. The disclosures of the widespread use of torture by US military personnel at the Abu Ghraib prison in Iraq following the American occupation of that country (2004) added more fuel to the fire.

As a consequence of these developments—some intended by the Bush administration others apparently not—the American left was able to derive some benefits. The principal benefit has been the formation of a substantial constituency of citizens concerned about the erosion of civil liberty protections and human rights violations linked to the 'war on terror'.

What about the right? What about the reaction of American conservatives to the 9/11 attacks? As in the case of the left, we are dealing with a heterogeneous cast of characters with different points of view.

The initial reaction of some religiously inspired conservatives was, like their left-wing counterparts, to blame the United States itself for the catastrophe that had befallen it. The Reverends Jerry Falwell and Pat Robertson initially claimed the attacks were a sign of God's displeasure with the mortal sins they detected in American society, e.g. abortion, gay marriage, the American Civil Liberties Union. Like the initial public reactions of left-wing academics to 9/11, Falwell and Robertson's remarks were not well received. Other religious conservatives imposed a millenarian explanation.[8] The 9/11 attacks were a "sign" of the imminent final battle between good and evil. The Book of Revelation was cited.

This is hardly the end of the story, however. More mainstream conservatives stressed the need for retaliation. To quote presidential adviser Karl Rove, 'Conservatives saw the savagery of 9/11 in the attacks and prepared for war; liberals saw the savagery of the 9/11 attacks and wanted to prepare indictments and offer therapy and understanding for our attackers.'[9] In the aftermath of the attacks major figures in the conservative movement defined the situation as the beginning of a war, one requiring the engagement of American

---

8   Michael Barkun, *A Culture of Conspiracy* (Berkeley, CA, 2003), pp. 158-9.

9   In "Democrats Demand Rove Apologize for 9/11 Remarks" *The New York Times*, 4 June 2005.

military forces in Afghanistan and elsewhere. Those 'liberals' who suggested other means were characterised as weak and misguided. The partisan rhetoric bore some resemblance to the 'soft on communism' discourse conservatives directed against Democrats so successfully during the Cold War era.

Modern conservatism in the United States has had a strongly anti-statist bent. For the followers of Ronald Reagan, after all, government was not part of the solution, it was part of the problem. Some conservatives, the lobbyist Grover Norquist for example, saw in the war on terror serious threats to the right of privacy and individual liberty. Opponents to some provisions of the Patriot Act included figures in the conservative movement as well as the liberal left. Waging a war on global terrorism meant 'big government', stronger police powers, the prospect of higher taxes and foreign military adventures, not policies that libertarians at the Cato Institute looked on with favour.

The neo-conservatives, on the other hand, were more single-minded in their reactions to 9/11. William Bennett wrote a book calling for moral clarity, entitled *Why We Fight*, a title borrowed from a popular World War II pamphlet.[10] Writing in *Commentary* Norman Podhoretz saw the United States as engaged in World War IV and warned against the dangers of appeasement advocated by the 'guerrillas-with-tenure in the universities.'[11] The United States was at war with an enemy as blood-thirsty, implacable and vicious as the Axis powers in World War II.

It did not go unnoticed by a few observers that several of the visible neo-cons calling for war with Iraq were Jews (e.g. William Kristol, editor of the *Weekly Standard*). For anti-Semites and other opponents of Zionism, Jews almost always have a self-serving agenda. In this instance, the agenda was support for Israel. According to this allegation, the major reason the neo-conservatives were so committed

---

10  William Bennett, *Why We Fight* (New York, 2002).

11  Norman Podhoretz, "World War IV: How it Started, What it Means, and Why We have to Win," *Commentary* (September 2004) p. 41.

to the Bush administration's war on terror was because this conflict would involve the deployment of American forces against Israel's enemies in the Middle East and the Muslim World more generally. For example: the right-wing columnist and former presidential candidate Pat Buchanan accused the neo-cons of 'dual loyalty', of mistaking Tel Aviv for Washington.[12] The fact that a number of key figures within America's defence establishment (e.g. Paul Wolfowitz, Douglas Feith, Richard Perle) were Jews did not pass without mention by Buchanan and others.[13]

## *The 'inside the beltway' game*

Policies may be proposed and debated by writers for such journals as *The American Prospect, National Review, The New Republic,* or *Commentary,* but it is only 'inside the beltway' of Washington that policies, having the force of law, are actually made. Nevertheless the game of the intellectuals and the 'inside the beltway' game do not occur in separate 'silos'. Instead they represent different arenas of a nested game. Many of the individual players are different; nevertheless there is significant overlap. Washington abounds with 'think tanks' (e.g. the American Enterprise Institute, the Heritage Foundation, the Brookings Institution, the CATO Institute), 'beltway bandits' (i.e. private firms that do research for government agencies on a contract basis), public interest lobbying groups (e.g. People for the American Way) and law firms whose job it is to formulate and convey liberal, conservative, libertarian and neo-conservative ideas to public officials who have the ability to transform them into laws and regulations. Not uncommonly many of the intellectuals mentioned above belong to one or another of the 'think tanks' and other advocacy organisations.

In fact one of the major developments following the 9/11 attacks was the enormous proliferation of terrorism experts inside the belt-

12 Cited in Stefan Halper and Jonathan Clarke, *America Alone: the Neo-Conservatives and the Global Order* (New York, 2004), p. 72.

13 For an assessment see, Gilles Keppel, *The War for Muslim Minds* (Cambridge, MA, 2004), pp. 47-69.

way and beyond. Large numbers of academics, foundation fellows and intellectuals of various kinds transformed themselves, often overnight, into terrorism specialists. A faculty member at an illustrious research university reported that within a week of 9/11 her institution's website displayed the names and pictures of 'terrorism experts' on the faculty, none of whom to her knowledge, had ever studied the subject before. Scholars whose careers had been devoted to excoriating the Soviet Union or theorising about the prospects of nuclear war, for example, changed, almost instantaneously, into terrorism specialists. The fact there were often tangible benefits that went along with such transformations cannot be totally discounted as a motive. Among these benefits was the opportunity for many to offer advice to policy-makers about the best ways to eliminate the terrorist threat to the country.

We should remember though that the public officials involved are not simply the passive recipients of ideas proposed by these terrorism advisers and 'inside the beltway' organisations. In the case of 9/11 many had their own views about what had gone wrong, why and what should be done. Those officials elected to public office were not reluctant to express their views about the intelligence and law enforcement failures that led to the attacks. On the other hand, lower-ranking civil servants or upper echelon executive appointees who had reason to be reticent often relied on the technique of the 'leak' to convey their views to an audience. Others waited until they left government service before making known their views in books, articles and television appearances.[14]

The 9/11 attacks have brought about the most substantial changes in government organisation and focus of American foreign policy since the early years of the cold war more than five decades earlier. These changes were reflected in *The National Security Strategy of the United States*, a document prepared by the National Security Council and

---

14  See, for example, the former CIA agent Robert Baer, *See no Evil* (New York, 2002); and the national security council adviser Richard Clarke, *Against all Enemies* (New York, 2004).

published by the White House in September, 2002. The statement begins by defining the new situation in which the country finds itself:

Defending our Nation against its enemies is the first and fundamental commitment of the Federal Government. Today, that task has changed dramatically. Enemies in the past needed great armies and great industrial capabilities to endanger America. Now, shadowy networks of individuals can bring great chaos and suffering to our shores for less than it costs to purchase a single tank. Terrorists are organised to penetrate open societies and to turn the power of modern technologies against us… To defeat this threat we must make use of every tool in our arsenal—military power, better homeland defences, law enforcement, intelligence, and vigorous efforts to cut off terrorist financing. The war against terrorists of global reach is a global enterprise of uncertain duration.[15]

Later in the document, as part of its discussion of weapons of mass destruction (WMD), the activities of terrorist groups with a global reach are linked to the dangers posed by 'rogue states', governments that do not abide by the conventional rules of international conduct and that the document identifies as the patrons of the former. In view of the potentially devastating effects of WMD in the possession of rogue states (i.e. Iraq, Iran and North Korea) with terrorist groups as clients, American foreign policy required a new 'proactive' approach. 'We must be prepared to stop rogue states and their terrorist clients before they are able to threaten or use weapons of mass destruction against the United States and our allies and friends.'[16]

America's new national, and by extension, homeland security policies were redefined in exceptionally ambitious terms. For a Republican administration following in the steps of the Reagan 'revolution' with its opposition to 'big government', the *National Security Strategy of the United States* was a statement calling for a substantial expansion of the federal government's role in the international arena and in the domestic sphere. What sorts of changes were involved?

---

15 The National Security Strategy of the United States of America, www. WhiteHouse.gov/nsc/nss.html p. 1.

16 Ibid., p. 14.

The most dramatic change from an organisational perspective was the creation of the Department of Homeland Security (DHS) to co-ordinate the activities of twenty-two agencies responsible for domestic protection and terrorism prevention.[17] Agencies that previously had belonged to other departments, e.g. the Secret Service (Treasury), Immigration and Naturalisation (Justice), Nuclear Incident Response Team (Energy), Transportation Security administration (Transportation), along with previously independent organisations, e.g. the Coast Guard, were relocated and placed under the control of a single cabinet level DHS secretary.

Following 9/11 there were widespread criticisms of the country's domestic and foreign intelligence agencies. The failures of the FBI and CIA, taken separately, attracted enormous public attention, as did their long-standing inability to co-operate with one another. In the years following 9/11 the Bush administration created the new post of Director of National Intelligence (DNI) to co-ordinate the government's intelligence-gathering function, a job that had nominally been in the hands of the CIA director for decades. To improve co-operation between the FBI and CIA, Congress and the Bush administration established the joint National Counterterrorism Center to build a common data base and better analyse and co-ordinate counterterrorism operations.

Since President Bush defined the response to al-Qaeda and the 9/11 attacks as a 'war on terror', the Department of Defense was clearly assigned a central role in waging it. Donald Rumsfeld, the Secretary of Defense, and his principal civilian assistants, stressed the importance of an aggressive role for the Special Forces (Delta Force, the SEALS, Gray Fox), not only in providing help to the Northern Alliance in defeating the Taliban regime in Kabul and forcing the flight and dispersion of al-Qaeda cadres from Afghanistan in November/December of 2001, but also in conducting manhunts for that

---

17 For a discussion see Donald Kettl, *System Under Stress: Homeland Security and American Politics* (Washington, DC, 2004), pp. 33-56.

organisation's leaders.[18] To quote Seymour Hirsch: 'We now know that the Bush administration decided in late 2001 or early 2002 to assassinate, capture, or otherwise 'disappear' suspected al-Qaeda and terrorist operatives wherever they could be found, in secrecy, with no due process.'[19] Sometimes these 'kill or capture' assignments have been carried out by forces on the ground, often in co-operation with other governments, but sometimes via the use of missiles launched from remote-controlled Predator aircraft. These manhunts also represented a significant reversal of policy. Since the Vietnam era, American presidents, beginning with Gerald Ford, had prohibited American forces, including the CIA, from targeting individual enemies of the United States for extra-judicial retribution.

Most of the structural and personnel changes undertaken in the Pentagon following 9/11 were largely generated internally. The Defense secretary and his civilian advisors wanted to modernise and streamline US forces following the end of the cold war and what they perceived at least to be the overly cautious approach to the deployment of these forces that they identified with the Clinton administration. The 9/11 attacks accelerated a process that was already underway.

Changes in the civilian agencies, the Department of Homeland Security, the CIA and FBI, often took place in response to post-9/11 investigations. In 2002 the Senate Judiciary Committee, for example, held public hearings in the course of an extensive investigation of the failure to anticipate the attacks. But it was the independent and bipartisan National Commission on 9/11 that had the greatest impact, both in terms of public awareness of its work and the willingness of the Bush administration to put its recommendations into practice. For instance, it was on the basis of the Commission's recommenda-

---

18 See, for example, Seymour Hirsch, *Chain of Command* (New York, 2004), pp. 249-86.

19 Ibid., p. 261.

tions that the National Counterterrorism Center and a Director of National Intelligence post were created.[20]

Taken together the game played inside the beltway following 9/11 has resulted in the most substantial structural and policy changes in American government since the period 1946-1947 when an integrated Department of Defense, the National Security Council and a Central Intelligence Agency were formed in response to the emerging Cold War challenge posed by the Soviet Union and it East Bloc allies.

The winners of the 'inside the beltway' game are to be found, unsurprisingly, inside the beltway. Those who favoured the strengthening of America's domestic and national security apparatus following the 9/11 attacks have been the clear winners. This particularly significant part of our nested game has been won by those think-tank advocates and policy-makers who support a more intrusive role for the federal government in the lives of American citizens and a more aggressive, more proactive stance for Washington in defending the country's interests abroad. The irony in this outcome is that an ostensibly conservative movement, now dominant inside the equally dominant Republican Party, has strengthened the very powers of government its most eloquent spokesmen, Ronald Reagan, vowed to weaken. For Reagan and his followers the whole purpose of the modern conservative movement was to take power from Washington and restore it to the states and to the people from which it had originally come. In effect, by winning the 'inside the beltway' game, the neo-cons and the conservative movement more generally have defeated the very purpose that brought them into being in the first place. This development should not have come as a surprise. For many years such conservative philosophers as Bertrand De Jouvenal have warned that modern warfare typically leads to an expansion of state power.[21] A small federal government with power dispersed to the states and

20  *The 9/11 Commission Report* (New York, 2004), pp. 403-15.
21  Bertrand De Jouvenel, *On Power* (Boston, 1962), pp. 254-79.

plans to wage a global 'war on terror' seem incompatible with one another.

## The election game

For many key political figures inside the beltway, winning the next election is the most important factor governing their behaviour. It is, in effect, the 'name of the game'. In this regard, Osama bin Laden and the nineteen suicide skyjackers were a major help to President Bush. The al-Qaeda terrorists played a significant role in helping, unintentionally we presume, the President win re-election in November 2004.

According to the Gallup poll, the President's job approval rating on 10 September 2001 stood at 51 per cent. At the next survey taken after 9/11 the level of popular support soared to 86 per cent, the largest poll-to-poll percentage swing since Gallup began polling on this question. The *Washington Post-ABC News* poll showed a parallel boost in presidential approval.[22] Americans were rallying around their president in a time of heightened anxiety and tension.

Karl Rove and other presidential advisers and Republican Party strategists quickly recognised the advantages to stressing Bush's vigorous response to the 9/11 attacks. In fact, not only could Bush benefit, but, as Rove pointed out to a meeting of the Republican Party National Committee in 2002, Repubilcan congressional candidates would be helped by depicting their party as better able to protect the country against the terrorist threat than the rival Democrats.[23] Stress 9/11 and win. The tactic appears to have worked. Before 9/11 the Democrats held a slim majority in the US Senate; following the 2004 elections, the Republicans held a ten seat majority in the same body.

Further evidence for the positive impact of the terrorist threat on President Bush's support may be found in popular reactions to

---

22  Cited in Robb Willer, 'The Effects of Government-Issued Terror Warnings on Presidential Approval Ratings,' *Current Research in Social Psychology* 10:1 (2004) p. 2.

23  Ryan Lizza, 'Storm Surge' *The New Republic*, 19 September 2005, p. 19

government-issued terror warnings. Following 9/11 various government agencies (e.g. FBI, Justice Department) issued public warnings
concerning the status of terrorist threats to the United States. The
most widely discussed of these warnings has been the Department of
Homeland Security's colour-coded (orange being the highest) current threat level. Robb Willer tested a series of models to evaluate
the impact of these warnings on President Bush's popular approval.
Based on this analysis, he reports a consistent boost in presidential
performance ratings in the periods following the issuance of the
warnings. The more the public perceived a terrorist threat, the more
they supported Bush. Furthermore, the warnings had a halo effect.
After terrorist threat warnings, the American public also raised its
level of support for the President's handling of the economy.[24]

In the 2000 election Bush lost the popular vote to then Vice-
President Al Gore by half a percentage point. In the 2004 balloting
he defeated the challenger John Kerry by 2.5 per cent. What role did
the terrorist threat play in Bush's victory?

The evidence is substantial that the public's perception of Bush's
ability to lead the 'war on terror' provided him with a distinct advantage over Kerry and the Democrats. A Gallup poll conducted in late
August 2004, before the election campaign was really under-way,
found Bush to be preferred over Kerry in his ability to handle the terrorist threat by a margin of 54 to 37 per cent. Exit polls a little more
than two months later showed an almost identical result. The Kerry
campaign's effort to depict their candidate as a highly decorated and
battle-tested Vietnam War veteran had virtually no effect. The same
observation may be made about the two competing political parties.
When asked whether the Republicans or Democrats could do a better job in 'handling terrorism', the public preferred the Republicans
by a margin of 45 to 27 per cent (27 per cent said both parties were
equally competent).[25]

---

24 Willer, 'The Effects of Government-Issued Terror Warnings on Presidential
   Approval Ratings,' *Current Research in Social Psychology* 10:1 (2004) pp. 5-7.
25 James Campbell, 'Why Bush Won the Presidential Election of 2004,' in

In Spain the terrorist attacks on Madrid-bound commuter trains on 11 March 2004 contributed to the defeat of Prime Minister Aznar's conservative government. In the United States, on the other hand, the 9/11 attacks and President Bush's response to them helped him gain re-election. Why the opposite effect? What was the difference?

A number of answers to these questions seem plausible. The Madrid bombings happened a few days before national elections and the Aznar government apparently misled Spanish voters about their perpetrators. The 9/11 attacks occurred only eight months after Bush took office. He had more than three years to perform before facing another election. Be that as it may, the war in Iraq must be taken into consideration. Spanish participation in the fighting was very unpopular and no doubt contributed to Aznar's defeat. The situation in the United States was more complicated.

In Spain, as in other Western European countries, there was widespread popular opposition to the American administration's decision to invade Iraq on 19 March 2003. Protesters marched in Madrid, London, Amsterdam, Paris, Rome, Berlin and other major European cities. Opinion[26] surveys reflected the fact that the protesters were not isolates, but in fact expressed the views of many of their fellow citizens. By supporting the American war effort in Iraq the governments of Western European democracies were jeopardising their own popular support. They also risked, as in the case of the British Labour Party, defections from within the government and the ruling party. At both the elite and mass levels, then, support for the war, especially if it involved the deployment of military forces, was a high risk policy. The downside was significant while the benefits were not all that easy to discern.

---

Robert Shapiro Ed., *The Meaning of American Democracy* (New York, 2005), p. 211.

26 Amy Gershkoff and Shana Kushner, 'Shaping Public Opinion: The 9/11-Iraq Connection in the Bush administration's Rhetoric,' *Perspectives on Politics* 3:3 (2005) pp. 525-37.

In the United States, on the other hand, public opinion surveys taken at the war's outset showed Americans to be very supportive of military action against Saddam Hussein and his Baathist dictatorship: some 70 per cent of those surveyed indicated they supported waging the war. Why the gap between European and American perceptions of the conflict? After all, in terms of blood and treasure, the peoples of Western Europe risked little while the Americans were risking quite a bit.

According to Gershkoff and Kushner's recent analysis of the way the Bush administration framed the war, the speeches its spokesmen delivered and the rhetoric they used, Americans came to believe the attack on Iraq was part of the 'war on terror'. The Bush administration successfully framed the war in Iraq as an extension of its response to September 11 and the war on terror. The administration juxtaposed allusions to Iraq with the terms *terror, bin Laden,* and *al-Qaeda.*[27] More than fears about weapons of mass destruction, it was the ability of the administration to identify Iraq with global terrorism that persuaded a substantial majority of Americans that by defeating Saddam's regime the US was also reducing the terrorist threat to domestic American targets. If we don't defeat them in Baghdad, the terrorists will defeat us by staging more 9/11 type attacks within the United States.

In successfully linking the war for Iraq to the 'war on terror' the administration was also taking a risk. Since President Bush's popularity hinged to a significant extent on the widespread perception that he was an effective leader in the fight against terrorism, and this fight was involved in the successful prosecution of the war in Iraq, what would happen if that war did not turn out as planned?

## Payoffs

Let us assume, as we did initially, that the responses of American intellectuals to 9/11, the events that played out subsequently 'inside

---

27  Gershkoff and Kushner, Ibid., p. 526.

the beltway' and the 2004 presidential election contest between Bush and Kerry were part of a single nested game played out in different arenas. If we make this assumption, we may then calculate who won and for how long.

In the short run, it would require a wilful suspension of disbelief to deny that the principal beneficiaries of the 9/11 attacks were those conservatives, neo-conservatives especially, who helped shape the administration's response. This response defined the country as engaged in war with al-Qaeda and the forces of global terrorism. President Bush's decisions aimed at a vigorous pursuit of the terrorists and those who supported them helped him win exceedingly high levels of support among the American people. Bush's victory in 2004 along with those of Republican congressional candidates was helped substantially by the voters' judgment that the President and his party were better at fighting terrorism than John Kerry and their Democratic adversaries.

The longrun, though, may produce a different outcome. By linking the war on terror to the conflict in Iraq, the Bush administration's defence establishment, the conservatives, neo-conservatives and perhaps even the Republican Party itself may have made themselves hostage to the future of that country. If, prior to the next presidential election in 2008, Iraq undergoes a successful transition to democracy and American troops withdraw under benign conditions, and if these developments result in a decline in terrorist violence in the Middle East—elsewhere, if the US seems to be winning the war on terror in other words—then the payoff to these players will continue to be substantial. On the other hand, the game may very well produce a very different payoff if the situation in Iraq deteriorates, and American casualties increase while terrorist attacks against American targets around the world continue to mount.

To a considerable extent, in the 1960s the Democrats were driven from power and advocates of welfare-state liberalism discredited by the Vietnam War and its domestic fallout (e.g. the breakdown of 'law and order'). Could a similar fate be in store for the conservative movement, including the neo-conservatives, who were the major beneficiaries of this defeat? It seems too early to tell for certain. It is, though, at least a possibility worth considering.

# 8

# THE POLITICS OF FEAR: WRITING THE TERRORIST THREAT IN THE WAR ON TERROR

## Richard Jackson

There is little question that terrorism is now the pre-eminent security preoccupation of western states. Issues surrounding the 'war on terror' have infused recent electoral contests in America, Spain, Australia, and Britain, and the terrorism threat is arguably the central prism through which both domestic and foreign policy is now formulated. Polling data indicates that a great many people in western countries live in fear of imminent terrorist attack and believe it poses a significant risk to personal and public safety. Largely as a consequence, there is now unquestioned social acceptance of anti-terrorist security precautions across virtually every area of social and economic life: commercial travel, sporting and cultural events, banking, computing, policing, entertainment, and education—to name a few. Arguably, western publics are also predisposed to accept a great many security practices previously considered unnecessary or morally abhorrent, such as vastly increased military spending, preventive internment, the suspension of *habeas corpus*, the coercive interrogation of suspected terrorists, shoot-to-kill policies, and pre-emptive war. Across all major sectors of society—the political establishment, the security services, the media, the emergency services, trade and industry, religion, and the academy—there are few individuals who do not accept that international terrorism is currently the greatest security threat facing western states. It could in fact be argued that for many western societies the fear of terrorism has become normalised in social and political life.

There are a number of explanations for this existential condition, a condition that has been called 'ontological hysteria' in which societies are constantly anticipating the next attack, just 'waiting for terror'.[1] Sociologists have suggested that it reflects broader cultural developments, namely, the emergence of an 'age of anxiety', a 'culture of fear', or 'risk society'.[2] According to this perspective, and due in large part to the erosion of social bonds, individuals (and society at large) are prone to moral panics and increased anxiety about a vast array of potential and actual dangers, from mad cow disease to global warming, 'stranger danger', paedophiles, prescription medicines, viruses, mobile phones, weapons of mass destruction, and the like. In response, public officials have taken up the role of societal risk managers: highly sensitive to public opinion about the latest social panic and lacking an ideological vision of positive social transformation; the precautionary principle has come to dominate the policy formulation process. From this perspective, the terrorism scare is merely the most recent moral panic to afflict an increasingly anxious and directionless culture.

More prosaically, security managers (among others) argue that current levels of social anxiety are a reasonable response to the 'reality' and magnitude of the terrorist threat facing western societies. It is undeniable that seemingly random violence, packaged as media spectacle, creates an initial shock that is difficult to transcend. The paralysing effect of terrorist violence was magnified many times over

---

1   Joseba Zulaika and William Douglass, *Terror and Taboo: the Follies, Fables, and Faces of Terrorism* (New York, 1996).

2   Ulrich Beck, *Rick Society: Towards a New Modernity* (London, 1992); Ulrich Beck, 'The Terrorist Threat: World Risk Society Revisited', *Theory, Culture & Society*, 19, 2002, pp. 39-55; Frank Furedi, *Culture of Fear: Risk-Taking and the Morality of Low Expectation*, (revised edition) (London, 2002); Barry Glassner, *The Culture of Fear: Why Americans are Afraid of the Wrong Things* (New York, 1999).

in the case of the globally televised September 11, 2001 attacks, the most devastating and horrifying terrorist attacks of all time. From this vantage point, the widespread fear of terrorism appears natural and rational; and the effort and expense of the authorities to enhance security seems only responsible politics and is, in any case, demanded by an anxious public.

Despite their undoubted veracity, there are reasons to doubt that these approaches provide anything more than a superficial explanation of present levels of social fear. In the first place, acts of political violence are always mediated through dominant social discourses and are prone to contestation, reinterpretation, and the renegotiation of political and social meaning over time. Even an apparently obvious event such as the Japanese attack on Pearl Harbor has been subject to competing interpretations over the past few decades,[3] not to mention the atomic attack on Hiroshima, the assassination of John F. Kennedy, the sinking of the Belgrano, and others. Second, public fears are social, political, and cultural constructions that only rarely correspond to the actual level of risk. While there are 'real' dangers in the world that have life and death consequences—disease, accidents, and violence, among others—not all dangers are equal and not all risks are interpreted as dangers.[4] In western society, illicit drugs are considered to be a greater threat than licit drugs for example, despite the fact that infinitely more people are killed or injured every year by the abuse of legally-prescribed medicines. In the case of terrorism, the gap between the level of social anxiety and the actual danger is especially pronounced: on a statistical scale of personal risk, terrorism ranks somewhere around the risk of being killed in a home repairs accident or being struck by lightening. Tens of thousands more people die every year from gun crime, suicide, hospital infections, and alcohol abuse or automobile accidents—not to mention diseases

---

3  See Emily Rosenberg, *A Date Which Will Live: Pearl Harbor in American Memory* (Durham, 2004).

4  David Campbell, *Writing Security: United States Foreign Policy and the Politics of Identity* (revised edition) (Manchester, 1998), p. 2.

like cancer—than from terrorism. Third and most importantly, these explanations fail to discern (and frequently function to obscure) the underlying political interests at work in the creation and maintenance of social fears such as terrorism or the danger of illicit drugs. Moreover, such fears are more than simply individual experiences of anxiety; rather, they emerge from, and are reflective of, underlying relations of power in society.[5]

The purpose of this essay is to analyse critically the social and political construction of the terrorist threat and the politics of fear that lies at its centre. The overall argument is fairly simple: the terrorism threat has been deliberately and purposefully exaggerated and maintained by political elites for the achievement of political goals; in this case, the social construction of fear is an exercise in power and domination. More importantly, from a normative perspective, the politics of fear are damaging to social values and democratic politics.

## Writing the terrorist threat after 11 September 2001

The war on terrorism is both a set of institutional practices (military and intelligence operations, diplomatic initiatives, special government departments and security bodies, standard operating procedures, new legislation, and so on), as well as an accompanying series of public political narratives designed to generate social consent for the counterterrorist campaign. At the centre of the legitimating discourse lies the notion that a ubiquitous and catastrophic terrorist threat justifies and necessitates a global 'war' against terrorism.

Apart from the almost daily generic warnings about the inevitability of another attack, the terrorist threat narrative is made up of a number of specific sub-narratives. The first of these is the notion that since September 11, 2001, a 'new' form of terrorism has arisen that is completely unlike the 'old' terrorism. What makes this new kind of terrorism so different, it is argued, is that it is deliberately targeted at innocent civilians, it is motivated by religious fanaticism rather

---

5    Corey Robin, *Fear: The History of a Political Idea* (Oxford, 2004), p. 179.

than political ideology, and it is aimed at causing mass casualties and maximum destruction. According to public officials, terrorists are determined to kill millions of westerners if they can, and are likely to employ weapons of mass destruction to do so. As American Vice-President Dick Cheney put it: 'The attack on our country forced us to come to grips with the possibility that the next time terrorists strike, they may well… direct chemical agents or diseases at our population, or attempt to detonate a nuclear weapon in one of our cities.' He went on to suggest that 'no rational person can doubt that terrorists would use such weapons of mass murder the moment they are able to do so', and the West is facing terrorists 'who are willing to sacrifice their own lives in order to kill millions of others'.[6] This kind of language, repeated endlessly by public officials, is clearly designed to generate maximum social fear. The visions presented are apocalyptic, reflecting the most terrifying of Hollywood dramas: the detonation of a nuclear bomb in a city, or the release of a deadly chemical or biological agent, as depicted in *The Sum of All Fears* and *Outbreak*, for example.

Related to this, public officials argue that terrorists are aided by rogue regimes and despotic states. One of the most powerful articulations of this particular sub-narrative came in George W. Bush's State of the Union address where he described the 'axis of evil' (the embodiment of the purported alliance between terrorists and 'outlaw states'): "States like these, and their terrorist allies, constitute an axis of evil, arming to threaten the peace of the world. By seeking weapons of mass destruction, these regimes pose a grave and growing danger. They could provide these arms to terrorists, giving them the means to match their hatred".[7] Similarly, as Colin Powell put it when Secretary of State, the terrorist threat resides in the "potentially

6   Vice President Dick Cheney, 'Remarks to the American Society of News Editors,' The Fairmont Hotel, New Orleans, 9 April 2003, http://usinfo. state.gov/topical/pol/terror/, accessed 29 August, 2003.

7   President George W. Bush, 'The State of the Union Address', Washington, DC, 29 January 2002, http://usinfo.state.gov/topical/pol/terror/, accessed 29 August, 2003.

catastrophic combination of a rogue regime, weapons of mass destruction and terrorists".[8] Incidentally, the rhetorical strategy of making terrorists and rogue states synonymous is an ingenious discursive slight of hand which allows for the re-targeting of the military from a war against a tiny group of dissidents scattered across the globe to a number of territorially defined states (who also happen to be candidates for 'regime change'). In sum, according to this sub-narrative, western societies face the threat of a 'new' kind of 'super-terrorism', 'mega-terrorism' or 'catastrophic terrorism' where hate-filled terrorists, aided by rogue states, seek weapons of mass destruction in order to try and kill millions of westerners.

Another sub-narrative is that the terrorist threat is so great that it creates the situation of a semi-permanent 'supreme emergency'. According to the political elite, terrorists threaten the entire western way of life, its values, democracy, and civilisation itself. Colin Powell, for example, stated that terrorism was a 'threat to civilization' and a 'threat to the very essence of what you do'.[9] President Bush frequently describes terrorism as a 'threat to our way of life',[10] a reiteration of a prominent cold war narrative. Cofer Black, Spokesman Coordinator for Counterterrorism, has gone even further to argue that 'the threat of international terrorism knows no boundaries'.[11] This is the logical

8  Secretary of State Colin L. Powell, Release of the 2002 'Patterns of Global Terrorism' Annual Report, US Department of State, Washington DC, 30 April 2003, http://usinfo.state.gov/topical/pol/terror/, accessed 29 August, 2003.

9  Secretary of State Colin L. Powell, 'Remarks by the Secretary of State to the National Foreign Policy Conference for Leaders of Nongovernmental Organisations (NGO)', Loy Henderson Conference Room, US Department of State, Washington, DC, 26 October 2001, http://usinfo.state.gov/topical/pol/terror/, accessed 29 August, 2003.

10 President George W. Bush, 'Address to a Joint Session of Congress and the American People', 20 September 2001, http://usinfo.state.gov/topical/pol/terror/, accessed 29 August, 2003.

11 Cofer Black, Spokesman Coordinator for Counterterrorism, US Department of State, Press Conference for 2002 Annual Report 'Patterns of Global Terrorism', Washington, DC, 30 April 2003, http://usinfo.state.gov/topical/pol/terror/, accessed 29 August, 2003.

conclusion of the language: it is in fact, an infinite threat, a 'super-emergency'. In this scenario, terrorism is as great as any threat the West has ever faced, including the threat of fascism during World War II and the threat of communism during the Cold War.

A final sub-narrative involves the notion of an ubiquitous and highly dangerous enemy who resides within western societies. According to public officials, there are enemies at home as well as abroad, hiding in 'sleeper cells', plotting and waiting to commit atrocities. The terrorist 'enemy within' is also highly trained, cunning, ruthless, and extremely dangerous. For example, John Ashcroft stated that the September 11 attacks proved that "terrorism is the activity of expertly organised, highly co-ordinated and well financed organizations and networks".[12] In the same speech, he suggested that terrorists "can kill thousands of Americans in a single day", and can mount "sophisticated terrorists operations". In a more detailed articulation, President Bush constructed a narrative which could have come directly from the pages of a popular spy novel, such as Nelson DeMille's *The Charm School*:[13]

Most of the 19 men who hijacked planes on September the 11th were trained in Afghanistan's camps, and so were tens of thousands of others. Thousands of dangerous killers, schooled in the methods of murder, often supported by outlaw regimes, are now spread throughout the world like ticking time bombs, set to go off without warning.

In a similar construction, John Ashcroft suggested that America confronted a 'terrorist threat that is both immediate and vast; a threat that resides here, at home, but whose supporters, patrons and sympathizers form a multinational network of evil.' He went on to state that terrorists 'live in our communities—plotting, planning and waiting to kill Americans again'.[14]

---

12  Attorney General John Ashcroft, 'Testimony to House Committee on the Judiciary', 24 September 2001, http://usinfo.state.gov/topical/pol/terror/, accessed 29 August, 2003.

13  Bush, 'The State of the Union Address', 2002.

14  Attorney General John Ashcroft, 'Prepared Remarks for the US Mayors

Importantly, the terrorist threat narrative has been discursively constructed in such a way as to completely de-politicise it. It is argued that unlike the 'old' terrorists such as the IRA, the PLO, or ETA, the 'new' terrorists are simply mindless fanatics who seek to maximise innocent casualties and cause mass destruction, and who are motivated by an extreme form of anti-modern, anti-western militant Islam with which there is no possibility of political compromise. Public officials constantly stress that the terrorists aim to destroy western civilisation and establish a global medieval caliphate, and that they have no other political agenda that might form the basis of negotiation. Western leaders are particularly quick to deny that the terrorists are motivated in any way by American or Coalition policies towards the Middle East or argue that this is a minor part of their aims and merely a convenient excuse for murder. In this way, the narrative predetermines the counterterrorism response: if there is no possibility of negotiation, and if this new form of terrorism does not belong to the political realm, then the only reasonable response is to eradicate it through massive counter-violence.

These public narratives have been incredibly successful in constructing social fear, not least because of the sheer volume of public speeches: senior government officials in America and Britain have made literally thousands of speeches on the subject of terrorism since the World Trade Center attacks,[15] most of which have been widely reported in the mainstream media. In addition, the narratives have been reproduced and amplified by an array of influential social institutions. In particular, the media, both in daily news making and entertainment programming (television shows such as *24* and *Spooks* consistently run storylines involving terrorist threats of nuclear or chemical attack), constantly amplify the official language of threat. Similarly, academics and so-called terrorism 'experts' have produced

---

Conference', 25 October 2001, http://usinfo.state.gov/topical/pol/terror/, accessed 29 August, 2003.

15 See Brigitte Nacos, *Mass-Mediated Terrorism: the Central Role of the Media in Terrorism and Counterterrorism* (New York, 2007), pp. 148-9.

literally hundreds of books and articles warning of the dangers posed by the 'new terrorism', as have risk management experts and public safety officials, religious leaders, school teachers, trade and industry officials, and others.

Of course, discourses are more than just words or texts; they are also actions and material practices which act as powerful symbols and message transmitters. In constructing the terrorist threat narrative, officials have also engaged in a conspicuous display of actions designed to reinforce the public language including: grounding passenger flights; placing armed sky marshals on passenger planes; flying jet fighters over major cities during periods of heightened alert; erecting massive steel and concrete barriers around public buildings; deploying tanks and other heavy military equipment around airports or at other public venues; mounting large-scale chemical or nuclear attack simulations; and institutionalising a national daily terrorist warning system, among others. These are very powerful discursive actions that reinforce the seriousness of the threat and send an unambiguous message to the wider public: if governments take this kind of action, then the threat must indeed be 'real', as no government would expend these kinds of resources on a spurious or imaginary threat. From this perspective, it can be argued that rather than reassuring the public (their proclaimed purpose), these kinds of actions actually serve to heighten the sense of societal insecurity.

In the end, the overall effect of these discursive processes is to generate and sustain a condition of widespread and intense social fear. The question is: why would public officials wish to create so much fear, or allow such high levels of anxiety to develop? Is this a natural and reasonable reaction to an actual threat, or are other forces at work?

## The politics of fear

There are a number of clear political advantages to be gained from the creation of social anxiety and moral panics. In the first place, fear is a disciplining agent and can be effectively deployed to de-legiti-

THE POLITICS OF FEAR

mise dissent, mute criticism, and constrain internal opponents. In an atmosphere of national peril, the appeal for political unity takes on greater moral force and voicing disagreement can be characterised as an act of disloyalty. Fear can lead ordinary citizens to act as the primary agents of censure themselves, both in terms of self-censorship (choosing to withhold their own doubts and disagreements in public discourse) and the censorship of others (expressing disapproval when confronted with dissenting or 'disloyal' opinions in others). This is because fear is corrosive of both political expression and moral courage. Either way, its primary function is to ease the pressures of accountability for political elites. An instrument of elite rule, political fear is in effect a political project aimed at reifying existing structures of power.

Fear also functions to distract the public from more complex and pressing social ills, thereby inhibiting transformative or counter-hegemonic pressures. Actually, some fears are better than others for this purpose, because some fear—such as the fear of being without healthcare or employment—are not amenable to quick-fix solutions and carry the risk of policy failure. The fear of terrorism on the other hand, is perfect because it is ubiquitous, catastrophic, and fairly opaque (reliant on government control of secret information). There is also little risk that the authorities will be seen to fail; every subsequent terrorist attack can be easily construed as a vindication of official warnings. As a consequence, more pressing and more complex threats to individual safety, such as crime, gun control, urban poverty, health insurance, and workplace conditions (to name a few), can be neglected while the government spends vast sums on countering the threat of terrorist attack. Disturbingly, in both America and Britain, the social distraction of the terrorist threat has allowed for the diversion of scarce resources into ideologically driven elite projects, such as National Missile Defence, rearmament and military expansion, military deployment in new regions, enforcing regime change, enacting doctrines of pre-emptive war, controlling strategic sources of oil, cutting welfare programmes, and increasing social surveillance, all

185

justified as a necessary response to the terrorist threat. In the end, political fear works to perpetuate elite rule by reifying existing power structures and controlling domestic challenges.[16]

At a material level, there are a great many vested interests in maintaining the widespread condition of fear, not least for the military-industrial complex which benefits directly from increased spending on national security. Large corporations with extensive ties to the political establishment have made extraordinary profits from government-sponsored anti-terrorism programmes. The organs of state security—the police, FBI, CIA, Department of Homeland Security, Department of Defence, MI5, MI6, and the like—also benefit from increased resources and an elevated status in times of national danger. In America, more than half of the federal budget for FY 2004 was devoted to national defence, with the Pentagon receiving $399 billion and spending on homeland security more than doubling from $18 billion to $38 billion.[17] In Britain, MI5 has been given a 50 per cent increase in its budget to £300 million per year and is set to increase its personnel numbers to the highest level since World War II.[18] In addition to these public bodies, private security providers have benefited greatly from the state of anxiety about terrorism: sales of security equipment have topped $50 billion per annum since the early 1990s.[19]

At a deeper level, it has been convincingly demonstrated that public discourses of fear and threat are an essential element in constructing large-scale political violence, particularly war which requires widespread social support.[20] Notably, the process of threat creation

---

16  Robin, *Fear*, p. 162.

17  William Hartung, 'The Hidden Costs of War', A Report Commissioned by Howard S. Brembeck and the Fourth Freedom Forum, 14 February 2003, http://www.fourthfreedom.org/php/t-si-index.php?hinc=Hartung_report.hinc, accessed 29 August, 2003.

18  Mark Evans, 'Idealists Rush to join MI5's Army of Spies', *The Times*, 2 March 2004.

19  Zulaika and Douglass, *Terror and Taboo*, p. 9.

20  See Vivienne Jabri, *Discourses on Violence: Conflict Analysis Reconsidered*

has been an evident feature of every intrastate war in the last two decades. In the Balkans for example, Slobodan Milosevic convinced the Serbian public that their culture, their way of life, and their very existence was under threat from Croatian and Bosnian designs; this led many to join the war to defend the Serb nation and many more to acquiesce or support it tacitly. Similarly, Rwandan elites in 1994 convinced ordinary Hutu citizens that the Tutsi-dominated RPF was making a bid to exterminate all Hutu people. The sense of threat generated by the political elite in both of these cases was sufficient to motivate ordinary people to engage in or support pre-emptive military attacks on their perceived enemies. A similar process has occurred in the war on terror: the social and political construction of fear and an overwhelming sense of danger have justified pre-emptive attacks on Afghanistan and Iraq, with the support of sizeable sections of the public.[21]

The politics of fear has another fundamental political function: constructing and sustaining collective identity. It is well known that groups unify in the face of external danger in a kind of instinctual psychological reflex. For sizeable and diverse collectivities such as states, the existence of abiding and multiple exogenous threats is indispensable for bolstering the unity of the 'imagined community'. While neo-realist scholars believe that the international system is by definition dangerous and threatening—thereby providing all states with pre-existing and permanent external danger—constructivists have demonstrated how state practices actually constitute or create this situation of anarchy through their discursive interaction.[22] From

---

(Manchester, 1996); Richard Jackson, 'The Social Construction of Internal War', in Richard Jackson, ed., *(Re)Constructing Cultures of Violence and Peace* (New York, 2004); Stuart Kaufman, *Modern Hatreds: the Symbolic Politics of Ethnic War* (London, 2001); Franke Wilmer, *The Social Construction of Man, the State, and War: Identity, Conflict, and Violence in the Former Yugoslavia,* (New York, 2002).

21 Jackson, *Writing the War on Terrorism.*

22 Alexander Wendt, 'Anarchy is What States Make of it,' *International Organization,* 46, 1992, pp. 391-425.

this perspective, external threats do not necessarily exist independently of states; rather, states deliberately construct them primarily for the purposes of disciplining the domestic sphere and sustaining national unity. Creating and maintaining a perennial 'discourse of danger' therefore, is a key function of foreign policy, designed to enforce inside/outside, self/other boundaries and thereby construct or 'write' collective identity.[23] Typically, states construct external threats by positing a rival state (the 'evil' Soviet empire, for example), an opposing ideology (fascism, communism, or Islamic fundamentalism), or 'national security' issues such as weapons proliferation, rogue states, illicit drugs, and terrorism.

More broadly, elites believe that fear can act as a tool of political renewal by providing an alternative sense of political purpose and establishing a new foundation for the national interest.[24] This is why the political use of fear has such a long genealogy; from the 'red scares' of the American frontier to the Palmer raids and McCarthyism, political fear has been deployed by elites to provide meaning and purpose during periods of destabilising social transformation. Creating a new national project based on a socially constructed fear of an alien 'other' is moreover, much easier than attempting to define a positive moral vision for society—especially in an era defined by the 'end of ideology' and its accompanying elite crisis of confidence. There is therefore, a moral economy of fear: it is self-legitimating and provides purpose and direction during moments of self-doubt. From this perspective, the war on terror, like its predecessor the Cold War, functions as 'a project of political and cultural reconstruction' for the body politic.[25]

The deliberate construction of a climate of fear by political elites is enabled by several pre-existing social, political, and cultural conditions. The aforementioned existence of a 'culture of fear'[26] for example,

---

23  Campbell, *Writing Security*.

24  Robin, *Fear*.

25  Ibid, p. 37.

26  Furedi, *Culture of Fear*.

and the widespread risk aversion expressed through the precaution-ary principle, makes the construction of a defensive fear of terrorism relatively easy for the entrepreneurs of anxiety. In addition, anthro-pologists have noted the way in which the official terrorism discourse articulates and amplifies a number of western cultural taboos and social fears, such as the fear of poison and contamination, of disorder and anarchy, the 'wild man' (the savage barbarian 'other'), and the fear of the 'mad mullah' figure.[27] In other words, there exists a ready-made set of cultural tropes and narratives about the threatening and alien 'other' which officials can graft onto the language of the 'enemy within'. More importantly, it has been eloquently demonstrated that political fear is actually integral to liberal doctrines of the state.[28] The doctrine of the social contract for example, is rooted in the fear of a violent and threatening state of nature, while the doctrine of separation of powers is rooted in the fear of unbridled and abusive executive power. Again, such deeply embedded political narratives provide the discursive raw material for the construction of an all-encompassing threat to the po-litical community. In essence, the public narrative of the terrorist threat is both an expression of an existing cultural politics of fear, and is in turn enabled by that culture. However, constructing and maintaining a condition of political fear requires deliberate and ongoing action by political elites. More than just a sociological condition, cultural fears are a form of deliberative politics.

## The dangers of the politics of fear

There are a number of palpable dangers inherent in the politics of fear. In the first instance, political fear is highly damaging to demo-cratic politics and civil society because it de-legitimises dissent, nar-rows the discursive space for political expression, and expands state coercive power at the expense of individuals and social institutions. The corrosive effects of the present discourse of danger are already

27 Zulaika and Douglass, *Terror and Taboo*.
28 Robin, *Fear*.

well documented: anti-globalisation protesters, academics, post-modernists, liberals, pro-choice activists, environmentalists, and gay liberationists have been accused of being aligned with the evil of terrorism and of undermining the nation's struggle against terrorism;[29] arms trade protesters have been arrested in London and animal rights campaigners have been banned from travelling to Britain under new anti-terrorism legislation;[30] blacklists of 'disloyal' professors, university departments, journalists, writers, and commentators have been posted on the internet and smear campaigns launched against them; critical voices have been kept away from speaking at public events or in the media; and political opponents of government policy are frequently accused of being traitors or of putting the nation at risk.

In the end of course, political fear furnishes no positive foundation for politics; it is ultimately vacuous and negative. In fact, it is a kind of anti-politics because it is corrosive of self-expression and morality. For its architects, the politics of fear is firmly rooted in the fear of politics: a confident, politically engaged, active citizenry would pose a challenge to elite power and structural inequality.[31] The real danger is that political fear can all too easily become a permanent condition, bleeding into every aspect of private and public life; the death of politics follows soon after and all we are left with is the self-perpetuating 'warfare state'.[32]

Apart from its effects on the democratic polis, the construction of the terrorist threat is also directly implicated in the very worst of the abuses of the global counter-terrorism effort, including: the

---

29 David Campbell, 'Time is Broken: The Return of the Past in the Response to 11 September', *Theory & Event*, 5, 2002.

30 On 31 August 2005, animal rights campaigner, Professor Steven Best, was prevented by the Home Office from entering the UK to attend an Animal Liberation Front event using the government's crackdown on hate preachers. Donald MacLeod, 'Britain uses hate law to ban animal rights campaigner', *Guardian*, 31 August 2005.

31 Robin, *Fear*, p. 145.

32 Barry Buzan, *People, States and Fear: The National Security Problem in International Relations* (Brighton, 1983), p. 240.

mass murder of Taliban prisoners during Operation Enduring Free-dom; the illegal rendition of terrorist suspects to countries which routinely practice torture; the public killing of an innocent Brazilian man, Jean Charles de Menezes, on the London underground; and the ongoing murder, torture, and inhumane treatment of prisoners at Guantanamo Bay, Baghram airforce base, Abu Ghraib prison and countless other detention facilities around the world.[33] Recent studies have convincingly demonstrated that these large-scale and systematic abuses of human rights, far from being aberrant or in any way exceptional, have instead been normalised and institutionalised in the day-to-day prosecution of the global war on terror.[34]

More importantly, the studies clearly demonstrate that the abuses were in many instances the direct result of the terrorist threat nar-rative. For example, the extreme forms of shackling seen in the photos of the initial Guantanamo Bay prisoners (in some cases, bound, blindfolded, gagged, and shackled to gurneys, detainees were wheeled to interrogations) were justified on the grounds that these were such dangerous individuals that they had to be restrained in this fashion for the safety of those guarding them.[35] Earlier, President Bush's Military Order of 13 November 2001 proclaimed that detain-ees in the war on terrorism were not entitled to protection under the Geneva Conventions and would instead be tried by special military commissions because, 'having fully considered the magnitude of the

---

33 See Richard Jackson, 'The Discursive Construction of Torture in the War on Terrorism: Narratives of Danger and Evil', paper presented at *The Barbarisation of Warfare* Conference, June 27-28, 2005, University of Wolverhampton, http://naspir.org.uk/members/richard_jackson/richard_jackson.htm.

34 Mark Danner, *Torture and Truth: America, Abu Ghraib, and the War on Terror* (New York, 2004); Karen Greenberg and Joshua Dratel, (eds), *The Torture Papers: The Road to Abu Ghraib*, (Cambridge, 2005); Seymour Hersh, *Chain of Command: The Road from 9/11 to Abu Ghraib* (London, 2004); Rachel Meerpol, ed., *America's Disappeared: Secret Imprisonment, Detainees, and the "War on Terror'* (New York, 2005); David Rose, *Guantánamo: America's War on Human Rights* (London, 2004).

35 Rose, *Guantánamo*, p. 2.

potential deaths, injuries, and property destruction that would result from potential acts of terrorism... I have determined that an extraordinary emergency exists for national defence purposes'.[36] Later, in correspondence regarding the treatment of prisoners, senior administration officials argued that 'the interrogation of such unlawful combatants in a manner *beyond that which may be applied to a prisoner of war* who is subject to the protections of the Geneva Conventions'[37] will be allowable because,

a detainee may possess information that could enable the United States to prevent attacks that potentially could equal or surpass the September 11 attacks in their magnitude. Clearly, any harm that might occur during an interrogation would pale to insignificance compared to the harm avoided by preventing such an attack, which could take hundreds or thousands of lives.[38]

What these excerpts clearly demonstrate is how the discursive construction of the terrorist threat was deployed to justify and normalise the systematic and institutional abuse of human rights.

One of the greatest dangers of political fear then is that it can lead individuals and societies to betray their own beliefs; that moral convictions about justice and human rights are abandoned in a desperate bid to allay fear.[39] The present politics of fear have to some extent already undermined the moral community: the relative public indifference to the preventive detention of thousands of terrorist suspects (the vast majority of whom are innocent of any crime), the illegal rendition programme, the Iraqi prisoner abuse scandal, and the shoot-to-kill policy are evidence of a creeping moral vacuity induced by the suffocating blanket of fear. And the relative impunity by which the authorities are gradually eroding civil liberties and legal

---

36  Military Order of 13 November 2001, in Danner, *Torture and Truth*.

37  Pentagon Working Group Report, 4 April 2003, in Danner, *Torture and Truth*, p. 188; emphasis added.

38  Memorandum for Alberto R. Gonzales, 1 August 2002, in Danner, *Torture and Truth*.

39  Robin, *Fear*, p. 168.

protections signals a further surrender of civic values to security values. In America, Britain, and Australia, governments committed to further drastic attacks on established rights have been returned to power in national elections.

Finally, within the pragmatic logic of counterterrorism, it seems obvious that the politics of fear can too easily become a self-fulfilling prophesy.[40] Exaggerating the terrorist threat and maintaining social fear actually emboldens and empowers terrorists; it provides them with incontrovertible evidence of their own ability to gain unlimited publicity and influence a terrified society through the threat of violence. Given that terrorism is essentially a form of political communication and therefore relies on the widest possible publicity, the politics of fear plays directly into the hands of militants. From this perspective, it is strategically counter-productive.

## Resisting the politics of fear

Despite the present hegemony of the politics of fear, the primary discursive constructions at the heart of the terrorist threat narrative are actually inherently unstable and vulnerable to deconstruction across a range of levels. An initial strategy of resistance lies in revealing the underlying politics of the discourse, as I have attempted to do in this chapter. That is, exposing the hegemonic forces at work in the public language of counterterrorism helps to de-invest it of much of its assumed moral authority.

On the other side of the coin, it is of vital importance to demonstrate the political basis of terrorism itself. It can be demonstrated that, apart from extremely rare instances of millenarian[41] and lone individual[42] terrorism, all sustained campaigns of terror are politically-motivated, including campaigns of suicide terrorism. A major empirical study at the University of Chicago, the Chicago Project on

---

40 Joseba Zulaika, 'The Self-Fulfilling Prophesies of Counterterrorism,' *Radical History Review*, 85, pp. 191-9.

41 The Aum Shinrikyo case is an example of millenarian terrorism.

42 The Unabomber is an example of a lone terrorist.

Suicide Terrorism, has examined every single suicide mission around the world between 1980 and 2003.[43] Its conclusions, based on rigorous analysis of 315 cases of suicide bombing, are revealing: there is little or no connection between suicide terrorism and religion; virtually all suicide attacks have secular, strategic goals such as attempting to force an occupying power to withdraw its military forces; suicide attacks are always a very minor part of a wider military campaign and are employed for a variety of logical, tactically determined reasons against a superior enemy; and thus far, once a group has achieved its political goals (such as Hezbollah's goal of driving American, French, and Israeli forces out of south Lebanon, or the LTTE's goal of preventing Indian reoccupation of Jaffna), the suicide campaign has been abandoned. The Chicago study convincingly demonstrates that even the al-Qaeda terrorist campaign against America and its allies since the early 1990s is principally aimed at expelling American troops from the Persian Gulf and reducing its interference in the region.[44] These findings reinforce the argument that there is no 'new' terrorism,[45] and that terrorism is a response to specific state policies rather than an expression of irrational belief, religious extremism, or non-political goals. Actually, suggesting that suicide terrorists are mindless fanatics plays into the hands of the terrorists by magnifying the fear and terror they induce.

Another strategy of deconstruction involves marshalling counter-evidence and counter-arguments that rebut the primary narratives or provide alternative viewpoints. For example, it is easily demonstrated that the actual risk posed by terrorism to personal and public safety

---

43  The findings of the study are presented in Robert Pape, *Dying to Win: the Strategic Logic of Suicide Terrorism* (New York, 2005).

44  This finding is supported by others who have examined the writings of al-Qaeda and interviewed its leaders. See for example, Peter Bergen, *Holy War Inc: Inside the Secret World of Osama bin Laden* (London, 2001); Jason Burke, *Al Qaeda: the True Story of Radical Islam* (London, 2004).

45  See Thomas Copeland, 'Is the "New Terrorism" Really New? An Analysis of the New Paradigm for Terrorism', *The Journal of Conflict Studies*, XXI, 2001, pp. 7-27.

is minute: in statistical terms the risk of being killed in a terrorist attack ranks somewhere near the risk of being killed by DIY accidents, lightning strikes, or bee stings.[46] Certainly, it does not even begin to compare with America's annual death toll from gun violence: since 1965 close to a million Americans have died from gunshot wounds, and in 2000 a total of 28,117 people died in weapons-related incidents, more than 10,000 of whom were murdered.[47] Even in 2001, America's worst year on record, the casualties from terrorism were still vastly outnumbered by deaths from automobile accidents and pedestrian deaths, alcohol and tobacco-related illnesses, suicides, and a great many diseases like influenza, cancer, rabies, and liver disease. At a global level, the estimated 1,000-7,000 yearly deaths from terrorism pales into insignificance next to the 40,000 people who die every day from hunger, the 500,000 people who are killed every year by light weapons, the 2 million who are killed around the world in automobile accidents, and the several million who die annually from diseases like influenza, HIV-AIDS, and tuberculosis.[48]

A study of the location of terrorist attacks themselves further confirms the view that terrorism actually poses a negligible risk to the personal safety of westerners. In geographical terms, the vast majority of terrorist attacks occur in a very small number of countries—Israel, Russia, Colombia, Kashmir, Saudi Arabia, Sri Lanka, Algeria, Spain, Afghanistan and, since May 2003, Iraq. Terrorism, in other words, is almost always associated with a relatively small number of ongoing intense political conflicts; the attacks on westerners in places like Bali, Casablanca, Karachi, Istanbul, Madrid, and London are likewise intimately linked to the ongoing war on terrorism, with all its geo-political dimensions. The reality is that not all countries are at risk of terrorism: the vast majority of the world's 200 or so states

---

46  Jonathan Barker, *The No-Nonsense Guide to Terrorism* (Oxford, 2002), p. 37.
47  Mick North, 'Dangers of the Armed Response at Home', in Phil Scraton, (ed.), *Beyond September 11: An Anthology of Dissent* (London, 2002), p. 162.
48  Peter Hough, *Understanding Global Security*, London, 2004, p. 155.

experience little or no terrorism at all and are unlikely to, unless they become entangled in a violent political conflict.

The nature of terrorist attacks reveals a similar picture: proportionally, most terrorist violence is directed at property rather than persons, the majority of attacks involve few or no fatalities at all, and attacks tend to be concentrated in politically symbolic locations such as capital cities or military installations. For example, of the fifty terrorist incidents reported for the entire Latin American region in 2003, forty-one of them were bombings of an American-owned oil pipeline in Colombia.[49] Significantly, of the more than 10,000 terrorist incidents between 1968 and 1998, fewer than a dozen involved more than hundred fatalities,[50] and only three per cent of terrorist incidents between 1980 and 2003 were suicide attacks.[51] The random mass casualty terrorism that we are constantly told to expect is actually extremely rare, although it has recently become a significant feature of the Iraq insurgency. Mass casualties are most often counterproductive to terrorist aims—they alienate their supporters and can provoke harsh reprisals from the authorities. In reality, most terrorist violence is directed at symbolic targets: its aim is to create a media spectacle in order to communicate some kind of political message; it is instrumental violence, or 'propaganda of the deed'.

For this reason, a number of respected academics have expressed doubt that terrorists would seriously consider using weapons of mass destruction,[52] or that regimes would ever sponsor such activities. Apart from the difficulties of obtaining and deploying such weapons (they are notoriously unstable and unpredictable), such attacks would

---

49 William Pfaff, 'Scaring America Half to Death', *International Herald Tribune*, 8 May 2003.

50 Brian Jenkins, 'Will Terrorists go Nuclear? A Reappraisal,' in Harvey Kushner, (ed.), *The Future of Terrorism: Violence in the New Millennium*, (London, 1998), pp. 244-5.

51 Pape, *Dying to Win*, p. 6.

52 See Jenkins, 'Will Terrorists go Nuclear?'; Ehud Sprinzak, 'The Great Superterrorism Scare', *Foreign Policy*, 112, 1998, pp. 110-24; Charles Townshend, *Terrorism: a Very Short Introduction* (Oxford, 2002).

likely be counter-productive, as they would undermine community support, distort the terrorist's political message, and invite overwhelming retaliation. Terrorists are rational political actors and are acutely aware of these dangers. The Gilmore Commission in 1999, a Clinton-appointed advisory panel that was assembled to investigate the threat of weapons of mass destruction falling into the hands of terrorists, agreed with this assessment. It concluded that "rogue states would hesitate to entrust such weapons to terrorists because of the likelihood that such a group's actions might be unpredictable even to the point of using the weapon against its sponsor", and because of 'the prospect of significant reprisals'.[53]

In a similar vein, the discursive construction of thousands of highly sophisticated al-Qaeda operatives around the world just waiting to strike can also be deconstructed as little more than myth-making: individual terrorists almost never reach the level of cunning and sophistication that officials ascribe to them. Information gathered since September 11, 2001 reveals that the characterisation of the al-Qaeda terrorists as brilliant professionals—the so-called 'superman scenario'—is misconstrued. In fact, they made a great many amateurish errors and only avoided detection and interception through profound failures in the American intelligence system.[54] Moreover, in relation to the mythology now surrounding al-Qaeda, it has been convincingly shown that the idea of a global Islamic terrorist organisation similar to the mafia, with Osama bin Laden at the head, is a fiction first advocated by the US Justice Department in the aftermath of the 1993 World Trade Center bombing. To the extent that al-Qaeda operated a number of camps on the fringes of the Islamist movement in Afghanistan in the 1990s, this rudimentary level of organisation was destroyed in December 2001 with the fall of the Taliban regime.[55] While there are extremist Islamic groups operating

---

53 Quoted in Dilip Hiro, *War Without End: the Rise of Islamic Terrorism and Global Response* (London, 2002), p. 391.

54 Hersh, *Chain of Command*, pp. 73-103.

55 See Burke, *Al Qaeda*.

locally and autonomously in countries like Saudi Arabia, Pakistan, Indonesia, Algeria, Egypt, The Philippines, and Yemen, they are for the most part fighting over locally-defined issues; the idea that they are unified in a global struggle against modernity and western values is a highly Eurocentric and misleading exaggeration, unsupported by serious scholarship. Certainly, the extremely small number of individuals convicted of mostly minor terrorism offences since September 11, 2001 in both America and Britain is hardly indicative of a massive global conspiracy against the West.

Related to this, even the most cursory knowledge of terrorism reveals that terrorists have never truly threatened a state, or democracy, or freedom, or the way of life of an entire people; nor have they ever threatened the peace of the world or the existence of any civilisation. This is so much demagoguery. Evidence from World War II, when cities on all sides were subjected to intense aerial bombardment in which hundreds of thousands of people were killed, demonstrates that society is far more resilient than officials are willing to admit. It is simply ridiculous to suggest that a few terrorist bombs could achieve what the Blitz was palpably unable to.

On the other hand, there are numerous examples where the reaction of the authorities to terrorist attacks has endangered democracy and freedom by seriously undermining civil and political rights, and where the state's eagerness to suppress dissidents has led to gross miscarriages of justice and human rights abuses by the security forces. Such acts have undermined public respect for political institutions, damaged the functioning of democracy, and demoralised society. In reality, it is not terrorism that threatens the essence of our societies—terrorists are tiny groups of isolated individuals able to do little more than commit symbolic acts of violence—but rather state-led counter-terrorism and the dangers of over-reaction by the authorities.

Lastly, it can be easily demonstrated that state terrorism—the use or threat of state-sponsored violence to instil fear for political purposes—remains a far greater threat to individual and societal security than the threat of dissident terrorism. Over the past few decades, states, including several liberal democracies, have tortured and murdered hundreds of thousands of political opponents and caused massive social destruction to communities in places like Vietnam, Cambodia, South Africa, El Salvador, Nicaragua, Cuba, Chile, Spain, Northern Ireland, Rwanda, Serbia, and Turkey—to name just a few. And government forces continue to employ violent repression and state terror in places like Chechnya, Palestine, Kashmir, Afghanistan, Iraq, Algeria, Saudi Arabia, Egypt, Uzbekistan, Zimbabwe, and Myanmar, among many others. State terror has always been a far greater threat to security than non-state terror; and yet, state terror is conspicuous by its absence from the public narrative of the terrorist threat—except of course, when it is cynically deployed to justify wars of 'regime change'.

## Political Fear is a social and political construction

I am not trying to suggest that there is no terrorist threat; the victims of 11 September Bali, Casablanca, Moscow, Madrid, Istanbul, London, and daily in Iraq and Israel, are all testament to the reality of the threat posed by political militants. Nor am I suggesting that governments do not have a responsibility to protect their citizens from attack. Rather, what I have attempted to demonstrate in this chapter is that the current official response to the threat—the politics of fear—is unnecessarily exaggerated, damaging to participatory democracy, and corrosive of the moral community. The official response has created an invidious and pervasive atmosphere of domestic anxiety—a chronic state of 'ontological hysteria' where political fear bleeds into the fabric of daily life. From one perspective, this is not surprising: a ubiquitous threat requires a ubiquitous response. I have also tried to show how the politics of fear functions as a political project. At a broad level, it is designed to reify existing structures of power and prevent social and political transformation; more specifically, it acts as a smokescreen for specific ideologically-driven projects at home and abroad.

199

Even if this was not the case, however, it seems obvious that the inherent discursive logic of the politics of fear prevents clear and creative thinking about how democratic societies should respond to politically-motivated campaigns of terror. Instead, as we have seen after three years of a massive global war on terror, the discourse of danger institutionalises an approach to counterterrorism which is proving to be both counterproductive and highly damaging. In large part, this is because the moral absolutism of the discourse induces political amnesia about the failures and lessons from other counterterrorist campaigns.[56] For example, a clear lesson from other campaigns in Israel, Kashmir, Spain, Sri Lanka, Northern Ireland, Chechnya, Peru, Algeria and many others, is that terrorism can never be defeated by military force or coercion alone; it only eases when political compromise takes place on the divisive issues that first instigated it. At the very least, the politics of fear actually misconceives and misunderstands the nature of the terrorist threat and the strategies required to deal with it—it is poor 'threat assessment' and poor 'mission definition', to use military parlance. By deliberately obfuscating the underlying history and politics of terrorism, the actual nature and causes of terrorism and the real motivations and aims of the terrorists, the search for more effective and long-term policy solutions is effectively cauterised.

Given the intellectual cul-de-sac of the politics of fear, it is not surprising that the present policies of the war on terror are actually making terrorism worse and intensifying those global conditions that encourage, nurture and sustain endemic violence.[57] It now seems clear that the global war on terror is entrenching an ever deepening cycle

---

56  Campbell, 'Time is broken'.

57  See Rahul Mahajan, *Full Spectrum Dominance: US Power in Iraq and Beyond* (New York, 2003); Alex Callinicos, *The New Mandarins of American Power* (Cambridge, 2003); Carl Boggs, (ed.), *Masters of War: Militarism and Blowback in the Era of American Empire* (New York, 2003); Noam Chomsky, *Hegemony or Survival: America's Quest for Global Dominance* (London, 2003); Aftab A. Malik, (ed.), *Shattered Illusions: Analyzing the War on Terrorism* (Bristol, 2002).

of violence and counter-violence similar to that which has already occurred at a micro-level in Israel, Chechnya, Kashmir, Colombia, and Algeria, for example where neither side can win decisively but no party is willing to abandon the military option. In strategic terms, it is now widely accepted that the wars against Afghanistan and Iraq have created a whole new generation of terrorists and made terrorism an even greater problem by creating new sources of grievance and decentralising the operations of terrorist networks across many more countries. The occupation of Iraq in particular is providing a new training ground for militants, much in the same way that Afghanistan did in the 1980s, when volunteers from various Muslim countries fought against Soviet occupation before returning to their countries of origin to launch violent campaigns against western-supported regimes. These two wars, as well as the abuses at Guantanamo Bay and Abu Ghraib, have turned many moderate Muslims towards the extremist camp, fuelling anti-Americanism and anti-western imperialism, and providing militant groups with an even bigger pool of potential recruits and supporters. It is also the case that the invasion of Iraq and its aftermath has been highly damaging to the institutions of global governance, right at the moment when they are needed most.

In large part, it was (and still is) the nature of the politics of fear that has prevented the consideration of alternative paradigms and approaches to counter-terrorism; the inbuilt logic of the language of threat and the privileging of only certain kinds of knowledge has circumvented the kind of in-depth, rigorous, and informed debate that a complex political challenge such as terrorism requires. Unless we break out of the stultifying confines of the current terrorism discourse, more effective policies will continue to prove elusive; unless or until both politicians and the wider public learn to speak and think in a language outside of the official rhetoric, we will be condemned to live in a perpetual condition of fear and violence.

In the final analysis, responding effectively to the actual terrorist threat requires an alternative politics based on realistic assessment, proportionality, and genuine social involvement in democratic debate. It requires authentic participatory discussion about what political and social values are worth preserving, and what policy options are available for dealing with the roots and causes of terrorism itself. Unfortunately, such a politics cannot come from the present leadership; they have too many vested interests in maintaining political fear and are too committed to the present course of action to go back. A new political vision must come instead from individual citizens, social movements, and civil society—and it must begin with a demolition of the current discourse. In order to bring down the stultifying and immoral edifice of anxiety, it will need to be dismantled brick-by-brick: the media will need to challenge the language of exaggeration by politicians; academics will need to debunk official (and cultural) fallacies and falsehoods; religious groups will need to contest the ethics of torture and abuse; the legal profession will need to confront the erosion of civil liberties; and individual citizens will need to march, shout, petition, write letters, vote judiciously, and make themselves heard. Political fear is a social and political construction; there is nothing to stop it from being torn down, if we have the moral courage to act.

# 9

# POLITICS vs TERRORISM: THE MADRID CASE

## Javier Jordan and Nicola Horsburgh

The terrorist attack in Madrid (11-M) constitutes an interesting case study especially for a book such as this. The attack occurred three days before the general election, in which the ruling party, the Partido Popular (PP) lost despite forecasts of a narrow victory. Empirical studies since then demonstrate that the attack did influence the vote, very probably handing victory to the main opposition party, the Partido Socialista Obrero Español (PSOE) led by José Luis Rodríguez Zapatero[1].

It is very likely the terrorists who planned and timed the attack took into account the political impact of their actions. In December 2003, two documents published on jihadi websites analysed the political situation in Spain following government support for the United States over Iraq. Both documents called for hostilities against and the withdrawal of Spanish troops from Iraq[2]. In one of these documents, attacks in Spain were discussed[3]:

---

1   Narciso Michavila 'War, Terrorism and Elections: Electoral Impact of the Islamist Terror Attacks on Madrid,' Real Instituto Elcano, Working Paper 13/2005, see: http://www.realinstitutoelcano.org/documentos/186.asp.

2   Brynjar Lia and Thomas Hegghammer, 'Jihadi Strategic Studies: the Alleged Al Qaeda Policy Study Preceding the Madrid Bombings,' *Studies in Conflict & Terrorism*, 27 (2004) pp. 355-75.

3   Reuven Paz, *A Message to the Spanish People: the Neglected Threat by Qa`idat al-Jihad,* Global Research in International Affairs (GLORIA) Center, Prism Special Dispatches, vol. 2, 2 (18 March 2004) in http://e-prism.org/images/

We believe that the Spanish government will not support more than two or three hits…before feeling obliged to withdraw following popular pressure. If its troops remain following the hits the victory of the socialist party will be practically guaranteed… and the withdrawal of the Spanish troops will be listed on its electoral project.[4]

Following 11-M, it was speculated that future terrorist attacks would be timed around general elections so as to wreak havoc on western governments[5]. However, the opposite can be true: a terrorist attack can strengthen a government, as with 9/11. Therefore, this chapter will examine the main factors in the political breakdown following 11-M. Attention will be paid to the first three intense days of the crisis (11-14 March) and the key actors during this period: the government, political opposition, media, security agencies, social movements and the terrorists.

The main argument of this essay is two-fold: firstly, any understanding of the electoral outcome must take into account the social malaise that existed in Spain: an agitation related to the war in Iraq and military operations there between March and April 2003. When the investigation began to broaden its inquiry into the perpetrators of 11-M many linked the attack to Spanish involvement in Iraq and personally blamed José María Aznar's government. Secondly, both the PP and PSOE sought, amid impending elections, to capitalise politically on 11-M. Both parties supported the line of inquiry that best served their respective interests, using the media to do so. They resorted to playing politics with terrorism, in the process seriously tarnishing the legitimacy of the political system in Spain.

To give a sense of structure to the chapter, there are three main sections. The first section will explore social and political consensus on ETA and the massive anti-Iraq war protests that took place in

---

PRISM_Special_dispatch_no_2-2.pdf .

4    A translation in Spanish of the document can be found at: http://www.realinstitutoelcano.org/materiales/docs/Hegghammer_traduc.pdf.

5    Fred Burton, 'Re-Examining the Odds of a Pre-Election Attack,' 1 October 2004, http://worldterrorismreport.stratfor.com/.

Spain. The second section will focus on the initial police investigation into 11-M. A chronological approach will be adopted so as to appreciate the political manoeuvres as they took place during this period. The last section will examine the key actors and the implications of their actions upon the political landscape in Spain.

## ETA and the political and social consensus prior to 11-M

ETA has been active in Spain for over forty years and is responsible for almost 1,000 deaths. Anti-terrorism was therefore a key priority during Aznar's government (1996–2004). In this time, several objectives were met:

a) Political and judicial efficiency: Spanish security services had disbanded tens of terrorist cells. Since 2000, 60 per cent of arrests were made before cells had become active or established. The security services possessed a high level of intelligence on ETA, complicating its ability to regenerate as an organisation. From an operational perspective, ETA's impact was at an almost unprecedented low. Major indentations had been made to its financial infrastructure. In addition, the introduction of and social support for tougher anti-terrorist laws widened the scope for prosecution.

b) Political consensus: in recent years, the PP and PSOE, both targets of ETA, shared a consensus on the Basque terrorist organisation. This political consensus culminated in the Anti-terrorist Pact in December 2000. Under the pact, both sides recognised terrorism as a state concern and pledged to forgo political confrontation in the interest of anti-terrorism.

c) Social consensus: according to opinion polls conducted by the Centre for Sociological Investigation (CIS), ETA was one of four key concerns within Spanish society[6]. There existed general social opposition to ETA[7]. A key factor in this is the July 1997 kidnap-

---

6  CIS is an official organisation dependent on the Ministry of the President. The studies to which we refer can be found at: http://www.cis.es/.

7  ETA enjoys some tactical support in the Basque country from the radical left (Abertzale). This group has a political wing that won 150, 188 votes and

ping and assassination of Miguel Angel Blanco, a PP councillor. As a ransom ETA demanded the transfer of ETA convicts to prisons in the Basque Country. Millions of Spaniards marched in protest, calling for the liberation of Miguel Angel Blanco and condemning the terrorist blackmail. The march was one of the largest in Spain's history as a democracy. Ultimately, the government did not cede to ETA's demand and Miguel Angel Blanco was assassinated. The tragedy spawned several anti-ETA movements like ¡Basta Ya! (That's enough!), Manos Blancas (white hands) and the Ermua Forum. The Spanish media were also united in their rejection of ETA and supported Aznar's anti-terrorist strategy.

Therefore, when the Madrid attacks took place the government enjoyed clear social, political and media support in its anti-terrorist struggle. Anti-terrorist politics hardly featured on the electoral agenda and then only to highlight government success. In this context, the government miscalculated that 11-M would bolster its chances at the polls.

## Political and social agitation over the Iraq war

If in the struggle against ETA the PP had achieved significant social and political success, Aznar's support of the United States over Iraq provoked the opposite reaction.

From late February to April 2003, Spain was witness to widespread social mobilisation against the war in Iraq and government support for George W. Bush. In Madrid and Barcelona over a million marched on the streets. Initially, the anti-war movement consisted of environmental and pacifist groups operating mainly in cyberspace (see: Platform Against the War http://www.culturacontralaguerra.org/, No to War http://noalaguerra.com/, and La Haine http://lahaine.org/). The movement later incorporated artists, actors and student groups. The media, apart from those with close ties to the government, were critical of state policy, even more so when a cameraman from a private

---

nine seats in the July 2005 Basque parliamentary elections.

television channel was killed by an American tank in Baghdad. In a survey conducted by CIS at the time, 91 per cent were against the administration's position over Iraq and in March 2003 the Iraq crisis was rated as the second most important state issue, with one in five considering the war one of their top three concerns.

In the political sphere, the PP was left isolated. No political party supported its position. In March 2003, support for the party declined (21.9 per cent of those surveyed maintained their support for the PP but the PSOE gained its best results with 27.4 per cent)[8]. The PSOE capitalised on PP decline, with a number of party members fronting the anti-war manifestations. The PSOE also enjoyed a united position on Iraq, improving the image of their party leader, Zapatero. This was a reversal of fortune for Zapatero, his leadership having been questioned both inside and outside his party. Indeed, during this period the PSOE leader for the first time received greater support in opinion polls than Aznar[9].

However, as the weeks passed, social concern waned and the damage to the government was contained. In June 2003, a Gallup poll gave Aznar a three point advantage over Zapatero as the most valued political leader[10]. By early March 2005, social agitation over Iraq was just a memory. The war in Iraq was now a concern to less than 2 per cent. The most recent CIS barometer before the attack gave the PP an electoral advantage of over five points[11].

## The initial police investigation

Between 7.01 and 7.14 a.m. on 11 March 2004, an undetermined number of terrorists (probably ten) boarded four short-distance trains[12]. After depositing thirteen rucksack explosives the terrorists

8   Narciso Michavila (Working Paper 13/2005).

9   Canal Sur, 30 March 2003.

10  Gallup, June 2003. Available at: http://www.gallup.es/encu/opp/jun03/intro.asp.

11  *El Mundo*, 4 March 2004.

12  The trains were *Cercanías*, connecting surrounding villages to the capital.

abandoned the trains at stations en route to Madrid. Between 7.37 and 7.39 a.m., ten of the rucksacks exploded, killing 191 and injuring almost 1,800 people.

In the first meeting on 11 March between senior political leaders, the civil guard and the national police it was concluded that ETA was responsible for the attack. The meeting took place between 12 noon and 1p.m. The National Centre for Intelligence (CNI) released a note at 15.51 p.m. identifying ETA as the group most likely responsible for 11-M[13]. This initial error in identification may surprise outside observers. The attacks were simultaneous, indiscriminate and against soft targets, typical characteristics of al-Qaeda. It is therefore important to highlight the reasons behind this mistaken analysis.

To begin with, ETA was the predominant terrorist organisation in Spain. Furthermore, the timing (around elections) and location (capital city) of the attack were also characteristics of ETA operations. A few days prior to 11-M, the civil guard stopped an armed ETA command unit (carrying 536kg of explosives) on route to Madrid. Under interrogation, it emerged that ETA had plans to attack a ski station used by the royal family and senior government officials. Twelve backpacks containing explosives would be used to carry out the attack. In addition to these plans, in 2003 ETA placed a suitcase bomb on a train, set to explode upon arrival at Chamartin, another major station in Madrid. Fortunately, the plan was foiled. Furthermore, although ETA usually pre-warns before an attack, there are exceptions: in 1987 ETA attacked a shopping centre in Barcelona without any forewarning, killing 21[14]. At the same time, ETA's future had been severely undermined by police efficiency in recent years. In this light, 11-M might represent a desperate attempt to return to the headlines, to regenerate and bring forward new tactics.

---

13 Jorge Dezcallar, ex-director of the National Centre for Intelligence at the Parliamentary Commission investigating 11-M, 19 July 2004.

14 Office of Information and Social Relations, Ministry of Interior, Spain, *España contra el terrorismo de ETA*. Available at: http://www.mir.es/oris/inforETA/actividad.shtm.

A splinter group might even be responsible for the attacks. The will to carry out an attack like 11-M was underlined by past declarations made by ETA threatening indiscriminate and mass killing. 11-M was an unprecedented attack by a jihadist terrorist group on Spanish soil. Since 9/11 almost seventy presumed jihadis were under arrest in Spain, leading experts to consider the jihadi infrastructure as significantly weakened[15]. Finally, an error in communication could have contributed to the initial faulty analysis regarding the perpetrators of 11-M. At a meeting held on 11 March between anti-terrorist experts, a senior police official spoke to the head of the bomb unit and in conversation the explosives were mistakenly said to be Titadyne, used by ETA. This error, though, was soon corrected.[16]

However, one of the first leads in the investigation, and a potential indication of ETA's non-involvement, was the van used by the terrorists to transport the explosives to one of the stations. The van, stolen a week earlier, was found by the police thanks to a witness on 11 March. In the van, Goma 2 Eco of Spanish origin was found (a type of dynamite no longer used by ETA), along with detonators (different to the types used by ETA) and a cassette recording of the Koran in Arabic.[17] The tape was a distinctive indication as to the identity of the perpetrators but it also had to be considered as a deliberate red herring.

Following the van search, the police opened a second line in the investigation, led by specialists in Islamic terrorism. According to police investigators, all options were open[18]. In truth however, ETA's

15 Mariano Rayón, Chief of the Central Unit for Exterior Information of the National Police at the Parliamentary Commission investigating 11-M, 7 July 2004.

16 Díaz-Pintado, former Subdirector General Operative of the general police at the Parliamentary Commission investigating 11-M, 8 July 2004. Available at http://www.congreso.es/.

17 Yousef Nedal Ziad, police translator, at the Parliamentary Commission investigating 11-M on 25 October 2004. Available at: http://www.congreso. es/.

18 Rafael Gómez Menor, head of the Brigade of the Central Unit of Exterior

involvement had been entertained by the investigating authorities for only a few hours.[19] When Islamist terrorism experts at CNI received word of the van and its contents, jihadist involvement was not doubted. A second translation of the tape by these experts revealed that the recorded passage was an aggressive piece, a characteristic not noted in the initial police translation.[20]

Later that day, another remarkable event took place. An Arab newspaper based in London published a document attributed to Abu Hafs al-Masri Al-Qaeda, claiming responsibility for the attack. The document itself was not remarkable since the group had previously claimed responsibility for attacks that were later proven to be false. Both UK and Spanish intelligence services questioned the credibility of the claim. Nevertheless, this further weakened the initial hypothesis that ETA had orchestrated 11-M.

The day after the attack, an unexploded bomb was discovered among the remains of the victims. The police deactivated the bomb using a mobile phone as the timer. By 13 March the police investigation had uncovered the source of the phone sim cards used in the attack and the individual who had bought them, the Moroccan Jamal Zougam. Zougam was already known to the Spanish police for his connections to the Abu Dahdah jihadist network.[21] Jamal Zougam was arrested within hours.[22] Three weeks later, further tracking of the mobile phones led to an apartment in Leganés (a small town south of Madrid) where core members of the 11-M network were hiding

---

Information of the National Police at the Parliamentary Commission investigating 11-M, 25 October 2004. Available at: http://www.congreso. es/.

19 Jesús de la Morena, former General Commissioner of Information of the National Police at the Parliamentary Commission investigating 11-M, 7 July 2004. Available at: http://www.congreso.es/.

20 Ibid.

21 This network was dismantled in November 2001 and key members were sentenced in September 2005.

22 Information and Social Relations Office, Ministry of Interior, Spain, 13 March 2004.

out. Upon discovering the raid and encircled by police, the terrorists committed suicide.[23]

## The Political Exploitation of 11-M

The attack took place three days before a general election for which the PP held a healthy lead. Electoral victory seemed guaranteed[24]. Following 11-M, political leaders were conscious that the attack would influence the elections, tilting the balance one way or another. The following section will examine the actors and strategies used to manage the impact of 11-M.[25]

Both the government and the opposition failed to manage the crisis adequately. Most of the actors involved attempted to de-legitimize their adversaries, using the media to do so. The main political parties abused the information vacuum following the attack, using supposedly privileged information to defend their postures. Paradoxically, the government maintained a policy of transparency when reporting on any developments in the investigation. These new developments often weakened, if not radically contradicted, its official position that ETA was involved in the attack. Overall, as will be demonstrated below, one can only provide a disappointing overview of what should have been responsible state action by the main political actors during a crisis.

---

23 Ibid., 3 April 2004.

24 But an absolute majority to form a single-party government was not guaranteed.

25 To study the events in a chronological manner, we have used two main books written by journalists: José María Irujo, *El Agujero. España invadida por la Yihad* (Madrid, 2005). Irujo is a journalist from *El País* (and thus critical of PP); and Miguel Platón, *11-M. Cómo la yihad puso de rodillas a España* (Madrid, 2005). Platón was director of information at the EFE News Agency during Aznar's administration and his book provides the most favourable assessment of the PP government. A graphic chronology of events between 11-14 March can be found on the *El Mundo* site at: http://www.elmundo.es/elmundo/2004/graficos/mar/s3/minuto.html.

## *The government*

In the first instance, most Spaniards and members of government attributed the attack to ETA. Even leaders of the political opposition originally considered ETA as the perpetrator. In fact, the first politician to blame ETA was PSOE leader Zapatero, in an interview with radio COPE at 8.45 a.m. on 11 March. Minutes later, Gaspar Llamazares, leader of IU, Izquierda Unida (a coalition of parties linked to the old communist party) made a statement to the press condemning the 'Nazi barbarism committed today by ETA'.[26] At 9.30 a.m., Juan José Ibarretxe, president of the autonomous government in the Basque Country attributed the attack to ETA.

So, in the early hours of 11 March when many considered ETA the perpetrator of 11-M, the Aznar administration was confident and led the way. The initial strategy employed by the government consisted in reproducing a scenario akin to July 1997 when ETA assassinated Miguel Angel Blanco. According to this strategy, the PP would be able to win the elections by absolute majority, on a strong proven record of anti-terrorism; strengthen its position towards the nationalist Basque party, which had recently launched an independence-driven agenda; and further isolate ETA and its political apparatus. The end of the terrorist organisation would be nearer than ever.

Because the government wanted to remain the dominant player in any anti-terrorist action Aznar chose not to summon the Delegated Commission of the Government for Situations of Crisis or the Delegated Commission of the Government for Intelligence. In their place, an internal cabinet was summoned at 11.00 a.m. Jorge Dezcallar, the director of the CNI, was not invited, complicating the synchronicity of information. Aznar also rejected an offer by Zapatero for a permanent commission of the Anti-terrorist Pact. Instead, the administration called for a demonstration, rather than a cross party initiative, to which it invited other parties. In the demonstration it adopted the slogan "with the victims, the constitution and

---

26  *El País*, 11 March 2004.

to the defeat of terrorism." The inclusion of the constitution was a clear reference to Basque separatism and engendered protest from nationalist elements in Catalonia.

However, when the ETA hypothesis began to breakdown amid growing evidence of jihadi involvement, the PP began to realise that the opposition would surely establish a link to Iraq. A worst case scenario was feared: the resurgence of anti-war protests. From then onwards, the government lost the initiative. It became reactive and inflexible. They persisted in claiming that ETA was the perpetrator, despite growing evidence otherwise.[27] When speaking to the media, government officials would provide information on the progress of the investigation, tying in their hypothesis and thereby abusing information. This strategy even continued until midday on 13 March when the Interior Minister, Angel Acebes, spoke to the media despite being fully aware that a Moroccan with links to Spanish jihadist networks was about to be arrested in Madrid.[28]

## The opposition

The PSOE adopted a reactive stance in the first hours of the crisis. They were conscious that if ETA were responsible, this would contribute to a landslide electoral victory for the PP.

However, once doubts in the investigation emerged, PSOE supported the hypothesis that the attack was perpetrated by jihadists acting in response to the government's support for and involvement in Iraq. PSOE were now keen for the public to use their vote to punish the government for implicating Spain in Iraq. The Madrid bombings became a window of opportunity for the PSOE leaders. The connection between the attack and the Iraq war was a simplification that seduced many a Spaniard. Indeed, 64 per cent of those

---

27  José Antonio Olmeda, *Fear or Falsehood? Framing The 3/11 Terrorist Attacks in Madrid And Electoral Accountability*, Real Instituto Elcano Working Paper, 5 May 2005, at: http://www.realinstitutoelcano.org/documentos/195. asp#_edn22.

28  *El País*, 14 March 2004.

surveyed (of which 80 per cent support the political left) agreed that 11-M would not have occurred were it not for Aznar's support for the United States over Iraq.[29]

PSOE maintained that the government was lying. Senior PSOE members circulated rumours that the government was hiding information. PSOE also claimed that it had access to privileged police information which pointed to jihadi involvement in 11-M. This claim to information was credible: with a long history of government, PSOE has numerous contacts within the police force. From 11–14 March, PSOE consistently pushed this agenda of political delegitimisation.[30] In the pursuit of this agenda, PSOE was supported by the media, in particular the PRISA group, a leading force in the media industry.

Other minority parties in the opposition like the United Left, the Basque Nationalist Party and the independent Catalonian Ezquerra Republicana signed up to the PSOE agenda. They initially blamed ETA but once doubts emerged in the investigation they also sought to capitalise on the attack. These parties are ideologically opposed to Aznar's centre-right politics and it is traditionally in their interest for PP to lose a majority in Parliament.[31]

The political wing of ETA, Batasuna, was the only actor on 11 March to deny Basque involvement in the attack. In the morning of 11 March, Batasuna's spokesperson, Arnaldo Otegui, attributed blame to 'Arab resistance' acting in response to Spanish troops stationed in Iraq.[32] In intercepted communications that morning between Otegui and his party the CNI discovered that Batasuna had no credible or substantiated information on 11-M and its potential

---

29  Javier Noya, 'Del 11-M al 14-M: estrategia *yihadista*, elecciones generales y opinión pública,' *Análisis Real Instituto Elcano*, No. 132, 2004, at: http://www.realinstitutoelcano.org/analisis/562.asp.

30  Miguel Platón, p. 294, *11-M. Cómo la yihad puso de rodillas a España* (Madrid, 2005).

31  In the current PSOE government, support of these smaller parties is crucial.

32  *El Mundo*, 11 March 2004.

perpetrators; in fact, Batasuna displayed great concern that 11-M was the work of ETA.[33] Batasuna, like the other political actors, was thus abusing information. Soon after, the CNI transmitted details of the conversation to Aznar, who later made this information public, gravely endangering intelligence sources.

## The role of the social movements

Other key actors during this period include the social movements of the extreme left and the anti-globalisation groups that had taken part in past anti-war demonstrations. These groups participated in the government-organised demonstrations on 12 March. The demonstrations were massive, testimony to the social impact of the attack. In Madrid, 2 million protested, in Barcelona 1.5 million marched and in total over 11 million people took part, an impressive figure given that the national population stands at 40 million.[34] The social movements represented a minority and were positioned at the front, together with government officials and a large number of television cameras. These organised groups vociferously accused the government of lying and provoking the attack because of Spanish involvement in Iraq. In Madrid and Barcelona these groups attempted to attack members of the government standing in the front rows.[35]

On 13 March, armed with the same placards used in anti-war demonstrations, the groups protested outside PP offices throughout Spain, labelling the government a murderer and liar. Although initially small in numbers, the attention these groups received from the media (especially PRISA) had a snowball effect in mobilising others. The protest alienated the government, creating a sense that it was under siege and socially isolated. In contrast, there existed considerable interaction between the minority groups, the political opposition and some media in generating the protest. The PP later

---

33  Miguel Platón, p. 225.

34  *El País*, 13 March 2004.

35  *El País*, 12 March 2004.

accused PSOE of organising these demonstrations. Under electoral law, the day before elections is a day of reflection and demonstrations are prohibited.[36] Some members of PSOE and IU had sent text messages calling for a protest and the event was publicised on websites. Arguably a decisive factor in driving the protest and magnifying its outreach was the role played by the PRISA group, in particular radio SER and Canal Plus television.[37]

## The terrorists

Both the jihadists and ETA attempted to intervene directly in events post 11-M. On 12 March ETA released a communiqué in which it denied any involvement in 11-M. In the communiqué ETA took the opportunity to blame Spanish foreign policy for the attacks. The Spanish Interior Minister doubted the credibility of the communiqué and in retrospect this was a mistake as the communiqué was genuine.

On 13 March the jihadists recorded a video communiqué in which a masked individual representing 'Abu Dujan al Afgani, spokesperson of Al Qaeda in Europe' claimed responsibility for the attack. In the video, the presence of Spanish troops in Iraq and Afghanistan was cited as a key motivating factor for 11-M. The individual in the video threatened further attacks. The video reached government hands at the last hour on 13 March and it was televised during a press conference at the Ministry of Interior at 00.30 on 14 March. It could be argued that these efforts to claim responsibility just hours before the general election are a significant indicator that 11-M was intended to influence the vote.

---

36 This modus operandi is common among anti-globalisation activists. See John Arquilla, David Ronfeldt, (eds), *Networks and Netwars: The Future of Terror, Crime, and Militancy* (Santa Monica, 2001). Available at http://www.rand.org/publications/MR/MR1382/.

37 Miguel Platón (2005) p. 378-87. SER news coverage can be replayed at: http://www.cadenaser.com/static/especiales/2005/sonidos11_14/dia13.html.

## *The media*

Initially, key media elements attributed 11-M to ETA and a reproduction of events akin to 1997 was considered imminent. Had the ETA hypothesis been confirmed, it is probable that the media would have influenced the electoral victory of the PP.

However, by midday, when the van was discovered and the ETA hypothesis began to unravel, the media adopted different attitudes according to the ideology of their editorial lines. Many kept both hypotheses—ETA and jihadism—open whilst doubts emerged in the investigation. They simply limited their role to transmitting information every few hours when updated with government press conferences, witness statements, acts of mourning and anti-terrorism manifestations.

State-run media supported the government line. This position became increasingly difficult to justify as ETA's role in the attack rapidly lost currency. For example, public television in Madrid deliberately changed its evening programme schedule on 12 and 13 March to feature a film on ETA. The same film was projected again the next day on national public television, again as a change to the original programme schedule. By then it was public knowledge that Moroccans were in custody. On 13 March, suspects were under arrest and the Interior Ministry was set to announce this information. However, one news channel—EFE—reported that the CNI had confirmed ETA as the main line of investigation, distorting prior comments made by the director of CNI.

Those elements of the media that were close to the PSOE supported the strategy promoted by that party. This strategy consisted in linking the attack to the war in Iraq, accusing the government of lying, and resuscitating anti-government mobilisation. The key actors promoting this strategy included *El País* newspaper and radio SER; both of the PRISA group. *El País* is the bestselling national newspaper, with great influence among the intellectual elite. Radio SER has the largest audience in Spain.

Amid doubts regarding the identity of the perpetrators, on 11 March at 10.00 p.m. radio SER announced that the body of a suicide bomber had been found among the dead. According to SER, three anti-terrorist sources had confirmed the report even though it was denied by the Interior Ministry.[38] This story ran until the next morning, when it was finally proven to be false. Early on 12 March *El País* called for the government to be responsible should 11-M be the work of al-Qaeda or an alliance of al-Qaeda and ETA, given Aznar's support for the war in Iraq.[39] During 13 March, SER covered the demonstrations outside PP head offices and continued to accuse the government of lying. Even at the last hour, SER circulated rumours that the government was going to call the general election off. This story was false. In addition, on 13 March when existence of the terrorists' video became known, radio SER claimed that it was aware of the video earlier in the morning that day, but had held onto the information so as to not prejudice the investigation. This was false since the video was recorded in the afternoon of 13 March.

## *Conclusion*

The analysis so far suggests that 11-M incensed a minority of the electorate strong enough to change forecasted electoral results[40] but beyond this several further conclusions can be drawn.

Firstly, the terrorists encountered exceptional social and political circumstances in Spain because of the war in Iraq, and were able to take advantage of this situation. However, it has been argued here that the timing of the attack alone did not influence the result of the election; there were pre-established conditions which favoured the outcome. Given its strong past record on counterterrorism, had the Spanish government not supported the United States over Iraq and an attack of similar proportion had taken place perpetrated by

38  The story can be heard at: http://www.cadenaser.com/static/especiales/2005/sonidos11_14/dia11.html.

39  *El País*, 12 March 2004.

40  Narciso Michavila (Working Paper 13/2005).

jihadists[41] it is very likely that the government would have enjoyed unanimous social support.

Secondly, the timing sparked aggressive competition between the government and the opposition. This had an extremely negative effect on the political system in general. The primacy of partisan interests over the general interest meant that the crisis was managed in a deficient manner. This lack of state responsibility was demonstrated in the way certain information concerning the investigation was treated. The government placed several valuable sources of information in danger and provided information that could have been used by the terrorists to frustrate the police investigation. Fortunately, the terrorists were not professional enough to take advantage of this situation.

Ultimately, this attitude tarnished the image of the main political parties. For some, the government lied and for others the PSOE stole victory from the PP.[42] Together, this transmitted the impression that the political actors were not in control of events. For this reason, events from 11-14 March remain bitter, if not shameful, memories. The case is a disappointing example of how the main political actors can misbehave following a tragedy of such magnitude.

The way in which the crisis was mismanaged continues to impact upon political life in Spain. During the parliamentary commission that investigated 11-M, which ended in June 2005, the parties continued to de-legitimise their political adversaries rather than search for preventative measures to support the security services and avoid further attacks. Those sectors of the media with clear political ties have continued to de-legitimise opponents. Thus, the ultimate conclusion of events post-11-M is that those that play politics with terrorism are very likely to witness their legitimacy undermined.

---

41  In 2001, France almost faced a similar massacre in Strasbourg from the Meliani cell. See Rohan Gunaratna, *Inside Al Qaeda. Global Network of Terror* (New York, 2002), p. 130.

42  Miguel Platón (2005) p. 420-1.

# 10

# A CONJURER'S GAME:
# VLADIMIR PUTIN AND THE POLITICS
# OF PRESIDENTIAL PRESTIDIGITATION

*Robert Saunders*

Throughout the first decade of the twenty-first century, Russian President Vladimir Putin has consistently used the threat of terrorism as a fig leaf to cover his neo-authoritarian policy agenda. This is not surprising, as Putin—with the full co-operation of his predecessor and patron, Boris Yeltsin—manipulated perceptions of the terrorist threat from Chechen separatists to win the presidency in 2000. While the First Chechen War (1994–1996) had disastrous consequences for sitting President Yeltsin, the Second Chechen War (1999–present) guaranteed a tidy electoral victory for Yeltsin's heir-apparent, Putin. This is partly due to Putin's masterful framing of the war as a campaign against international terrorism rather than the quashing of a separatist movement. Some commentators, including the exiled oligarch Boris Berezovsky, have even gone so far as to suggest governmental complicity in the spate of apartment bombings in the late summer of 1999—events which served as a pretext for resuming the Chechen conflict.[1] Putting aside unproven conspiracies, it is clear that once the war resumed and Chechen guerillas initiated attacks on civilian targets, the discourse of terror played to Putin's

---

1   See, for instance, Stephen J. Blank, 'Putin's Twelve-Step Program,' *The Washington Quarterly*, 25(1), 2002, pp. 147–60 and Dmitry Shlapentokh, 'Trends in Putin's Russia,' *Society*, 41(1), 2003, pp. 72–80.

advantage. His approval ratings since taking office have rarely dipped below 70 per cent—this despite continued terrorist attacks which claimed nearly 1,000 Russian lives in the first six years of his presidency. During this time, Putin has deftly used his own popularity and the threat of terrorism to completely remake the political landscape of the Russian Federation and reorient Russia within the international community.

This essay explores the political maneouverings of the Putin administration in the immediate aftermath of three terrorist incidents: the 9/11 attacks (2001), the Nord-Ost theatre siege (2002), and the Beslan hostage crisis (2004). Each of these events precipitated rapid and drastic changes in Russian policies. In each case, the reforms that followed each attack served to solidify Putin's grip on power and weaken his critics inside and outside of Russia. In the wake of the September 11 attacks, Putin repositioned Russian foreign policy in such a way as to provide legitimacy to his policies in Chechnya and inure the West to his neo-authoritarian agenda. After the Nord-Ost debacle, he made provocative alterations to the country's military doctrine intended to make Russia a 'strong state' once again. Putin also took the opportunity to rein in his country's media for their 'irresponsible coverage' of the incident, effectively neutralising the press. This, in turn, paved the way for future reforms which might have been thoroughly scrutinised—and even challenged—in a freer media environment. Most dramatically, Putin utilised the grief and insecurity felt by the Russian people in the aftermath of Beslan to procure a sweeping reform of his country's federal system—changes that clearly contravened the constitution of the Russian Federation and eviscerated lingering opposition to presidential power. My thesis is that Putin, a master of political sleight-of-hand, used each terrorist attack as a tool of misdirection. Once inveigled, Putin's various audiences quietly capitulated to his agenda for remaking Russian politics—both on the international and domestic levels.

## An overview of terrorism in the Russian federation

The statistics of terror in Putin's Russia tell a grim tale. In 1999, a series of apartment bombings in Moscow killed roughly 300 people just a few months before Putin took office as president. Two years later, a bomb blast in Moscow's Byelorusskaya metro station wounded fifteen people. In 2002, Victory Day (9 May) celebrations in the Dagestani city of Kaspiisk were marred by a bomb explosion which killed forty-two and injured more than 130 people. On 19 October 2002, a bomb killed one person outside a Moscow McDonald's restaurant. Four days later, forty-two heavily-armed men under the leadership of the Chechen guerilla leader Movsar Barayev took over the Dubrovka Theatre where the play *Nord-Ost* was being staged. In the ensuing gas attack on the Moscow theatre and raid by Russian Special Forces (*Spetsnaz*), all the terrorists were killed along with 130 hostages. 2003 was a particularly bloody year: in May, dozens died in bombings in Chechnya. On 5 July, fifteen people were killed by a bomb attack on a Moscow rock concert by female suicide bombers—an event which was dubbed the 'Black Widow' bombing by the Russian press. Later that summer, explosions killed more than fifty people in an Ossetian hospital and seven people on a train in southern Russia. In December, another train bombing in the south claimed nearly fifty lives and a blast in Moscow killed six. On 6 February 2004, a bomb in the Moscow metro left forty-one dead. The bombings of two domestic flights claimed ninety lives on 24 August, and on the last day of the month a suicide bomber killed ten and injured thirty at a northern Moscow metro station. The next morning, the Beslan hostage crisis began when terrorists stormed School Number One during opening day celebrations; when it was over, 344 civilians were dead—of which the majority were children. In 2005, Chechen rebels attacked federal buildings and police stations in Nalchik, Kabardino-Balkaria; the conflict took the lives of 137, including ninety-two guerillas.

According to the National Memorial Institute for the Prevention of Terrorism's (MIPT) terrorism database, there have been a total of 273 terrorist attacks, 2,811 injuries, and 941 deaths in the Russian Federation since Putin assumed the presidency on 1 January 2000.[2] These statistics put Russia ahead of India in injuries (2,150) and fatalities (885) during the same time period. While the Russian Federation experienced fewer deaths than Colombia's total of 1,177, it leads the Latin American country in injuries (1,981). Russia trails Israel in the number of attacks (460) and injuries (3,726), but actually leads the country in fatalities as only 709 have died due to terrorism in Israel since 1 January 2000. During the same period, only Iraq leads Russia in all categories with 4,067 incidents producing 16,773 injuries and 10,485 deaths.[3] Consequently, Russia clearly ranks as one of the most terrorism-prone countries in the world today.

While many of the terrorist incidents have occurred in the ethnic republics of the northern Caucasus region (e.g., Chechnya, North Ossetia, and Dagestan), the violence has also impacted the metropole with a number of high profile attacks in the capital, Moscow. As a consequence, the level of visible security precautions in Moscow remains high in the metro, tourist sites, shopping areas, and in the vicinity of government buildings. The proliferation of privately-armed bodyguards during the 'wild 1990s' has been supplanted by the presence of similarly-armed, uniformed officers representing the military, federal agencies, and local police. According to Irving Louis Horowitz, the former director of the first research task force on terrorism for the Council on Foreign Relations, Putin has rapidly adopted the 'Israeli model' of response to the terrorist threat which places the goal of 'ensuring humanity's survival' over certain aspects of perfect governance associated with modern democratic and plural-ist societies.[4] The conditions which have given rise to such policies

---

2  All figures are from 1 January 2000 through 31 March 2006.

3  While the United States had 2,990 fatalities and 2,386 injuries resulting from terrorism during the same period, there were only 98 attacks—of which 9/11 accounted for the bulk of the casualties. Russia had about twice as many fatalities as the West Bank/Gaza, and slightly more deaths from terrorism than both Pakistan and Afghanistan.

4  Irving L. Horowitz, 'Terrorism and the Return to a Bi-Polar World',

represent a sharp break from the Soviet past (though not tsarist Russia where anarchist, leftist, and nihilist terrorism reached stunning levels in the waning decades of the Romanov regime).

During the 1970s and 1980s, Russia enjoyed its longest respite from mass violence in memory. However, during this same period, much of Western Europe grappled with 'red' terror propagated by such groups as Action Direct (France), Brigate Rosse (Italy), Rote Armee Fraktion (West Germany), and Revolutionary Organisation 17 November (Greece). Meanwhile, various separatist terror organisations such as the Irish Republican Army (IRA), Euskadi Ta Askatasuna (ETA), and the National Liberation Front of Corsica conducted bombings, assassinations, and robberies in the UK, Spain, and France, respectively. France, alongside its left-wing and regionalist terror threats, also saw the rise of Islamist terrorist networks and fell victim to several attacks during the 1980s. The disruptive effects of terrorism did not go unnoticed in the Soviet Union and Eastern Europe. In fact, the underlying causes for such political violence were a point of pride for Soviet propagandists who argued that the West—through its capitalist system and imperialist proclivities—had only itself to blame for the phenomenon of terrorism, a threat which by the 1970s was virtually unknown within the Soviet sphere of influence. However, such self-congratulatory palaver was somewhat disingenuous considering the aid and comfort provided to many of these terrorist organisations by friendly regimes in the Warsaw Pact Organisation.

Beginning in 1989, the collapse of communism dampened the ideological sustenance of left-wing terrorist organisations. Similarly, popular support (which had hitherto been slim but palpable) faded away with the abandonment of Marxism-Leninism by Poland, Czechoslovakia, Romania, and eventually the USSR itself. The 1990s also saw significant progress on settling long simmering issues between regional separatists and their metropole adversaries. Local support for regionalist terrorist groups can be partly attributed to

*Society*, 42(1), 2004, pp. 7-9.

changing economic and political conditions across the continent. The European Community's 1992 Maastricht Treaty pushed Europe closer towards a political and economic union, and created a milieu where regionalism could be promoted though legal and peaceful means (rather than by the gun and the bomb). By the end of the decade, only Islamist terrorism represented a sustained threat to European stability. During the same time period, however, a Pandora's box of ethnic antagonism opened across post-Soviet space. In the wake of the Afghan War (1979–89), various styles of asynchronous warfare worked their way into the once impervious geopolitical space of the former Soviet Union through the agents of transnational Islamists trained in the madrassahs of western Pakistan. Although methods of political violence that might be characterised as terror have been employed in a number of conflicts in the former USSR (e.g., in the Nagorno-Karabakh conflict between Armenia and Azerbaijan, in the Ferghana Valley which stretches across Uzbekistan, Kyrgyzstan, and Tajikistan, and by Russian nationalists in northern Kazakhstan), the Chechens have emerged as the face of post-Soviet terror.

## Chechnya: Russia's fountainhead of terrorism

The history of Russo-Chechen relations is littered with conflict, controversy, and mutual vilification. Tsarist Russia's conquest of the northern Caucasus represents the bloodiest chapter in the empire's centuries-long period of expansion to the east, south, and west. Today, Russian military policy in the Great Caucasian War (1817–64), when Chechnya was incorporated into the Romanov Empire, would have certainly been labelled as genocide. Forced conversion, eradication of whole villages, and a scorched earth policy forever stained relations between the conquering Russians and the subdued Muslim nations of the mountainous territory between the Caspian and Black Seas. In the wake of the 1859 surrender of Imam Shamil—the charismatic Dagestani leader who built a formidable multi-ethnic Muslim army of resistance, many

225

Chechens suffered from the policy of *mukhadzhirstvo* (deportation) which resulted in their removal to Turkey and other parts of the Middle East.[5] In the ensuing decades, Chechnya languished under the Russian yoke. After a brief flowering of nationalist sentiment in the early days of the Bolshevik regime, the country was once again brought under tight control by Moscow. In 1936, Chechnya was joined with neighbouring Ingushetia and granted the status of an Autonomous Soviet Socialist Republic within the Russian Federated Soviet Socialist Republic, thus guaranteeing a moderate level of self-government for the Chechens. However, World War II proved especially traumatic for the Chechens and undid the moderate successes gleaned under the Bolsheviks. At Joseph Stalin's order, the entire nation—along with five other Caucasian peoples as well as the Volga Germans and the Crimean Tatars—was packed into cattle cars and deported en mass to Central Asia. About a third of all Chechens died en route or as a result of poor conditions upon arrival in Kazakhstan and southern Siberia. Chechen oral history now had two great traumas around which the community's identity was constructed. During the 'thaw' which followed Stalin's death, the Chechens (and the other Caucasian peoples—though not the Tatars, Meskhetian Turks, or the Germans) were rehabilitated and allowed to return to their homeland. The displacement and debilitation of the nation, however, produced multiple generations of marginalised and discontented Chechens, as well as resulting in their 'criminalisation', as many Chechens turned to 'grey' and 'black' market activities to sustain themselves in exile.[6]

The twin policies of *glasnost'* ('transparency' or 'openness') and *perestroika* ('restructuring') provided an aperture for Chechen elites to begin to escape the effects of Russian domination. Inspired by the devolution of power from Moscow to the Soviet Socialist Re-

---

5   John Russell, 'Terrorists, Bandits, Spooks and Thieves: Russian Demonisation of the Chechens before and since 9/11,' *Third World Quarterly*, 26(1), 2005, pp. 101-16.

6   Russell, 'Terrorists, Bandits, Spooks and Thieves,' pp. 103-5.

publics (SSRs) at the end of the 1980s, the Chechens unilaterally declared the creation of the Chechen-Ingush Republic in 1990. This was done in hopes of raising the country to a co-equal status with Lithuania, Estonia, and the other SSRs which were beginning to move in the direction of independence from the Soviet Union. In the autumn of 1991, the Supreme Soviet of Chechnya-Ingushetia, at the direction of the Soviet air force general Jokar Dudayev, voted itself out of existence. A Chechen Republic of Ichkeria was declared and a less-than-fair presidential election put Dudayev in power. This move effectively paved the way for independence from Russia. The Kremlin—fearing a second round of decolonisation which might free Tatarstan and other integral parts of the newly-formed Russian Federation from its control—balked at the move, rejecting the declaration of independence as illegal and the election of Dudayev invalid. After 1991, Chechnya held an ambiguous status; the country possessed de facto sovereignty without international or Russian recognition of its independence. The uncomfortable union lasted until 1994 when Boris Yeltsin, in a risky gamble, sent in troops to reintegrate the breakaway province. Purportedly, Yeltsin had been advised that the war would be short, decisive, and popular, and would shore up his position going into the 1996 presidential elections. The war went badly with atrocities regularly committed by both sides. After two years, Yeltsin declared a unilateral ceasefire leaving the Chechens once again to their own devices, though still without formal independence.

Putin, unlike his predecessor, had the political advantage of being able to make a discernable link between international terrorism and the Chechens. During the troubled peace that followed the first Chechen War, the local leadership of the secessionist movement fractured. Once a clearly nationalist affair under Jokar Dudayev, by the end of the decade the political landscape included revolutionary Islamists—personified by the notorious figure of Shamil Basayev, who converted to the transnational Islamist cause during the first Chechen War. Following Dudayev's death at the end of the first

war, his successor Aslan Maskhadov attempted to project a secular, nationalist façade in order to maintain support among western
advocates. However, Maskhadov's inability to rein in paramilitaries
like Basayev demonstrated the chaotic conditions that ruled the
country. The 1995 declaration of jihad by Chechnya's supreme
mufti, Akhmat Kadyrov, attracted numerous Islamist combatants
from across the Caucasus, as well as experienced 'Afghan-Arab'
mujahideen and would-be jihadis from around the Muslim world.
The influx of foreign fighters, an expansion of terror attacks, and the
limited application of Islamic law (including Shari'a court-ordered
executions beginning in 1996) rapidly changed the nature of the
conflict. Though Kadyrov would later publicly revoke the decree,
ally himself with Putin, and condemn the 'Wahhabification' of his
country, his call to jihad permanently reordered Chechen politics
and provided grist for those in the Kremlin wishing to frame the
conflict as a war against the forces of international terror.

From the end of the first Chechen War, the Islamists were no
longer content with an independent Chechnya. Instead this increasingly prominent clique articulated its aim of creating a mini-
caliphate in the Caucasus where Shari'a rather than secular law
would prevail. After taking over Chechnya, the goal was to expand
the boundaries of the theocratic state to include all the Muslim
regions of southern Russia, parts of Georgia, and potentially even
oil-rich Azerbaijan. Basayev's quixotic raid into neighbouring
Dagestan in August 1999 provided a threatening salvo in this new
struggle for ideological supremacy in Chechen politics. Occurring
the same month as the Dagestani incursion, the apartment bombings in Moscow provided a clarion call for Russian action. On 24
September 1999, the then Prime Minister Putin stated: 'We'll
chase down the bandits everywhere. If we catch them in the toilet,
then we'll bloody them in the outhouse'. By using the underworld
slang, *mochit'* ('make bloody'), Putin signalled that his intentions
were violent and non-negotiable. So began the Second Chechen
War and Putin's campaign of playing politics with terror.

## 11 September: the internationalisation of Chechnya and Russia's return to great power status

As the second Chechen war began, Putin—both as prime minister and president—employed a strong hand in dealing with the 'terrorists' and 'bandits', a strategy which provided him with a good deal of credibility among Russians who feared that the secessionist drive in the northern Caucasus presaged a new wave of territorial losses reminiscent of the breakup of the USSR in 1991. Putin's tough talk and unmitigated resolve to maintain the integrity of the Russian Federation played well to those who saw Washington and London behind a grand conspiracy that would result in independence for the resource-rich republics of Tatarstan and Sakha, if not the whole of the Russian Far East and perhaps even Siberia. Not surprisingly, Putin's rise to power was a vagary for the West. His tenure in East Germany as an intelligence officer, his disciplined and abstemious lifestyle, and his rapid ascent from obscurity provided few clues about the direction in which he would take the country.

In 2001, George W. Bush assumed the presidency of the United States. He moved quickly to develop a cordial relationship with his Russian counterpart who had only been in office a few months longer than he. In their first meeting in Ljubljana, Bush, after probing the depths of Putin's soul, came away with the impression the Leningrader was a man who could be trusted. Though the US-Russian relationship had been somewhat compromised by events in the Balkans, the Baltics, and the Middle East, Putin and Bush seemed ready to begin the new millennium on the right foot during the summer of 2001. However, the tentative first steps in Slovenia neither hindered, nor necessarily helped the development of the US-Russian relationship. Only when an al-Qaeda cell brought down the Twin Towers and ripped a hole in the Pentagon on the morning of September 11 2001, did a vibrant and multivariate Bush-Putin relationship actually materialise.

In the immediate wake of the September 11 attacks, Putin called a meeting of the most influential members of the Duma represent-

229

ing a cross-section of Russian politics. He posed the eternal Russian question to them: 'What is to be done?' The vast majority argued for neutrality or even condemnation of American foreign policy; only a tiny, marginalised minority of liberals and 'westernisers' suggested support for the Americans. Putin, whose initial blush of popularity had been jeopardised by his administration's clumsy handling of the accidental sinking of the *Kursk* submarine during the summer, could have been forgiven for conceding to the majority. Instead, he decided to unequivocally support the Americans in their plight against 'international terrorism'. Putin, in fact, was the first world leader to speak with the American president in the aftermath of the attacks. His televised address made clear his intentions to frame Russia as a major victim of terror: 'Russia knows directly what terrorism means and because of this we, more than anyone, understand the feelings of the American people. In the name of Russia, I want to say to the American people—we are with you'.

In the coming months, Putin even took the unprecedented (and domestically unpopular) step of permitting US military bases within Russia's southern sphere of influence. American installations quickly materialised in Kyrgyzstan, Tajikistan, and Uzbekistan—all former republics of the Soviet Union. In policy circles, Putin's failure to demur to the Americans was instantly recognised as a 'tactical move to exploit the political situation for his own benefit'.[7] Moscow also began an unprecedented programme of information sharing with Washington in an effort to root out transborder networks that connected former mujahideen from the Afghan War who had now dispersed around the globe. Putin even took it in stride when the US began deploying near the Pankisi Gorge along the Georgian-Russian border—an area of special sensitivity to Moscow due to the presence of Chechen rebels. Bush and Putin even went on to issue a Joint Statement on Counterterrorism Cooperation (24 May 2002) which stated: 'We reaffirm our commitment to working with the

---

7   Oleg D. Kalugin, 'Window of Opportunity: Russia's Role in the Coalition against Terror,' *Harvard International Review*, 25(3), 2002, pp. 56-60.

Government of Georgia on counterterrorism issues, while upholding Georgian sovereignty, and hope that the presence of terrorists in this country will be eliminated'. The statement also committed Washington and Moscow to co-operate on reincorporating the breakaway republics of Abkhazia and South Ossetia back into Georgia—despite Russia's long support of secessionists in both regions.[8] Dmitri Trenin, deputy director of the Moscow Carnegie Center and Soviet/Russian veteran, characterised the post-9/11 shift as a 'revolution' in Russia's foreign policy, and Putin himself refers to September 11 as a 'turning point' in Russia's relations with the world.[9]

As Stephen J. Blank, professor of national security studies at the US Army War College, contends, 'everything flows from or is connected to Chechnya'.[10] Putin's sophisticated response to 9/11 allowed him to remake the chessboard of international politics by placing Chechnya at the 'epicenter of the global war on terror'.[11] While Putin's behavior seemed magnanimous, he quickly reaped a host of benefits including an expanded role for Russia in European security through the NATO-Russia Council (NRC); a pledge of full membership in the G-8; and commitments of greater Western consumption of Russia's oil and natural gas. Russia also emerged—almost overnight—as a key global player in the fight against terrorism. According to Dov Lynch, lecturer in war studies at King's College:

After September 11, counterterrorism became quickly—and far less problematically—a prominent element of Russia's relationship with the United

---

8   However, according to the *Financial Times*, 'Georgia accuses Russia of doing everything it can to undermine attempts of its reformist government to reintegrate two breakaway regions and revive its shattered economy.' See Arkardy Ostrovsky, 'Georgians reap grapes of Russian wrath,' *Financial Times*, Col. 1, p. 6, 26 April 2006.

9   Jill Dougherty, '9/11 a "Turning Point" for Putin,' CNN Web site, 10 September 2002. Available at: http://archives.cnn.com/2002/WORLD/europe/09/10/ar911.russia.putin/index.html [accessed on 5 April 2006].

10  Blank, 'Putin's Twelve-Step Program,' p. 150.

11  John Kampfner, 'A President Craves Understanding,' *New Statesman*, 133(4704), 2004, pp. 10-13.

States. Based on similar visions of threats and countermeasures, US-Russian relations progressed quickly, as George W. Bush's early concerns about Chechnya and the development of Russian democracy dissipated.[12]

Russia's location, expertise in combatting Islamic extremism, and extensive intelligence-gathering capabilities allowed the state to don the mantle of 'great power' once again.

[Russia] sought to activate the diplomatic assets that history and geography gave it: it tried to restore something of the neglected Soviet-era friendship with Arab states; endeavored to persuade Central Asian states to abandon their post-independence policies of distancing themselves from Russia; and sought to use its relatively sizable Muslim population to justify admission (currently as an observer) to the Organization of the Islamic Conference.[13]

For ordinary Russians, this new posture was not a trivial development since it partially banished the shame of the tumultuous 1990s when Russia went from superpower status to ranking somewhere between South Korea and Luxembourg on the world stage.

The most important gain for Moscow was, however, discursive. In the wake of 9/11, Putin was effectively able to redress international perceptions about the conflict in Chechnya: what the international community had once seen as a brutal war of attrition by an occupying power against a hopelessly outnumbered minority nationality prior to 9/11 was now rebranded as the most important front in the war between 'civilisation' and the faceless threat of international terror. As early as the summer of 2000, Putin had been telling the European press that his country was straddling an 'arc of instability extending from the Philippines to Kosovo' and was alone in its fight against the shock troops of Islamic fundamentalism.[14] It took a brazen act of terrorism conducted by Osama bin Laden's henchmen the next summer to lend weight to his arguments. Putin subsequently pounced on

---

12  Dov Lynch, '"The Enemy is at the Gate": Russia after Beslan,' *International Affairs*, 81(1), 2005, pp. 141–61.

13  'Terrorism, Shaper or Fuel for Kremlin Policy?' *Transitions Online*, 27 February 2006. Retrieved via *Factiva*.

14  Russell, 'Terrorists, Bandits, Spooks and Thieves,' p. 109.

the opportunity to reaffirm his arguments on Chechnya's role in the global terror nexus. While not all of Europe's elites were dazzled by the political sleight-of-hand, Washington was thoroughly convinced by the arguments put forth by the Kremlin. According to Russell, Western media likewise fell under Putin's spell. The "rebels, armed resistance and freedom fighters" of the first [Chechen] war have been replaced in the public perception by the "Islamic terrorists" of the second'.[15]

In addition to the benefits of rebranding the Chechen conflict, Putin secured the enduring patience of Washington vis-à-vis his reform process. In the years following the attacks on the World Trade Center and the Pentagon, Russian participation in the coalition against international terrorism has served as a powerful prophylaxis against American criticisms of neo-authoritarianism. Washington's muted stance on the Russian political order is especially noticeable when one considers the pivotal role of Condoleezza Rice—a notoriously anti-Soviet/Russian academic—in both Bush administrations. Understanding the demands of a political marriage, George W. Bush was forced to overlook many of the faults of his new partner. The farcical case surrounding the murder of *Forbes Russia* editor Paul Klebnikov, the arrest of Mikhail Khodorkovsky and nationalisation of Yukos, revanchist policies in the south Caucasus and Ukraine, and the unflinching abrogation of much of Russia's hard-won freedom of the press escaped US censure (though the obligatory criticisms were made at the appropriate levels). Such tolerance can be partially attributed to President Putin's political prestidigitation surrounding the tragic events of 9/11.

---

15 See Russell, 'Terrorists, Bandits, Spooks and Thieves,' p. 102. It can further be argued that September 11 and the subsequent confluence of Moscow's policies in the north Caucasus with the 'global war on terror' provided Russian society with some level of retroactive validation for the disastrous effects of two wars, countless collateral deaths, and perpetual underdevelopment and economic trauma in the country's southern tier. This is in part due to the growing perception by the end of the 1990s that Chechnya had moved beyond a geographic conflict and had become the frontline against global Islamist terror.

## Nord-Ost: overcoming Bespredel and the taming of the press

On the evening of 23 October 2002, forty-two gunmen who claimed allegiance to the Chechen separatist movement stormed a crowded Moscow theatre during a performance of the musical *Nord-Ost*. After taking hostage some 900 spectators, the terrorists demanded the withdrawal of Russian forces from Chechnya. In a predawn raid on the third day of the crisis, Russian *Spetsnaz* entered the building after filling it with an unknown airborne agent which rendered hostages and their captors unconscious. All of the terrorists were killed, along with 130 of the hostages; there were no *Spetsnaz* casualties. The principal cause of fatalities was the mysterious aerosol anaesthetic used by *Spetsnaz* rather than gunfire or explosives. The government blamed the separatists for the loss of life arguing that they had begun assassinating hostages when the Kremlin failed to meet the 6:00 a.m. deadline on 26 October 2002 to withdraw federal forces from Chechnya. However, it is clear that the assault was planned well before its execution as was evidenced by the notification given to foreign diplomats in advance of the siege.[16] Despite the fact that members of Putin's alma mater—the Federal Security Service (FSB)—killed all but two of the hostages, the Russian people strongly supported their president's actions. He was also absolved of guilt by his western allies, especially the US State Department which quickly moved to add more Chechen groups to its list of terrorist organisations.[17]

The generally forgiving orientation of the Russian masses to Putin's actions owes much to how he publicly couches his policy decisions—and the way in which he projects a persona of control, confidence, and rationality. The lyrics of the 2002 pop ballad 'I Want a Man like Putin' reflect some of the popular perceptions of Putin the man: energetic, abstemious, protective, and loyal.[18] Taking the helm

---

16 Torrey Clark, Oksana Yablokova and Andrei Zolotov, Jr., 'Commandos Strike, Death Toll Hits 167', *The Moscow Times*, 2553, pp. 1-2, 28 October 2002.

17 See Russell, 'Terrorists, Bandits, Spooks and Thieves,' p. 112.

18 And now I want a man like Putin.

of Russian politics after the tortuous reign of Boris Yeltsin, Putin quickly made the elimination of *bespredel* (literally 'beyond the limits', but usually translated as 'anarchy', 'chaos', or 'disorder') a centrepiece of his administration. While the events of October 2002 might easily have besmirched his record in bringing order to Russia, Putin turned the calamity into political capital. By refusing to negotiate with the terrorists holding nearly a thousand people hostage and acting decisively—even when it meant scores of dead innocents—Putin snatched victory from the jaws of defeat. Lawmaker Boris Nemtsov lauded Putin's resolve stating, 'I think this was the moment of truth, and it is of utter importance that President Putin did not succumb and did not begin to talk with them... This was the moment we preserved the Russian state'.[19] In the wake of the attack, Putin focused like a laser to strengthen the Russian state and prevent its various enemies—overt and surreptitious—from doing the country further harm. His popularity proved nearly unassailable.

The *Nord-Ost* tragedy was quickly and clumsily framed as 'Russia's 9/11', and, not surprisingly, the analogy rang hollow. Unlike the surprise attacks on the World Trade Center and the Pentagon, the hostage-taking in the outskirts of Moscow allowed the perpetrators to make demands to the Russian government and to link their actions to the Kremlin's policies on Chechnya. The videotaped message issued by Movsar Barayev's gunmen stated:

Every nation has the right to their fate. Russia has taken away this right from the Chechens and today we want to reclaim these rights, which God has given us, in the same way he has given it to other nations. God has given

---

A man like Putin, full of energy.
A man like Putin who doesn't drink.
A man like Putin who wouldn't hurt me.
A man like Putin who wouldn't run away from me.
I saw him in the news yesterday.
He was saying the world was at the crossroads.
It's easy with a man like him at home or out and about.
~ Lyrics by Russian pop band *Singing Together*, 2002.

19 See Clark, Yablokova and Zolotov, 'Commandos Strike, Death Toll Hits 167,' pp. 1-2.

us the right of freedom and the right to choose our destiny. And the Russian occupiers have flooded our land with our children's blood. And we have longed for a just solution…And therefore, we have chosen this approach.[20]

The nearly 3,000 deaths in New York resulted directly from the terrorist attack itself whereas the vast majority of the 130 *Nord-Ost* fatalities[21] stemmed from the gassing of the theatre. The deaths resulted from a miscalculation on the part of FSB Special Forces, who failed to take into account the stress, dehydration, and undernourishment which had gripped the theatre's occupants in the three-day long crisis.

The political after-effects of *Nord-Ost* and September 11 also differed markedly. Following the debacle, Putin stated 'Russia will respond with measures that are adequate to the threat to the Russian federation…striking on all the places where the terrorists themselves, the organisers of these crimes and their ideological and financial inspirers are…I stress, wherever they may be located'. Just as the American President George W. Bush had done after September 11, Putin publicly and boldly declared a pre-emptive strike doctrine and proclaimed the freedom to act without regard for international norms in cases of terrorist threats on the homeland. Unlike the Americans, however, such posturing failed to materialise in tangible external action. While the Kremlin identified the countries from which Chechen terrorists received their funding and support (a senior aide to President Putin, Abdul-Khakim Sultygov, stated in the wake of *Nord-Ost* that Chechen militants received financing from groups based in Turkey), Russia has yet to engage in any meaningful confrontations with Turkey, Turkish Cyprus, Azerbaijan, or the various 'Arab states' which maintain purported links with Chechen terrorists. Only Georgia—a country barely able to make a claim to

---

20 See 'Gunmen release chilling video', *CNN* Web site, 25 October 2002. Available at: http://archives.cnn.com/2002/WORLD/europe/10/24/moscow.siege.video/ [accessed on 9 April 2006].

21 This number includes only civilians; 42 hostage-takers were also killed—many of whom were shot dead by *Spetsnaz* as they stormed the theatre.

territorial sovereignty—has suffered under the new doctrine. Such meddling in the country does not represent a break from past actions as Russia has long supported the breakaway republics of Ajaria, Abkhazia, and South Ossetia. As such it is reasonable to conclude that Putin's new military doctrine was crafted for a domestic audience and not as a tool to shape international perceptions of Russia's intentions for military action or to change the behaviour of those wishing Russia harm.

In addition to the changes in Russia's military doctrine, the *Nord-Ost* crisis resulted in a precipitous acceleration of Putin's campaign to rein in his country's media. Upon his ascent to the presidency, Vladimir Putin began the process of nationalising the country's various television stations. Prior to *Nord-Ost*, Russia's media system could easily be described as neo-authoritarian.[22] Such a system is characterised by limited autonomy among state-owned media, a Byzantine system of economic pressures to silence critics, and the arbitrary or quasi-legal persecution of owners and editors for issues relating to interests of the state.[23]

The unique feature of the neo-authoritarian media system is that while there are tight reins placed on television, there may exist, in spite of periodic harassment, violence and closures, a vibrant print media that is independently owned (by individuals, parties, or foreign corporations), relatively autonomous, accessible to the population and highly critical of the regime.[24]

Putin's focus on the medium of television proved a wise strategy in post-Soviet Russia. As Ellen Mickiewicz, renowned scholar of Russian media and director of the DeWitt Wallace Center for Communications and Journalism at Duke University, states: 'from the very first appearance of television on a mass scale, it soon became the principal source of information and news, easily superseding the

---

22 Jonathan Becker, 'Lessons from Russia: A Neo-Authoritarian Media System', *European Journal of Communication*, 19(2), 2004, pp. 139–63.

23 Ibid,. p. 149.

24 Ibid., p. 150.

hallowed newspaper...political elites held a view of television as a persuasive instrument without peer'.[25]

During the Yeltsin era, Russian media closely resembled that of Italy—a system often referred to as the 'division of the spoils' as it reflected a segmentation which mirrored the distribution of economic power within the country.[26] Various stations and media outlets tended to represent the interests of their economic backers or patrons. For Putin, the nationalisation of television media functioned as an integral part of reducing the political—though not necessarily the economic—influence of the country's oligarchs. Putin's strategy was not to end press freedom altogether, as such a move would inevitably sour relations with Europe and America. Instead, Putin played a subtle game where television would become the mouthpiece of the Kremlin, while print publications and online sources would operate with relative impunity.[27] Putin's endgame for media policy seemed to be the de-politicisation of mainstream media outlets—thus undoing the 'Italianisation' of the media which occurred during the turbulent Yeltsin years. By removing controversial subjects from the airwaves, the Kremlin's strategy was to produce a more effective—or effectively managed—system of governance, i.e., one in which politicking is left to the closed circle of elites who already have the president's ear. As Masha Lipman, editor-in-chief of the Russian-language journal *Pro et Contra*, points out, 'With all national television networks tightly controlled by the Kremlin, nothing that government authorities deem "inappropriate", unexpected, or unpleasant may appear on the

25 Ellen Mickiewicz, 'The Election News Story on Russian Television: A World Apart from Viewers', *Slavic Review*, 65(1), 2006, pp.1-23.

26 John Dunn, (2006) 'Where Did It All Go Wrong? Russian Television in the Putin Era.' Paper presented at The Mass Media in Post-Soviet Russia International Conference, University of Surrey, 6 April 2006.

27 The Kremlin's suspect acquisition of NTV through the agent of the Kremlin-friendly energy giant Gazprom in 2001 served as a powerful symbol of this new policy. As the last independent station and owned by the oligarch Vladimir Gusinsky, NTV's nationalisation signalled a sea change in television content and ownership.

television screens of the major networks. In the summer of 2004 the last live TV political talk show was shut down, as well as the last political satirical show'.[28]

Putin's strategy for media reform was pushed into high gear by *Nord-Ost*. From the very start of the crisis, the Kremlin seemed overly preoccupied with media coverage of the event. As the siege progressed, various efforts were made to control reporting of the situation. The government temporarily closed the private Moscow television station *Moskoviya* for allegedly promoting terrorism. The Kremlin also threatened to shut down the independent radio station *Ekho Moskvy* for its airing of an interview with a hostage-taker. The government-dominated NTV refused to do likewise, wisely heeding warnings from its government handlers. Furthermore, the Media Ministry also issued a warning to the government-run newspaper *Rossiyskaya Gazeta* for publishing an image of a hostage killed by the terrorists.[29]

*Nord-Ost* produced a rather macabre media spectacle which Putin skilfully employed for his own designs. A master at the art of political prestidigitation, the president turned the deaths of more than a hundred people at the hands of his precious FSB into a reason for hobbling the press. After the end of the crisis, new legislation was proposed which curtailed even the most innocuous forms of coverage in similar situations. As a result of the new media environment, Russian journalists now face increasing hurdles to reporting other sorts of news and criticising Russia or its president. The generally responsible, though often sensational coverage, of the *Nord-Ost* siege marked an ominous milestone in the rollback of Russia's press freedoms. When the Beslan hostage crisis occurred less than two years later, Russian television barely interrupted its regularly scheduled

28  Masha Lipman, 'Constrained or Irrelevant: The Media in Putin's Russia', *Current History*, 104, 2005, pp. 319-24.

29  See Ann Cooper, 'CPJ Urges Putin Not to Sign Amendments', *Global Policy Forum* Web site, 14 November 2002. Available at http://www.globalpolicy.org/wtc/liberties/2002/1114cpj.htm.

programming during the first day. While CNN, FOX News, the BBC, and other non-Russian media outlets buzzed with speculation and actual reporting from the region, Russian TV delivered its standard line-up of soap-operas and light entertainment fare. 'By the time the hostage-taking tragedy at a Beslan school occurred...the Kremlin was fully protected against the detrimental effects of professional journalism, at least as far as national television was concerned...There were no survivors' accounts, no stories of desperate people who lost loved ones, no independent experts' analysis, and no public discussion whatsoever'.[30] The lessons of *Nord-Ost* had clearly been learned.

## Beslan: Yeltsin's legacy, Putin's 'vertical of power', and the remaking of Russian democracy

As stated earlier, Putin comfortably won the 2000 elections by playing up both real and imagined threats. Under the banner of ending *bespredel*, he then began steadily to dismantle Yeltsin's bureaucratic *bricolage* that he blamed for the country's current weakness. Yet, even with the threat of global Islamic networks operating in Russia's southern hinterlands, Putin was unable to reverse many of the democratic reforms of the Yeltsin era, specifically the direct election of regional governors and half of the lower house of parliament. But through a careful policy of weakening opposition sources (the oligarchs, the media, and 'real' political parties), he created the groundwork for a *coup de grâce* in remaking Russian democracy. An opportunity to strike the final blow came with the Beslan 'spectacular' of late summer 2004. Although Putin's post-Beslan reforms—restricting direct elections in the regions and a proportional system for the lower house of parliament—were linked to terrorism in only the most superficial of ways, these radical alterations proved surprisingly uncontroversial among all but a few of the country's political elites. As such, Putin's

---

30  Lipman, 'Constrained or Irrelevant', p. 320.

boldest act of political legerdemain was pulled off without anyone bothering to see through the illusion.

Even before taking office, Putin had made clear his intentions to dismantle Russia's asymmetrical federal system that relied on the direct election of regional governors—some of whom like Kirsan Ilyumzhinov, President of Kalmykia, wield near total power over their bailiwicks. Writing prior to Putin's rollback, Dmitry Shlapentokh of Indiana University identified a steady increase in provincial separatism in the regions where corrupt elections produced governors-for-life. These elites understood their role as 'little fathers' taking care of their flock, while simultaneously fostering 'local animosity toward the center' to increase their own political capital.[31] 'Unless the centre puts the election of these governors to an absolute end, anti-center sentiments will play an increasing role in shaping the local polity.'[32] This curious structure was very much a vestige of Yeltsin's weak presidency which was only perpetuated through constant deal-making with sometimes unsavoury regional and economic elites (Yeltsin once told the regional governors 'Take as much sovereignty as you can swallow'). Yeltsin came to power as a charismatic figure who climbed tanks and faced down the entire Soviet system, yet as soon as his reforms ran foul of the populist Russian Duma, he reacted like a despot shelling the parliament and locking up his adversaries. His alcoholism and chronic poor health did not help his image. With his popularity flagging, Yeltsin began buying off powerful allies. The 1993 Constitution of the Russian Federation—a document which itself brought the country to the brink of civil war—created a convoluted and asymmetrical federal system comprised of twenty-one ethnic republics, forty-nine provinces, six territories, ten autonomous regions (*okrugs*), two federal cities (Moscow and St Petersburg), and one autonomous province (*oblast*).[33]

---

31  Shlapentokh, 'Trends in Putin's Russia,' p. 75.

32  Ibid.

33  The system has since been reduced by one, as two regions merged—an event which foreshadows numerous other consolidations that have either been

Exemplifying the Byzantine structure of the system, one of the ethnic republics—Tatarstan—signed a special agreement with Russia in 1994 which recognises the 'state sovereignty' of Tatarstan and grants the republic the right to conduct direct economic relations with foreign states (during the 1990s Tatarstan refused to pay federal taxes or contribute troops to the Russian army). Two years later, Yeltsin's desperate re-election campaign—punctuated by a heart attack at a crucial point—required an acceleration of the devolution of power to the regions. Sakha, Bashkortostan, and other ethnic republics, as well as regions like Nizhny Novgorod and the Pacific maritime province Primorskiy Krai, truculently played the system to gain ever greater independence from Moscow. Regional leaders crafted laws and constitutions that contravened the Russian constitution and federal law, including Tatarstan's citizenship law that permitted Tatar citizenship without Russian citizenship. [34] By the end of the decade, the Russian Federation's political structure functioned as a network of satrapies and fiefdoms, many of which thumbed their noses at Moscow and kept the spoils of their resource wealth to themselves. [35]

Putin's new deal for Russia involved an unflinching reassertion of sovereignty and sharp recentralisation of authority which he deemed the 'vertical of power.' Editor of the Russian-European journalism review *Sreda*, Alexei Pankin parsimoniously describes Putin's mandate:

Putin had no practical choice but to try to start with creating what we call in Russia a vertical of power. It meant that he had to take measures that on appearance looked undemocratic. He had to rein in the oligarchs who

---

approved or proposed since 2005.

34 Olga Oliker and Tanya Charlick-Paley, *Assessing Russia's Decline: Trends and Implications for the United States and the US Air Force* (Santa Monica, 2002), p. 13.

35 According to Oliker and Charlick-Paley, *Assessing Russia's Decline*, p. 13: 'In fact, over the course of the 1990s, Russia's regional governments signed over 1000 agreements with partners in dozens of countries and many sent official representatives abroad'.

viewed Russia as their war spoils. In doing so he inevitably had to rein in the media. That is because the Russian media served not the public. The media were used by the oligarchs as weapons for plundering public resources, and as instruments for blackmailing the state. Putin had to reign in the governors, many of whom had turned into semi-independent feudal lords. And, in the absence of functioning democratic parties, he hardly had any choice but to create a loyal and obedient party and let it have a working majority in the parliament.[36]

As early as August 1999, Putin had already made clear his intentions to reduce regionalism and promote economic cohesion across the Russian Federation.[37] Unable to move very quickly against embedded interests in the provinces, Putin instead began his sovereignty reclamation project by reining in the political ambitions of the unpopular industrial tycoons in the summer of 2000. Bullying the oligarchs—men who had come to symbolise the rape of the Soviet system—won Putin allies among the disaffected Russian public. The majority of ordinary Russians suffered greatly under the chaotic 'shock therapy' economic reforms of the 1990s which were characterised by Strobe Talbott, US President Bill Clinton's advisor on Russia, as involving too much 'shock' and not enough 'therapy'.[38] The devaluation of the ruble in 1998 compounded the already dire economic conditions of much of Russian society creating a painfully evident gap between the 'haves' and 'have-nots'. Putin's taming of the oligarchs was not just lauded in popular circles; clamping down the anarchic environment of foreign direct investment, crony capitalism, and corruption in the country was not unwelcome among many Russia-watchers in the West who may have admired Yeltsin's demo-

---

36 Alexei Pankin, 'A Look at Russia behind the Headlines'. Speech made at the World Affairs Council in Philadelphia, PA, April 2006.

37 Ildus G. Ilishev, 'Nation-Building and Minority Rights in Post-Soviet Russia: The Case of Bashkortostan,' in Y. Ro'i ed., *Democracy and Pluralism in Muslim Eurasia* (London, 2004), pp. 307–28.

38 See Strobe Talbott, *The Russia Hand: A Memoir of Presidential Diplomacy* (New York, 2003).

cratic leanings but also understood the mess he made of his country and his failure to live up to his own principles.

Marginalising the tycoons proved a wise foundation for the re-centralisation of power in Russia. By forcing these vested interests from the political arena, Putin effectively deprived the regional governors of their most powerful allies. The media reforms which followed Putin's ascendancy also created an environment which buttressed Moscow's position on reform. However, popular support continued for many of the 'little fathers' during the Putin administration, but the growing support for a reassertion of state power soon challenged even this measure of strength. Putin's strategy during the first two years of his presidency centred on economic reform and juridical management to curtail the power of the regional governors, however, he was still somewhat hamstrung by Moscow's weak position vis-à-vis its periphery.[39] So when Chechen, Ingush, and (according to the Russian government) Arab hostage takers precipitated a bloodbath in the railway junction town of Beslan, North Ossetia[40] in September 2004, Putin used the event to steamroll any opposition to his plans for the 'vertical of power'. In a speech on 13 September 2004 at the Enlarged Government Meeting with the Government and Heads of Regions, Putin stated:

I believe that in the current situation, the current conditions, the system of executive power in the country must not simply be adapted to work in crisis situations, it must be fundamentally reorganised, in order to strengthen the unity of the country and stop crises from arising...I am certain that the unity of the country is the main condition for conquering terrorism.

---

39  See Oliker and Charlick-Paley, *Assessing Russia's Decline*, pp. 11-23.

40  Ossetians, the titular majority of the republic, are an Indo-European people whose language is related to Persian. Under Georgian influence, most Ossetians converted to Eastern Orthodoxy during the early Middle Ages. When the Muslim Chechens and Ingush were deported to Central Asia, many Ossetians occupied their vacated homes and businesses. Upon the return of the exiles, ethnic rivalries flared and continue to colour relations in the region.

Putin unequivocally linked expanded presidential power and re-duction of regional autonomy to a future free of terrorist violence, although according to Lynch, 'Putin's words produced more puzzle-ment than clarity' among the political elite.[41] By creating what he deemed an 'integral co-subordinate single organism', Putin projected his confidence to avoid future Beslans and *Nord-Osts*. Putin went on to reaffirm his 'first strike' doctrine promising to get the 'criminals... in their own lair, and if the situation requires it, to get them from abroad'. Other reforms that have been proposed include a re-intro-duction of the death penalty (in cases of terrorism), tougher visa re-strictions, stricter residency registration requirements, and increased regulation on buying, selling, and borrowing automobiles.

Putin also used Beslan to lurch the political structure of the Rus-sian Federation closer to a pure presidential system, calling for a party list system to be instituted in the Duma. In recent elections, the Kremlin has been able to craft ad hoc parties and party coalitions to marginalise the communists and liberals in parliament. By shifting towards a proportional system, Putin is effectively guaranteeing that the Duma will function as a rubberstamp rather than a balance to presidential power. Not surprisingly, Putin's critics from the liberal Yabloko Party to the Communist leader Gennady Zyuganov im-mediately condemned the reforms. Perhaps the sharpest criticisms came from Garry Kasparov—international chess champion and chair of 2008: Free Choice Committee, a group trying to field a liberal candidate for the next presidential election in Russia. In a 16 Sep-tember 2004 statement where he called Putin's post-Beslan reforms a 'constitutional coup', Kasparov stated:

Vladimir Putin proposes to establish an authoritarian regime, one that is ca-pable neither of ensuring the safety of Russian citizens nor of guaranteeing the integrity of the Russian state. Quite the opposite: The enactment of such plans will, actually, mean that Russia capitulates to terrorists, after being intimidated into the destruction of its constitutional system. The terrorists

---

41 Lynch, 'The Enemy is at the Gate', p. 142.

could not dream about such rapid and easy success as the Russian authority now presents them.[42]

While Kasparov has a political axe to grind, his fears about Putin's use of the Beslan tragedy for political purposes were echoed in other quarters of Russia's political elite. In a statement to *The Moscow News*, the last Soviet premier Mikhail Gorbachev stated, 'Under the motto war on terror, there are suggestions of sharply limiting democratic freedoms; citizens are stripped of the opportunity to directly express their attitude toward the government by giving up elections in single-seat constituencies. This comes now when we have mostly government-sponsored pet parties'.[43] Former President Boris Yeltsin, however, was more conciliatory in his mild—if not gossamer—criticisms of Putin. While affirming his wishes that Russia remain a democratic country, he spoke for the Russian people stating: 'The Beslan tragedy has become a watershed. We are all different now'.[44] Like the Americans after 9/11, Russians were truly reeling from the effects of Beslan and looked to their leader for guidance. He was more than happy to explain the changed world to them.

Putin stated in a televised address to the nation on 4 September 2004: 'We showed ourselves to be weak, and the weak get beaten.' In his subsequent statements, he wisely equated Beslan with September 11 (conveniently forgetting the earlier characterisation of Nord-Ost as Russia's 9/11). According to Lynch, such discursive practices have created a 'black and white situation, in which it becomes more difficult to utter any criticism of Russian actions'.[45] Beslan simultaneously undermined any false perceptions of Russian strength, while paradoxically paving the way for the *siloviki* ('the strong ones', i.e., Putin's inner circle of FSB cronies and former military) to increase Russia's strength at the cost of democracy. By framing his reforms as

42  See 'Russia and Chechnya: President Putin's Response to the Beslan Tragedy', *International Debates*, 2(7), 2002, pp. 214–23.

43  Ibid., pp. 219–21.

44  Ibid., pp. 221–23.

45  Lynch, 'The Enemy is at the Gate', p. 158.

a panacea for the country's weakness, Putin has effectively silenced his critics within Russia.

Putin's calls for a rollback of the purportedly debilitating elements of democratisation enacted during his predecessor's tenure were not so well-received outside of Russia. He, however, quickly moved to counter external criticisms and actually met with a number of foreign journalists and foreign policy makers within several days of the Beslan massacre to articulate his plans for the future and defend his policies. The basic messages were clear: Chechnya remains a hotbed of Islamic extremism; there is no legitimate authority to bargain with; Chechnya could lead to a domino effect in the Caucasus; and, Russia will no longer be a victim of its own weakness.[46] While many in the West continue to decry the erosion of democracy, few bemoan Moscow's efforts to quell the sources of terror that resulted in the deaths of hundreds of schoolchildren in its southern periphery.

## Putin as illusionist extraordinaire

Putin's reforms—though criticised by a handful of political elites—went over surprisingly well among the masses. This begs the question of why Russians have been so lackadaisical about the ebbing of democracy since Putin's ascension. Some commentators claim that 'Russians are predisposed—by Orthodox Christianity, by the paternalistic mores of village life, by centuries of tsarist rule, and, most recently, by cradle-to-grave socialism—to favor authoritarianism'.[47] This predilection has, in part, been used to provide a cultural explanation for the anti-democratic leanings of twenty-first century Russians.[48] However, one must also consider the impact of what I call 'chaos fatigue'. Putin has skilfully played on Russians' antipathy

46  Kampfner, 'A President Craves Understanding,' pp. 10–13.

47  Timothy J. Colton and Michael McFaul 'America's Real Allies,' *Foreign Affairs*, 80(6), 2001, pp. 46-58.

48  A recent poll of Russians found that roughly one-quarter of adults would vote for Stalin if he were alive today and running for president. See Sarah H. Mendelson and Theodore P. Gerber, 'Failing the Stalin Test,' *Foreign Affairs*, 85(1), 2006, pp. 2-8.

towards unpredictability and disorder in politics and has been re- warded with a pliable public. And like those who attend carnivals to escape their 'reality fatigue', Russians are looking for a bit of escape from the *bespredel* which characterised the Yeltsin years. In fact, a study of elites by the Institute of Sociology found that one of Putin's greatest virtues in the minds of influential Russians is that he is a '"normal president" in a country which had grown accustomed to considering itself "abnormal"' with nearly 80 per cent of those polled affirming this contention.[49]

As such, it is not surprising that Putin has been able more ef- fectively to play politics with terror than his counterparts George W. Bush, José Mariá Aznar, and Tony Blair who all experienced major terror attacks on their own countries during the same period. While the Bush administration's manipulation of terror in the wake of 9/11 is comparable in scope and scale to Putin's, a robust criticism of the American president's terror-linked policies soon developed after the invasion of Afghanistan. It is now clear that George W. Bush clearly over-played his hand by launching an invasion of Iraq in response to purported links between Al Qaeda and the Saddam Hussein regime and exaggerated threats to the American homeland stemming from Baghdad. Bush is now regularly lambasted for his massaging of the truth and his approval ratings are at historic lows.

Aznar's feckless attempts to blame the Basque separatists for the Islamist train bombings in 2004 proved a spectacular failure of play- ing politics with terror. The Spanish population easily recognised his fumbling attempts to gain political capital out of the event by placing the blame at the feet of ETA and repaid him by voting his ruling party out of office in one of the biggest election upsets in recent European history. Tony Blair, though perhaps the least manipula- tive of the bunch, has also seen his attempts at playing politics with

---

49  Olga Kryshtanovskaya, 'In Putin, Populace Sees What It Wants to See,' *The St. Petersburg Times*, 908(76), 7 October 2003. Available at: http://www. sptimes.ru/index.php?action_id=2&story_id=11166 [accessed 17 April 2006].

terror pan out less effectively than President Putin's. Blair's resolute denial that the 7/7 terror attacks could be linked to his country's Iraq adventure seemed preposterous to most Britons; in fact, a *Guardian* poll found that more than half of the country thought that Blair's decision to go to war in Iraq was at least partially responsible for the attacks. In the wake of the bombings, Blair's own reform agenda has become mired in difficulties and, at the time of writing, he seems to be the parliamentary equivalent of a lame duck.

Perhaps Americans, Spaniards, and Britons are less easily beguiled by political prestidigitation than Russians, or possibly Putin is just a more seductive sleight-of-hand artist. In either case, it is clear that Putin is both the ringleader and the illusionist extraordinaire of Russia's bloody carnival. His alternatively subtle and ham-handed use of the threat of terrorism—when combined with the pervasive loathing of chaos among the Russian population—has endowed the president with a prodigious mandate for change. In any country which has suffered as much from terrorism as Russia has over the past few years, the government's ability to safeguard its people and to bring the perpetrators of violence to justice should be expanded. However the measures undertaken must—at a minimum—correspond to the threats posed. In Russia's case, the reaction to terror has been a strange farrago of administrative reforms, media restrictions, and doctrinal posturing. Putin's traducing of the press, Western ignorance of the Chechen threat, and of his regional governors for the various attacks on his country has done little to address the actual threat of terrorism. Yet, his actions seem to have been well-received by his various constituencies. Rather than prompting a public outcry, Putin's curious efforts to combat terrorism have only solidified his popularity.

# 11

# A RETURN TO THE MIDDLE AGES? AUSTRALIA'S COUNTERTERRORISM LAW AND POLICY IN A POST-9/11 WORLD

## Christopher Michaelsen

On inaugural day 1933, at the height of the Great Depression, US President Franklin D. Roosevelt galvanised the dispirited American people with a simple declaration of faith: 'This great Nation will endure as it has endured, will revive and prosper. So, first of all, let me assert my firm belief that the only thing we have to fear is fear itself—nameless, unreasoning, unjustified terror which paralyses needed efforts to convert retreat into advance.'[1] Roosevelt's reading of the situation at this critical juncture of history could hardly be more pertinent to the state of affairs today. International terrorism creates fear, individually and collectively. Terrorists gain power only if they inspire fear in the minds of their audience, either because an atmosphere of terror enhances their rational political leverage or because it satisfies the irrational dictates of the fanatical, ideological and/or religious doctrine they espouse.

The atrocities of 9/11, Bali, Madrid and London understandably inspired fear in the minds of many Australians, and the desire to escape from an atmosphere of fear into a climate of greater security is

---

1  Quoted in Joseph M. Siracusa and David G. Coleman, *Depression to Cold War: a History of America from Herbert Hoover to Ronald Reagan* (London, 2002), pp. 21-2.

a natural reaction. Besides, as terrorism often violates the most basic aspects of human security, there is a duty for the state to respond. But the relentless pursuit of absolute security also brings great danger as an ill-conceived and fear-driven response may well damage the integrity and value of the state and have severe consequences for the very way of life one is actually trying to defend. It is also obvious that a climate of fear can be fertile political ground for any incumbent government. And indeed, since international terrorism became a major political issue on 9/11, the Australian government, led by Prime Minister John Howard (Liberal Party), a close personal ally of US President George W. Bush, has sought to capitalise politically on the public fears arising from the terrorist threat. The Howard government is not the only incumbent government to have done so, of course. But it has (successfully) attempted to reap electoral benefits in a particularly aggressive and morally most dubious manner.

Two months after 9/11 and a mere four days before Australia's federal election of 11 November 2001, for instance, Prime Minister Howard claimed that 'Australia had no way to be certain terrorists or people with terrorist links were not among asylum seekers trying to enter the country by boat from Indonesia'.[2] Although such claims have been subsequently discounted by senior intelligence officials, they nonetheless achieved their political purpose at the time. Linking the threat of terrorism to the highly political (and election-deciding) issue of refugees and the coalition's vigorous and uncompromising campaign focusing on immigration policy in the wake of the MV Tampa incident more generally have been widely cited as the main reasons for Prime Minister Howard's last-minute victory at the 2001 federal elections.[3]

---

2   Dennis Atkins, 'PM links terror to asylum seekers,' *Courier Mail* (Brisbane), 7 November 2001.

3   David Marr and Marian Wilkinson, *Dark Victory* (Sydney, 2003); David Solomon (ed.), *Howard's Race: Winning the Unwinnable Election* (Sydney, 2002). On the MV Tampa incident see http://en.wikipedia.org/wiki/MV_Tampa; Peter Mares, *Borderline: Australia's Response to Refugees and Asylum Seekers in the Wake of Tampa* (Sydney, 2002).

The threat of international terrorism has also been unduly employed by the Howard government to attack and ridicule the opposition and to justify draconian anti-terrorism legislation. During a 27-hour parliamentary debate in December 2002, for instance, the Coalition went so far as to accuse Labor of wearing the blame for any blood spilt in a terrorist attack that occurred because of the deadlock on new anti-terrorism legislation.[4] This was but one example of the government's attempts to play politics with terrorism in order to rush through Parliament unprecedented laws. Since September 2001, the Coalition has introduced no fewer than twenty-eight new (federal) 'security laws' dealing with a broad range of issues.[5] And while it is always wise and prudent to reassess existing legislation in the light of the changing threat of international terrorism, it is equally questionable whether the introduction of wide ranging repressive domestic laws could ever contribute to the defeat of that threat. What is more, constant changes to the law not only create a degree of uncertainty in the legal system but may also perpetuate the very atmosphere of fear in the society itself.

This essay will commence by outlining briefly some of the main legislative measures introduced by the Howard government in the aftermath of 9/11. While the bulk of anti-terrorism laws was enacted in 2002 and 2003, further significant changes were made in 2004 and 2005, both at the federal and the state level. Most of the more recent amendments were introduced as a direct response to three particular incidents—the Willie Brigitte affair, the Jack Roche trial, and the Bilal Khazal bail hearing. Consequently, the analysis will focus specifically on each of these three cases and seek to illustrate that the corresponding legislative responses derived mainly from the government's attempts to play politics with terrorism and national security rather than from an urgent need to reform the law. What the new measures fully have in common is that they break with long-standing

---

4   Cynthia Banham, 'Howard, Crean to go to war on terrorism,' *Sydney Morning Herald*, 14 December 2002.

5   As of 13 October 2005; see 'Legislation', http://www.nationalsecurity.gov.au.

judicial traditions and curtail civil and political rights to a previously unseen extent. Whether they can provide any protection against the dangers of international terrorism, however, remains problematic.

## Australia's anti-terrorism laws

Before 9/11 there were no Australian laws dealing with terrorism specifically. A first package of anti-terrorism legislation passed both Houses of Parliament in early March 2002. This package contained the Security Legislation Amendment (Terrorism) bill 2002, the Suppression of the Financing of Terrorism bill 2002, the Criminal Code Amendment (Suppression of Terrorist Bombings) bill 2002, the Border Security Legislation Amendment bill 2002, and the Telecommunications Interception Legislation Amendment bill 2002.

The most important of these first five bills was the controversial Security Legislation Amendment (Terrorism) bill 2002. The bill drew notably on the British Terrorism act 2000 and passed the House of Representatives (the lower house) and the Senate (the upper house) only after it had been amended substantially to include recommendations by the Senate Legal and Constitutional Legislation Committee. It added a host of new terrorism offences to the Criminal Code act 1995. In particular, it provided a definition of a 'terrorist act' and introduced criminal sanctions for involvement with a 'terrorist organisation', including for providing support or funding, recruiting members, directing its activities or being a member. The bill also introduced new powers for the attorney-general to outlaw terrorist organisations and organisations that threaten the integrity and security of Australia or another country. A common criticism of many of these new measures has been that they are considerably broad-defined and that they criminalise actions that go far beyond the kind of terrorist attacks that motivated the legislative amendments in the first place.[6]

---

6  Jenny Hocking, 'Counterterrorism and the Criminalisation of Politics: Australia's New Security Powers of Detention, Proscription and Control,' *Australian Journal of Politics and History*, 49(3), 2003, pp. 355–57; Michael Head, 'Counterterrorism Laws Threaten Fundamental Democratic Rights,'

The second cornerstone of Australia's new anti-terrorism legislation is the Australian Security Intelligence Organisation Legislation Amendment (Terrorism) act 2003. The ASIO bill was first introduced into the House of Representatives on 21 March 2002 and subsequently subject to one of the most bitterly fought campaigns in Australian parliamentary history. After sixteen months of exhaustive debate, three parliamentary committee reports and extensive expert contribution, a revised bill finally passed the (then) Labor-controlled Senate on 26 June 2003. Nonetheless, the act remains highly controversial, partly because it vests a domestic intelligence agency with powers of arrest and detention that in Australia are traditionally held by the law enforcement agencies.[7]

The main purpose of the ASIO Amendment Act, then, was to authorise the detention by ASIO of persons for questioning in relation to terrorism offences. In particular, the new arrangements allow the intelligence agency to detain any person—Australian or otherwise—without judicial warrant for up to seven days and interrogate them for up to 24 hours within that seven-day period. In contrast to comparable legislation in the US, the United Kingdom, Canada and other liberal democracies, persons detained do not need to be suspected of any offence and can be taken into custody without charges being laid or even the possibility that they might be laid at a later stage. What is more, during the interrogation detainees are required to answer all questions and provide any material or face up to five years imprisonment. This means that the person detained and questioned bears the burden of proof to establish that he/she does not have the information sought. While a

---

*Alternative Law Journal*, 27(3), 2002, pp. 121–3; Christopher Michaelsen, 'Australia's Antiterrorism Legislation: a Proportionate Response to the Terrorist Threat?' *Studies in Conflict & Terrorism*, 28(4), 2005, pp. 322–5.

7 For a detailed critique of the ASIO Act see Jenny Hocking, *Terror Laws: ASIO, Counterterrorism and the Threat to Democracy* (Sydney, 2004), pp. 212-39; George Williams, 'Australian Values and the War against Terrorism,' *University of New South Wales Law Journal*, 26(1), 2003, pp. 191-9; Joo-Chong Tham, 'ASIO and the Rule of Law,' *Alternative Law Journal*, 27(5), 2002, pp. 216-21.

detainee may ask for a lawyer of his/her choice, counsel is not allowed to intervene in the questioning process and cannot challenge any aspect of the detention warrant in a court of law. In effect, these provisions abandon several fundamental principles of the rule of law: they dilute the prohibition of arbitrary detention, they obliterate the right to habeas corpus, they remove the right to silence, and they reverse the onus of proof. Needless to say, they also raise serious concerns in relation to Australia's obligation under international human rights law.[8]

The Howard government has since continued to enact further anti-terrorism laws. Several significant legislative amendments were introduced as a direct response to the Brigitte affair, the Roche trial and the Khazal bail hearing. These three cases will be the subject of closer analysis below. Similar to the legislative responses in other western democracies, a common feature of almost all of Canberra's legislative measures has been that they curtail civil liberties and encroach upon the rule of law to an unprecedented extent. What is unique about the Australian legislation, however, is the fact that both judicial and parliamentary oversight and review of the new laws is extremely limited. And in the very few instances where such review is possible, the measures in question cannot be checked against any substantial human rights standards. The reason for this lack of human rights protection is simple: Australia has neither a constitutional bill of rights nor an act of parliament codifying the very basic civil rights and fundamental freedoms of its citizens.[9]

## The Willie Brigitte affair

Willie Brigitte was born on the Caribbean island of Guadeloupe in 1968 and moved to Paris as a teenager in the 1980s. After dropping out of high school and deserting from the navy he worked in general

---

8   Christopher Michaelsen, 'International Human Rights on Trial: The United Kingdom's and Australia's Legal Response to 9/11,' *Sydney Law Review*, 25(3), 2003, pp. 281–6.

9   George Williams, *The Case for an Australian Bill of Rights: Freedom in the War on Terror* (Sydney, 2004).

labouring occupations throughout the 1990s. In 1998, Brigitte converted to Islam, changing his name to Mohammed Abderrahman, or Abderrahman the West Indian. According to Radio Europe 1 correspondent Alain Acco, it was around this time that Brigitte first became known to the Directorate for Territorial Surveillance (DST), the French security and counterintelligence service.[10] He attended regularly the Omar and Abou Bakr mosques in the poor and immigrant Paris suburb of Couronnes and allegedly associated with people who had links to the Salafist Group to Call and Combat, an Algerian-based extremist group. Subsequently, in 1999 and 2000, Brigitte and 'carloads of bearded Muslims' were observed heading off on several 'strenuous camping trips' in the Fontainebleau Forest just outside Paris. The group, dubbed 'the camper group' by DST, was also seen departing for hiking excursions on remote Normandy beaches.[11]

Two years later, after September 11, 2001, DST reportedly noted that members of the same 'camper group' were reappearing in Afghanistan fighting with the Taliban.[12] Brigitte apparently also headed for Afghanistan in late 2001. However, due to the US-led military campaign, he was unable to cross the Afghanistan-Pakistan border. Instead, he remained in Pakistan where he allegedly spent four months in a Lashkar-e-Taiba training camp in the mountains of the Punjab.[13] According to transcripts of an interrogation conducted by French anti-terrorism magistrate Jean-Louis Bruguiére, Brigitte admitted his presence at the Lashkar-e-Taiba complex near Lahore, Pakistan, in

---

10 Alain Acco's report was derived from what Brigitte is alleged to have told DST under interrogation. His account depended entirely on information supplied by an unnamed 'senior member of the French police' and an equally anonymous 'Parisian anti-terrorist magistrate'. Acco's report was virtually the sole basis of the subsequent wave of sensational and embroidered media reports in Australia.

11 Australian Broadcasting Corporation (ABC), Transcript TV Program, *Four Corners—Willie Brigitte*, at http://www.abc.net.au/4corners/content/2003/transcripts/s1040952.htm.

12 Ibid.

13 Lashkar-e-Taiba, or LET, is a Pakistani group formed to fight for the liberation of Kashmir from India.

2001–2002. He then returned to Paris and, in May 2003, obtained a tourist visa to visit Australia where he arrived on 16 May.[14] Settling in a suburb in Sydney's south-west, Brigitte worked in a halal restaurant in the city. In August 2003, he married Sydneysider Melanie Brown, an Australian Muslim convert. His motives for travelling to Australia, however, remain subject to wild speculation.[15]

Brigitte's trip to Australia and his presence in Sydney were not initially noticed by either the French or the Australian security services. On 16 September 2003, however, DST reportedly confirmed, through a Paris travel agent, that Brigitte had bought a one-way ticket to Australia using his original French name. About six days later, on 22 September, the Australian Embassy in Paris received a letter from DST requesting confirmation that the Frenchman was still in Australia. Although the letter indicated that Brigitte was possibly a member of an Islamist group and that he had received military training in Pakistan, ASIO appears to have treated it as a routine trace request.

Some ten days passed and the French received no reply to their enquiry. Then, on Friday 3 October 2003, the French authorities sent a second message warning that Brigitte could be in Australia in connection with terrorism-related activity and that he was 'possibly dangerous'. This time the information was sent directly to the ASIO headquarters in Canberra. The intelligence communiqué arrived in Canberra at 11 p.m., a time at which ASIO's communications area was apparently closed for the weekend. Since the following Monday

---

14  ABC, *Four Corners—Willie Brigitte.*

15  Brigitte's lawyers claimed that their client 'was off to Australia to start a new life'. Ibid. According to (then) ASIO Director-General, Dennis Richardson, 'Brigitte was almost certainly involved in activities with the intention of doing harm in Australia.' David Wroe, 'Ruddock restarts push for tougher law,' *The Age* (Melbourne), 4 November 2003. However, when ABC TV correspondent Tony Jones directly asked the attorney-general whether he believed that Brigitte 'was plotting some kind of terrorist action', Mr Ruddock's reply was simple and clear: 'No.' ABC, Transcript TV Program '*Lateline*'—*Intelligence delay has Ruddock asking questions*, 27 October 2003, http:www.abc.net.au/lateline/content/2003/s976417.htm.

was a public holiday, it was not before Tuesday 7 September—three days later—that ASIO finally received the message. Within two days, the Australian authorities located Brigitte and detained him for breaching his visa conditions. The newly adopted questioning and detention powers of the ASIO Act, however, were not invoked. Brigitte was subsequently deported to France on 17 October 2003.

The glaring failure of intelligence exchange and communication problems between the French and Australian authorities, resulting in a person with suspected links to an Islamic extremist organisation being granted a tourist visa, carried significant potential for political damage to the government, particularly with a federal election a mere eleven months away. The topics of 'national security' and 'counterterrorism' featured prominently in the government's campaign plans and were generally predicted to be ballot-winning issues for the October 2004 federal election. The government thus chose an aggressive response to the Brigitte incident. Rather than reviewing and addressing apparent administrative lapses, however, the Coalition's political rhetoric focused heavily on the assertion that Brigitte's presence in Sydney had highlighted the threat of terrorism to mainland Australia. And, as a consequence, the introduction of even 'tougher' anti-terrorism legislation was warranted.

Attorney-general Philip Ruddock, in particular, sought to capitalise politically upon the Brigitte incident. Emphasising the effectiveness of Australia's co-operative counterterrorism arrangements with France, Ruddock went so far as to claim that the Brigitte case had shown that ASIO's powers were 'clearly inadequate' and that Australia's anti-terrorism legislation ranked only 'third and fourth best'.[16] Without even attempting to apply ASIO's new questioning and detention powers to the Brigitte case, the attorney-general called for further amendments to the ASIO Act. A comparison with French anti-terrorism laws, so Mr Ruddock hinted, required Australia to

---

16 Cynthia Banham, 'ASIO laws inferior insists Ruddock,' *Sydney Morning Herald*, 4 November 2003.

introduce significant additional arrangements.[17] However, as Greg Carne has pointed out, comparing the ASIO Act with the French counterterrorism powers was not only inappropriate for inter-jurisdictional reasons, but also failed to acknowledge the systemic human rights abuses arising from those powers reported by the United Nations human rights treaty bodies, the European Court of Human Rights and Amnesty International.[18]

Seemingly unaffected by such criticisms the government moved quickly to expand the legislative counterterrorism framework and introduced into Parliament the ASIO Legislation Amendment bill 2003 on 27 November 2003. The legislation passed the Senate just eight days later. In contrast to the ASIO Act amendments of 2002 (enacted in June 2003), the November 2003 additions were not subject to scrutiny by any parliamentary committee. And although the Greens and Democrats called for the bill to be referred to the Senate Legal and Constitutional Committee, Labor, fearing once again to be seen as 'soft' on terrorism, supported the government's bill unconditionally.

The bill doubled the maximum time a person could be questioned under a warrant where an interpreter is needed from 24 to 48 hours. Despite strong criticism from a number of organisations, including the Australian Broadcasting Corporation and the Australian Press Council, the legislative amendments also tightened secrecy provisions preventing people from discussing information obtained during their interrogation for two years after the warrant has expired. These disclosure offences include unauthorised primary and secondary disclosures of an extensive range of information. The effect of these provisions criminalises media reporting of material within the broad terms of the prohibitions, including reporting of the fact that

---

17 ABC, Transcript TV Program *Lateline—Intelligence delay has Ruddock asking questions.* This comparison has also been used to explain the deportation of Brigitte on the grounds of the supposed inadequacy of the ASIO detention and questioning regime.

18 Greg Carne, 'Brigitte and the French Connection: Security Carte Blanche or a la Carte?,' *Deakin Law Review*, 9(2), 2004, pp. 604-10.

a detention and questioning warrant has been issued in relation to a specific matter.

The government's effort to turn the political negative of Brigitte's presence in Australia into a positive by claiming that recently enhanced ASIO powers were inadequate, is remarkable for several reasons. First, it confirmed an unapologetic shift to an overt, professionalised politicisation of counterterrorism issues, juggling partisan political advantage with the security of the nation.[19] Second, the attorney-general's call for legislative reform a mere four months after the conclusion of sixteen months of exhaustive debate, and three parliamentary committee reports highly critical of the government's proposals, was dismissive of the democratic contribution expended in that legislative process. Finally, the legislative response to the Brigitte incident included provisions that encroach upon fundamental freedoms such as the freedom of the press. It is difficult to see, however, how such amendments can constitute an essential tool for effective counterterrorism policy. If anything, they reduce democratic accountability and diminish the vital safeguard of free press reporting, without decreasing the risk of a terrorist attack.

## The Jack Roche case

Jack Roche was born as Paul George Holland in the Yorkshire town of Hull in 1953 and moved to Australia in 1978.[20] After working in various general labouring occupations throughout the 1980s, he accepted a job at a Sydney factory which also employed several Indonesian Muslims. Through the contact with his Indonesian workmates, Roche eventually converted to Islam in 1992 while trying to combat a drinking problem. He then spent several years in Indonesia learn-

---

19 Ibid., pp. 597-602.

20 Unless referenced otherwise, the information on Roche provided in this chapter is based on the sentencing remarks by Justice Healy, District Court of western Australia; Sentencing Remarks—IND 03/0622—(The Queen v. J Roche), http://www.districtcourt.wa.gov.au/content/files/binaryFiles/Roche_sentence.pdf.

ing about Islam and teaching English as a second language. Upon his return to Australia in 1996, Roche came into contact with the Indonesian twin brothers Abdul Rahman and Abdul Rahim Ayub who are believed to have headed the Australian branch of the Indonesian Islamist group Jemaah Islamiah (JI).[21]

In February 2000, Abdul Rahim Ayub delegated Roche to fly to Malaysia to meet with Hambali. Hambali is thought to have been the regional head of JI and the mastermind of the Bali bombings of October 2002. He encouraged Roche to travel to Afghanistan for basic military training. Roche agreed, and, a month later, flew to Karachi, Pakistan, where he met Khalid Sheikh Mohammed (Mukhtar), a senior al-Qaeda operative who is now in US custody. Mukhtar asked Roche about Israeli and American interests in Australia and gave him a letter addressed to 'the sheik'. Roche subsequently embarked on his trip to Afghanistan and delivered Mukhtar's letter to Abu Hafs and Saif, allegedly two deputies of Osama bin Laden. While receiving two weeks of military training in an al-Qaeda camp near Kandahar, Roche also briefly met bin Laden in person and later described him as 'really very nice'—so much for the elusiveness of bin Laden.[22]

After the completion of his military training, Abu Hafs and Saif ordered Roche to conduct surveillance on Israeli and US targets in

---

21 Abdul Rahman is a militant cleric and veteran of the 'Islamic holy war in Afghanistan' and a graduate of the infamous Ngruki School founded by radical Muslim cleric and alleged JI spiritual leader Abu Bakar Bashir. ABC, Transcript TV Program, *Four Corners—The Australian Connections*, http://www.abc.net.au/4corners/content/2003/transcripts/s878332.htm. Abdul Rahman applied for refugee status but lost his case in the Refugee Review Tribunal and was deported in 1999. Abdul Rahim left Australia for Indonesia in September 2002. Indonesia's national intelligence agency, BIN, located Abdul Rahim Ayub in West Java in early 2004. However, according to Indonesian officials neither Abdul Rahim, nor his twin brother Abdul Rahman, have been linked to any terrorist act in Indonesia or raised the interest of Indonesian counterterrorism police; See Martin Chulov, 'Indonesian agents track down JI's Australian "leader",' *The Australian*, 16 July 2004.

22 Roy Gibson, 'Bin Laden Very Nice: Roche', *The West Australian* (Perth), 21 May 2004.

Australia, and also to recruit other Australians to form a 'cell'. Roche returned to Perth in April 2000 and, according to his own account, was 'full of fervour for the Islamic cause'. However, he then found out, through an internet search, that some of the people who had given him orders in Afghanistan were on the FBI's most wanted list. It was around this time that Roche apparently began to realise and understand the enormity of what he had embarked upon. But since 'you just don't walk away from these kinds of people', Roche, fearing for his life, continued to carry out his orders to investigate Israeli interests in Australia.[23]

Two months later, in June 2000, Roche travelled to Sydney and took still pictures of the Israeli consulate. He then drove to Canberra and filmed the Israeli embassy. Instead of quietly video-taping the embassy compound, however, Roche wandered around behaving so conspicuously that an Australian Protective Services security guard walked up and had a conversation with him. A month later, he told Ibrahim Fraser, a friend and fellow Muslim-convert, that there were plans to bomb the Israeli embassy. After telling him about 'twenty-five times', according to Fraser's account, Fraser finally took Roche seriously and telephoned the Australian Federal Police (AFP). The AFP, however, ignored Fraser's call. On 14 July 2000, Roche contacted ASIO himself to report about his surveillance work, his trip to Afghanistan and the orders he had received from senior al-Qaeda operatives. The intelligence agency did not respond—a failure subsequently acknowledged by ASIO itself.[24]

In late July 2000, Roche travelled to Indonesia where he was told by JI's alleged spiritual leader, Abu Bakar Bashir, to comply with any order he was given by Hambali, 'whatever it happens to be'. Upon his return to Australia on 10 August 2000, Roche contacted ASIO again. Once more the intelligence agency did not reply. Roche then 'thought just leave it' and decided to wait for 'somebody to come

---

23 'Australian suspect "feared for life",' *BBC News (Online)*, 27 May 2004, http://news.bbc.co.uk/2/hi/asia-pacific/3753627.stm.

24 ASIO, *Report to Parliament 2003–2004*, Canberra, 2004, pp. 5, 26.

knocking on my door'.[25] Several weeks later, Bashir allegedly called Roche in Perth and told him to abandon any plans. Apparently there had been a fall-out between the Ayub brothers and Bashir over Hambali's interference in JI's affairs in Australia.

Two years later, shortly after the Bali bombings of October 2002 which killed eighty-eight Australians, Roche was tracked down by a reporter from *The Australian* newspaper and subsequently gave a series of taped interviews. These interviews provided the basis for ASIO raids on his home in Perth and later charges laid by the police. Roche subsequently co-operated fully with ASIO and the AFP and provided the full details of what he had been doing, his JI contacts in Indonesia and his al-Qaeda contacts in Afghanistan. It has been reported that this information contributed to the arrest of alleged Bali mastermind Hambali as well as to the capture of Khalid Sheikh Mohammed (Mukhtar). What is more, the information provided by Roche was instrumental in proving the Crown's case against him.[26]

The trial of Jack Roche commenced on 17 May 2004. Initially pleading not guilty, Roche changed his mind during the proceedings and, on 28 May, admitted to the charge of conspiring to:

commit an offence contrary to section 8(3C)9a) of the Crimes (Internationally Protected Persons) Act 1976 being to intentionally destroy or damage by means of explosive the official premises of internationally protected persons, namely the Israeli Embassy, with intent to endanger the lives of internationally protected persons by that destruction or damage contrary to section 86(1) of the Crimes act 1914.[27]

---

25 'Roche "lost interest" in bombing,' *Sydney Morning Herald*, 27 May 2004.

26 According to AFP officer Michael Duthie, it was Roche's own interview with the AFP which provided the evidence which led to his conviction. By taking part in the interview, he put 'a noose around his own neck.' Cameron Stewart, Paige Taylor, Belinda Hickman and John Kerin 'Terrorist tried to warn ASIO,' *The Australian*, 29 May 2004.

27 It has been falsely reported that Roche was the first person convicted under Australia's 'new' anti-terrorism laws; see e.g., 'Australian jailed for embassy plot,' BBC News (Online), 1 June 2004, http://news.bbc.co.uk/2/hi/asia-pacific/3765453.stm; Wikipedia Online Encyclopedia, 'Jack Roche,' http://en.wikipedia.org/wiki/Jack_Roche.

On 1 June 2004 he was subsequently sentenced to nine years imprisonment. Since Roche did not have a previous criminal record, he was declared eligible for parole after half of his sentence. According to Justice Healy, Western Australia's most experienced judge, his chances of re-offending were virtually non-existent.

Tabloid front pages and news reports were filled with fury at the court's treatment of Australia's 'first terrorist'. Sydney's *Daily Telegraph*, for instance, carried the front page headline: 'What a joke - free in three years'. 'Soft on terror' the Melbourne *Herald Sun* screamed, equally infuriated, and *The Australian* criticised Justice Healy for failing 'to get with the [anti-terrorism] program'. Unsurprisingly, the media's outrage was mirrored by the reaction of the public at large. In an instant internet poll conducted on TV Channel Nine's website (http://ninemsn.com.au), for instance, over two thirds of respondents thought the Roche sentence 'too lenient'.

Politicians and police officials quickly joined in the chorus of critics and put forward their own personal suggestions on how the courts—purposely independent of government—should deal with the 'terrorists'. According to federal Liberal MP Peter Dutton, for instance, the court should have 'put in place proper deterrents for terrorists'.[28] Similarly, the then New South Wales Shadow Minister for Police, Peter Debnam, insisted that the judges needed to 'get in step with community expectations and also what Parliament expects'.[29] Some of these community expectations were more drastic than others. For John Harrison, who lost his daughter in the Bali bombings, even the 25-year maximum sentence initially requested by the Crown would have been too light. Although Roche was not charged for any involvement in the Bali atrocities, Harrison's demand was blunt and simple: 'Hang the bastard!'[30]

---

28 'DPP may appeal Roche sentence: Ruddock,' *Sydney Morning Herald*, 2 June 2004.

29 'Ruddock flags national no-bail laws for terror suspects,' *ABC News (Online)*, 3 June 2004, http://www.abc.net.au/news/newsitems/s1122028.htm.

30 Christopher Michaelsen, 'A disturbing descent into paranoia,' *Canberra*

The public outrage over the court's sentence provided another convenient opportunity for the government to divert attention from the fact that—analogous to the Brigitte affair—the Roche incident had revealed serious administrative failures on the part of ASIO. ASIO's raids on Roche's Perth home in October 2002 and the charges subsequently laid by the police had followed an independent investigation by a newspaper journalist. What is more, Roche had attempted to contact the intelligence agency repeatedly over several months in 2000. ASIO, however, did not return the calls and the Perth resident apparently did not spark any further interest from the government authorities until late 2002.

Some commentators subsequently suggested that Roche's information on al-Qaeda and JI 'might have' prevented the Bali bombings from occurring.[31] Clive Williams, a former senior Australian intelligence official, pointed out, for example, that

[i]t would have perhaps been possible for us to have gained a much better understanding about what JI was all about, that it had operational plans, it did intend to conduct activities, because it then went on and perpetrated the December 2000 bombings [in Indonesia and the Philippines] and, of course, ultimately was responsible for the Bali operations. So had we known a bit more about JI and its linkages to al-Qaeda and what it was planning to do, maybe we could have put a bit more pressure on the Indonesians to put more effort into monitoring JI, which in turn might have made it more difficult for JI to actually conduct its operations'.[32]

Whether and to what extent Roche's information on JI and al-Qaeda would have in fact enabled ASIO and the Indonesian authorities to prevent the Bali attack, remains subject to speculation, of course. It is patently obvious, however, that any ASIO blunders remotely connected to the bombings that killed eighty-eight Australians about eighteen months earlier carried significant potential for an electoral

---

*Times*, 10 June 2004.

31  ABC Radio, Transcript, PM Program, *Does Roche's profile fit that of a terrorist?* 28 May 2004, http://www.abc.net.au/pm/content/2004/s1118493. htm.

32  Ibid.

backlash. At the time of the Roche trial, the Australian federal elections were a mere three months away and the government had already been under political pressure for a number of reasons. First, the opposition was calling for an inquiry by a royal commission into the intelligence agencies' apparent failures in the lead-up to the Iraq war of 2003. Second, tough questions were being asked about the government's knowledge of, and the Australian military's involvement in the Abu Graib prison scandal. Finally, despite the government's domestic counterterrorism and emergency response efforts, a review conducted by Australian emergency response personnel and several US officials involved in the September 11 recovery operations found that Australia still lacked a 9/11 rescue capability.[33] The review's publication coincided with the opening day of the Roche trial.

The government thus decided to go on the offensive and its response was in many ways similar to the one in the Brigitte affair. Declaring that any inquiry into potential ASIO failures would be 'indulgent' and 'disruptive', the attorney-general announced that he had instructed the Commonwealth (federal) director of public prosecutions (DPP) to consider appealing against the Roche sentence for being 'too lenient'.[34] The next day, however, Ruddock admitted under questioning in Parliament that the federal DPP had sent a letter to Justice Healy at the District Court of western Australia acknowledging Roche had co-operated with the authorities and therefore deserved a more lenient sentence than the 25-year maximum the Crown would ask for in open court.[35] (Incidentally, the DPP's appeal was crushed by the western Australian Court of Criminal Appeal and Roche's sentence upheld on 14 January 2005).[36]

---

33 'Australia lacks 9/11 rescue capability,' *Australian Associate Press*, 18 May 2004.

34 Cynthia Banham, 'Courts too "lenient" on terrorists,' *Sydney Morning Herald*, 3 June 2004.

35 ABC Radio, Transcript AM Program, *DPP appeals against the sentence of Jack Roche*, 28 May 2004, http://www.abc.net.au/am/content/2004/s1130575. htm.

36 'Jack Roche's nine-year sentence upheld,' *Sydney Morning Herald*, 14 June

In addition, the attorney-general also announced further changes to the federal anti-terrorism laws. In particular, he indicated that the government was looking at immediately introducing new legislation that would set a non-parole period for persons convicted of 'terrorist' offences. And indeed, on 30 June 2004, Parliament passed the Anti-terrorism Act 2004. The act provided for minimum non-parole periods for persons convicted of, and sentenced for, committing terrorism offences and certain other offences 'that are relevant to terrorist activity'.

The Anti-terrorism Act 2004 also amended the Proceeds of Crime Act 2002. Under the new arrangements the Commonwealth is entitled to seek a restraining order 'if there are reasonable grounds to suspect (sic) that a person has committed an indictable offence or a foreign indictable offence, and that the person has derived literary proceeds in relation to the offence.'[37] In effect, this provision enables the government to prevent persons from making money by selling books or memoirs about training and contact with banned organisations. As the amendment operates retrospectively, it potentially applies not only to the Roche case but also to the two Australian Guantanamo Bay detainees, David Hicks and Mamdouh Habib.[38]

The Jack Roche case is another remarkable example of the Howard government's ability to instrumentalise public sentiment in order to divert attention from serious administrative inadequacies in handling public line calls on the part of ASIO. It is self-evident that these inadequacies carried considerable potential for embarrassment for the government, with possible adverse effects on the outcome of the federal elections three months later. Particularly in light

---

2005.

37  Proceeds of Crime Act 2002, section 20(1)(d).

38  Indeed, when Mamdouh Habib returned to Australia from Guantanamo Bay in late January 2005 (without conviction or charge), attorney-General Ruddock initially indicated that he was looking into trying to prevent Habib from selling his story to Australian television. However, no application for a restraining order was made. Christopher Michaelsen, 'Why everybody should hear Habib's story,' *Canberra Times*, 3 February 2005.

of the fact that the Coalition had heavily invested in its election campaign on 'national security' which included the establishment of a 'national security hotline', guidance on 'how to spot a terrorist' and freely dispatched (to every household) fridge magnets advising Australians to be 'alert but not alarmed'.[39] The government thus chose an aggressive response to the Roche case that appears to have been primarily motivated by a desire to maintain an image of being 'tough on terrorism'. In effect, however, the measures introduced constituted a disturbing interference in the administration of justice and the courts' discretion to set parole. What is more, they unduly encroached upon the freedom of speech in an apparent attempt to silence 'alleged terrorists' from telling their part of the story. Again it is difficult to see how such legislative measures may contribute to decreasing the risk of terrorist attacks.

## The Bilal Khazal bail hearing

Born in Northern Lebanon in 1970, Bilal Khazal came to Australia as a three-year-old child. After living in Australia for several years, he moved back to Lebanon to spend time with his relatives. In 1989, Khazal returned to Australia settling in the outskirts of Lakemba, in Sydney's south-west, with his wife and two children. He found employment at Sydney airport and worked as a Qantas baggage handler for twelve years. In 2000, health problems forced Khazal to quit his job and he was given compensation and a payout.[40] While undertaking occupational retraining he intensified his involvement with the Islamic Youth Movement in Lakemba, which, among other activities, raises funds for relief projects in Islamic countries. Khazal edited the movement's magazine, Nida'ul Islam or Call of Islam, and also oversaw the administration of its website. Through this outlet he seems to have attracted attention, both from sympathisers and ASIO.

---

39 Kerrie-Anne Walsh, 'Be calm, but here's your "terrorist kit," *Sydney Morning Herald*, 2 February 2003.

40 'The Baggage of Bilal Khazal,' *Sydney Morning Herald*, 4 June 2004.

However, Khazal appears to have been known to ASIO for his extremist and Islamic fundamentalist views for more than ten years. According to ASIO documents reportedly sighted by ABC Radio correspondent Michael Vincent, Khazal came to the agency's attention after being stabbed in an apparent faction fight in Lakemba's Islamic community in 1994. Over the last decade, ASIO apparently interviewed Khazal at least a dozen times.[41] At first he was reported to be quite forthcoming, telling intelligence officers they could contact him any time.[42] Following 9/11, however, the relationship between ASIO and Khazal worsened. Khazal described Osama bin Laden as a 'good man' and allegedly told ASIO agents that 'civilians should not have been targeted but targeting US military would be all right'.[43] ASIO then intensified his surveillance and informed Khazal that 'he and people like him were now being monitored very closely'.[44]

In February 2002, Khazal booked a flight to Saudi Arabia in order to participate in the pilgrimage to Mecca. Australian authorities, however, prevented him from leaving the country and his passport was cancelled.[45] Four months later, in June 2002, the CIA issued a report claiming that Khazal was 'reportedly planning an explosives attack against some US embassies', including one in Venezuela, as well as against US interests in the Philippines.[46] Khazal, however, proclaimed his innocence and pointed out that the authorities had

---

41 ABC Radio, Transcript, PM Program, *ASIO had long-standing relationship with terror suspect*, 2 June 2004, http://www.abc.net.au/pm/content/2004/s1121635.htm.

42 At one stage Khazal agreed to ASIO taking his computer away. But when it came back from ASIO, the screen didn't work. As an apparent act of goodwill, ASIO decided to buy him a new one. 'The baggage of Bilal Khazal,' *Sydney Morning Herald*, 4 June 2004.

43 Ellen Connolly, Les Kennedy and Cynthia Banham, 'Fury at terror suspect's bail', *Sydney Morning Herald*, 3 June 2004.

44 'The baggage of Bilal Khazal,' *Sydney Morning Herald*, 4 June 2004.

45 ABC Radio, *ASIO had long-standing relationship with terror suspect*, 2 June 2004.

46 David Adams, 'CIA report unmasks Australian "terror boss",' *The Age* (Melbourne), 10 June 2004.

obviously targeted the wrong person because his middle name was wrongly given as 'Abdallah'.[47] No charges were laid against him in response to the allegations raised in the leaked CIA document.

Nonetheless, Khazal appears to have had an ability to attract trouble. In late 2003, he and his brother, Maher, were sentenced in absentia by a Lebanese military tribunal for donating money (A$ 1,800) to an Islamic group which orchestrated a string of bomb attacks in Lebanon. The Lebanon trial heard allegations that Khazal became friends with the leader of Khaliyat Trablus (The Cell of Tripoli), Mohammed Kaaka, in the late 1990s. Both Maher and Bilal Khazal have vigorously protested their innocence. Their lawyer in the matter, Adam Houda, pointed to statements from Mohammed Kaaka—corroborated by his mother—that the money had been for Lebanese charities.[48] Although Australia introduced laws allowing his extradition to Lebanon, no extradition request has been made to this date.

Then, on 2 June 2004, Khazal was arrested and charged with 'collecting or making documents likely to facilitate terrorist acts', an offence that carries a maximum of 15 years imprisonment. The arrest apparently stemmed from information obtained by ASIO staff while inspecting his computer's hard-drive under a search warrant on 6 May 2004. This information allegedly linked Khazal to a document posted on the internet from 26 September 2003 to 10 May 2004. The document, entitled *Provision in the Rules of Jihad-Short: Wise Rules and Organisational Structures that Concern every Fighter and Mujahid Fighting against the Infidels*, was written in Arabic and espoused radical views on severe violent action against so-called 'infidels'. Nonetheless, the electronic pamphlet was very general. It did not urge any particular action to be taken by any particular person at any particular time or at any particular place. And while some of its sections appear to have been written by Khazal personally, many

---

47  Graeme Webber, 'Ex-Qantas man denies terror link,' *Herald Sun* (Melbourne), 4 June 2004.

48  'The Baggage of Bilal Khazal,' *Sydney Morning Herald*, 4 June 2004.

paragraphs were 'cut and pasted' from other publicly available internet documents. When police brought the posting to Khazal's attention in late May 2004, he removed it from the internet immediately.

Khazal appeared before Local Court Central in Sydney on the afternoon of 2 June 2004 and applied for bail. While the Crown argued that it was 'inappropriate' to grant bail given the 'seriousness of the offence' and his 'overseas links', Khazal's counsel, Chris Murphy, maintained that the arrest was conveniently timed for political purposes, coinciding with the Prime Minister's departure to the US to see 'Mr Bush pat him on the head'.[49] Accusing the Government of conducting a 'one terrorist-a-week arrest program' in the lead-up to the federal election (of October 2004), Murphy claimed the case was all about 'bash a Muslim, buy a vote'.[50] Given that Khazal's passport had been withdrawn in 2002, the defence counsel also argued that his client did not pose any flight risk. Magistrate Les Brennan agreed with this latter view and held that while the Crown's case appeared strong, it had failed to convince him to overturn the (then) existing presumption in favour of bail. Consequently, the judge set bail at A\$ 10,000 and imposed the additional condition that Khazal report to a nearby police station daily. The Crown did not oppose.

Similarly to the response to the Roche judgment the day before, the magistrate's decision was followed by outrage on both sides of politics. In New South Wales (NSW), Labor premier Bob Carr called on the Commonwealth DPP to lodge an appeal against the bail decision immediately as the latter clearly was 'an example of a court failing to acknowledge that [it is] dealing with a new type of threat and a new type of offence'.[51] Carr's fury was matched by similar comments from other prominent NSW politicians and officials. For Police

---

49  Ellen Connolly, Les Kennedy and Cynthia Banham, 'Fury at terror suspect's bail,' *Sydney Morning Herald*, 3 June 2004.

50  ABC, Transcript TV Program, *7.30 Report—Khazal bail sparks law debate*, 3 June 2004, http://www.abc.net.au/7.30/content/2004/s1124145.htm.

51  'Khazal's Bail Must Be Appealed,' *Sydney Morning Herald*, 3 June 2004.

Minister John Watkins the bail decision was simply 'inexplicable'.[52] Police Commissioner Ken Moroney too was 'honestly astounded' and criticised the magistrate's ruling as 'inadequate on this occasion'.[53] And shadow Police Minister Peter Debnam claimed that he was totally 'dumbfounded' by the decision. He subsequently called on the 'judges and magistrates' to 'get real'.[54]

The next day, the NSW Parliament amended the (NSW) Bail Act 1978, (which applies to Commonwealth and state offences, both of which are prosecuted before state courts), bringing all federal 'terrorism-related offences' into the category of offences for which there is a presumption *against* bail.[55] The new legislation was also specifically allowed to operate retrospectively and thus applied to offences committed or bail decisions made before the commencement of the new Act. As a consequence, the new arrangements also applied retrospectively to the Khazal bail decision of 2 June.

Unsurprisingly the amendments were heavily criticised by several leading members of the legal profession, not only because they were rushed through Parliament without adequate deliberation, but also because they further diluted one of the fundamental principles of criminal justice, the presumption of innocence.[56] Dismissing these

---

52 'Minister critical of bail for terror suspect,' *ABC News (Online)*, 3 June 2004, http://www.abc.net.au/news/newsitems/s1121797.htm.

53 ABC Radio, Transcript PM Program, *DPP to appeal Khazal bail*, 3 June 2004, http://www.abc.net.au/pm/content/2004/s1124078.htm.

54 Ruddock flags national no-bail laws for terror suspects,' *ABC News (Online)*, 3 June 2004.

55 The presumption against bail places the burden on the applicant (rather than the Crown) to show that bail should not be refused alongside other serious offences involving drugs, weapons and violence.

56 The president of the Australian Bar Association, Ian Harrison, stated: 'I take exception to the furore at a political level. It itself strikes at the administration of justice. I'm not in favour of political reactions to the judicial process; the judicial process is well founded historically. It is supported by appropriate legislation and the application of those laws is a matter for the courts.' ABC, Transcript TV Program, *7.30 Report—Khazal bail sparks law debate*, 3 June 2004, http://www.abc.net.au/7.30/content/2004/s1124145.htm. Harrison's remarks were mirrored by those of Pauline Wright, chairperson of the

criticisms as baseless, NSW attorney-general Bob Debus, on the other hand, claimed that it was justified 'bringing the section dealing with bail forward today'. Moreover, it was 'necessary to give the public reassurance in the light of events in the last 24 hours'.[57]

Equipped with the new bail legislation, the Commonwealth DPP then launched an appeal against the magistrate's bail decision and the matter was referred to the NSW Supreme Court. Much to the federal and state government's disappointment, however, Supreme Court Justice Greg James formally dismissed the appeal on 24 June. In continuing the bail, Justice Greg James imposed stricter reporting and monitoring conditions on Khazal and increased the surety on his bail. Nonetheless, he found that the Lakemba resident 'posed no threat to the community' and that his actions in relation to the compilation of the internet pamphlet did not constitute an offence 'of the greatest seriousness'.[58]

A few hours after the Commonwealth had lost its appeal, Federal attorney-general Philip Ruddock subsequently blamed the NSW government for failing to enact adequate bail laws. 'If New South Wales had adopted the same standard that we are proposing', the attorney-general speculated, 'the case may have been dealt with differently'.[59] The federal government's standard Ruddock was referring to was then enacted six days later as part of the Anti-terrorism Act 2004. It provided that a bail authority must not grant bail to persons charged with, or convicted of terrorism-related offences unless it is 'satisfied that

NSW Law Society's Criminal Law Committee and John North, president of the Law Council of Australia, ABC Radio, Transcript AM Program, *Ruddock criticises NSW bail laws*, 25 June 2004. http://www.abc.net.au/am/content/2004/s1140214.htm.

57  Brendan Nicholson, 'Moves to alter law after suspect wins bail,' *The Age* (Melbourne), 4 June 2004.

58  *R v Khazal* [2004] NSWSC 548; see also 'Khazal free on strict bail conditions,' *Sydney Morning Herald*, 25 June 2004.

59  ABC Radio, Transcript AM Program, *Ruddock criticises NSW bail laws*, 25 June 2004.

exceptional circumstances exist to justify bail'.[60] Although the wording of this provision is undoubtedly stronger than the 'presumption against bail' terminology of the NSW legislation, it is likely that both arrangements have the same effect in practice.

The political and legislative response to the Khazal bail decision constitutes an illustrative example for a tendency on the part of the executive to play politics with issues related to 'terrorism' and 'national security'. Both the federal government in Canberra and the state government in NSW sought to capitalise politically on an incident, which had few, if any, important implications for the security of the nation, but potentially adverse effects on the way the major political actors were perceived by the electorate in relation to the politics of national security. Some commentators went so far as to claim that the Khazal arrest itself was motivated purely by political reasons, particularly given that the Lakemba resident had been on ASIO's watch-list for over ten years, and also in light of the fact that the electronic pamphlet that provided the basis for his charge had been removed from the internet four weeks earlier. While the timing of Khazal's arrest is dubious indeed, the case is also remarkable for the legislative action that followed at both the state and federal levels. The NSW government's unabashed admission of its intentions in amending the bail laws, for instance, is disturbing in particular. Similar to the Howard government's response to the Roche sentence, the immediate amendment of the NSW bail legislation showed blatant disrespect for the judicial system, its impartiality and fairness, and undermined the principles of due process in the criminal justice system. Whether and to what extent the amendments are of any value for effective counterterrorism policy, however, remains problematic at best.

## Partisan political benefit vs legal principle

The Howard government's recent domestic responses to the threat of terrorism, of which the Brigitte, Roche and Khazal cases

---

60 Crimes act 1914, (new) section 15AA(1).

are illustrative examples, are distinctive for their overt political approach in shifting responsibility for, and in seeking remedy of, a national security administrative and policy failure through the expansion of the legislative counterterrorism framework. At the same time, these responses have steadily eroded fundamental rule of law principles such as accountability and scrutiny of authority, due process, separation of powers, and coherent justification for the introduction of intrusive measures. This erosion is reflected in the attitudes of the legislative proponents as well as apparent in the legislative amendments themselves. At no point did the government demonstrate adequately that the changes in law were necessary, let alone effective in the fight against Islamic extremism. Indeed, it appears that many of the new measures were motivated by the government's aspirations for partisan political benefit rather than by legal principle. And one wonders why none of the legislative amendments that followed the Brigitte, Roche and Khazal cases had been included in the original anti-terrorism legislation if they were in fact indispensable in order to protect the public.

What is perhaps most worrisome, however, is the fact that the legislative and political responses to the Brigitte, Roche and Khazal cases followed a trend to regard every terrorism-related offence as a so-called '*crimen exceptum*', an exceptional crime that needed to be treated differently from all other offences. While the notion of '*crimen exceptum*' is unknown to any modern western legal system, it featured prominently in sixteenth and seventeenth century Europe to prosecute the crime of witchcraft. As 'exceptional offenders', people accused of witchcraft were not subjected to regular legal procedures. The rules of evidence, for instance, were set aside and torture was justified or indeed deemed desirable. A comparable process existed in medieval England and became known as outlawry. Persons designated as outlaws were placed outside the regular protection of the law with their lands and goods forfeited to the Crown. Although outlaws were personally liable upon all causes of action, they did not enjoy any civil rights and could not sue in a court of law. In contemporary Australia, persons suspected of, or charged with, terrorism-related offences have not yet lost all their regular judicial rights and guarantees. However, in the light of recent legislative amendments and corresponding political rhetoric it seems that alleged 'terrorists' have become the witches and outlaws of today. This is a deeply troublesome development which ultimately poses a greater threat to 'our way of life' than international terrorism itself.[†]

[†] I would like to thank Dr Joe Siracusa for his most generous and helpful comments on earlier drafts of this chapter. Thanks are also due to Dr Rob Ayson.

## 12

# TALKING TERROR: HYPE, FACTS AND THE MEDIA

### *Mark Huband*

'Why do they hate us?' In the wake of the terrorist attacks on New York and Washington on 11 September 2001, this was a question that many Americans asked themselves, each other and anybody who was prepared to listen. More than five years later, the answer may be as simple as: 'Because we give them lots of reasons to do so.' Equally, it could be: 'Because they hate each other and possibly even themselves. But they are looking for somebody else to blame for their woes.'

Whatever the answer, since that day when the United States found itself forced to face the consequences of its foreign policy choices, the difficulty its people, its thinkers and its policymakers have had in understanding what is confronting them has grown rather than diminished. Far from being contained or consigned to the margins as a 'radical minority' or an 'extremist fringe' or a group that 'hates our success and prosperity', the suicide bombers, extremist preachers and radicalised groups that together amount to the 'global jihad', are presenting a challenge that is likely to prove as profound and enduring as any in history.

'Why do they hate us?' was once the plaintive cry of a people that reckoned the trauma would eventually pass like the strong winds that batter the US during the hurricane season. National strategies would and could be put in place to deal with the consequences. Life would return to normal. The survival of the nation was—ultimately—not at stake.

But to convince themselves that there was no mortal threat to a way of life whose value ultimately lies in the opportunity to take it for granted, Americans cocooned themselves in a web of lies, deceits and misinformation about themselves and their place in the world.

Meanwhile, on the other side of the Atlantic Ocean, the opposite appeared to be true. In Britain the assumption since 9/11 had been that one day the counter-terrorism effort would fail and that the bombers would slip through the net and commit their crimes. The British knew they would be attacked, and prepared themselves. That it took until 7 July 2005 for the attackers to achieve their aims—after numerous plots aimed at Britain had been foiled by the police and security service—provided ample opportunity for the British to examine their national psyche. They talked of their *sang-froid*, their stoicism, and referred to the qualities that had seen them through Irish Republican Army terrorism during the 1970s and 1980s. Familiarity with IRA terrorism—smaller in scale but as disturbing when experienced over time—was regularly portrayed as proof the 'Brits' possessed the mettle that Americans were grappling to find after 9/11.

But not only were the British rumoured to be possessed of sterner stuff than their American allies; they also seemed to have the courage to admit that whatever measures were taken to thwart a plot, it was bound to happen sooner or later. They were not invincible, and were not tempted to pretend they were. The Prime Minister said so, the Mayor of London said so, and the Commissioner of the Metropolitan Police said so. Britons, it seemed, knew they were hated, and apparently had no reason to ask why it was so. Empowered by their realism, the British embarked on the process of waiting—a process that ended with the 7 July bombings in London.

## Telling it like it is?

The primary role of most media in both countries during the period between the 9/11 attacks and those in London almost four years later has been to provide definitions: what it is to be American or British; what it is to be democratic; what it is to be Muslim; what it is to be a suicide bomber; what it is to be 'hate-filled'. The media has facilitated the process of defining what the people involved in this drama are: some people are terrorists; some people are intelligence officers; some people are apologists while others are either moderates or extremists; some people are senior al-Qaeda operatives, while other people are footsoldiers; some people are victims; other people are western allies, while some are 'not with us, so they are against us'.

For the media, as for the political establishment with which its agenda is so closely entwined, everybody has had to become something. Without allotted roles, the 'war on terror' would have no shape. A shape was needed in order for bulletins and news reports to have a beginning, a middle and an end, for headline writers to grab the readers' attention for yet more of the same story, and for nations to feel that they were winning, that the 'war' was moving, and that all this would one day come to an end so that we could all get back to living normal lives.

Just as the people of America wrapped themselves in the Stars and Stripes, so the British sought to prove their *sang-froid* was not a hackneyed cliché but a national characteristic with real substance. But to really believe this of themselves they required the media. Unless the media flew the flag, the people would not know how to respond to the threat to the nation. Thus, the media had the role of defining the nation of which the people under threat needed to feel a part. The media would define who was a part of the nation and who was not. Those who were a part were the heroes; those who were not could be rightly reviled. In short, the media would become the window through which the people would see the correct version of themselves and their enemy.

To meet this formidable challenge required that the media was itself extremely well-informed. Not only would it have to identify accurately the source and purpose of the terrorist threat, but also accurately describe the nations that were being threatened. Why do they hate us? It was a question the media had to be able to answer accurately and without hesitation, because to explain why a bomb had been detonated or a person shot or a plot revealed, the media had to be able to provide context, historical perspective and genuine, well-judged, well-informed and sober explanation.

In these endeavours most media have completely failed. In fact, most have never sought to provide such a service to the public. This is either because having realised they were not up to the task they chose to deny it was ever their role, or because they could not conceal the superficiality of their self-appointed *expertise* on the issues that have arisen without making it obvious that they simply did not know what they were talking about. In place of information they opted to become the voices of popular indignation.

## *The 'oxygen of publicity'*

Among the more experienced journalists there has been a trend towards trying to avoid being the 'media' at all. Peter Preston, former editor of the *Guardian*, made this clear in 2004 when he wrote:

There is no limit to the targets that may be chosen by terrorists who expect to die but know that they will make a splash in the process. There is no limit to the soft touches that cannot be anticipated or defended. Frontiers are meaningless, because pictures have no frontier. Fear needs no visa. Two bleak things follow. One is that—whether or not it exists on any organised level—we shall gradually come to identify a force called international terrorism, a force defined not by the coordination of its strikes or creeds but by the orchestration of its inhuman propaganda. I manipulate, therefore I exist. The other thing is self-knowledge for media-makers and media-watchers. If the malignant message is itself a device, a weapon of mass hysteria, how do we defuse it? By a suppression that undermines free society, that gives terror its victory? Or by the realisation that we are not puppets, that we must see and explain for ourselves. That we have a duty of understanding.[1]

Preston is admitting a confusion that exists within the media, by suggesting ultimately that the terrorists only really do what they do because they know the media will report what they do. He further emphasises the confusion he clearly feels as a media professional by pointing out that the media have a 'duty of understanding' which necessitates that they do report what has taken place and thus risk becoming tools in the terrorists' propaganda war.

But would the terrorist threat from al-Qaeda and the adherents to its ideology die if the media started to ignore it? Of course it would not. For Preston to imply that the *jihadist-salafist* threat and the campaign that is currently underway under its banner could somehow be halted if western media—for it is they to whom he is addressing his comments—ignored them, betrays a major failure in the 'duty of understanding'.

There is no doubt that al-Qaeda and its affiliates are using the media to get their messages across. But the medium is not the message. The message is something far more profound. This is because it is a message that is ultimately not directed at the West but at Muslims in the heartland of Islam. A decision by western journalists to self-censor or not would make little difference in the big scheme of the jihadists' campaign because the real target of that campaign remains the Muslim world itself.

The determination of the Bush administration to portray al-Qaeda's campaign as *primarily* rather than *secondarily* a campaign against the United States has been a key test of the media's ability to distinguish propaganda from fact, fiction from political clap-trap, truth from lies. The 'malignant message' referred to by Preston is one that has powerful repercussions in the West because the West has the most dynamic and advanced media: most global television channels are controlled by western interests and are omnipresent. In order to

---

1    Peter Preston, 'Writing the script for terror: Media makers must defuse these weapons of mass hysteria,' *The Guardian* (London), 6 September 2004.

engage viewers and readers, western media needs to portray stories as essentially *relevant* to the West. Even though there is no doubt the West is under attack, this *relevance* is strengthened by portraying attacks on western targets and in western cities as being the *primary* ambitions of the terrorists and as attempts to destroy western civilisation and all it stands for. In fact this has not been the terrorists' aim, though the emergence of 'homegrown' terrorists in Western Europe may eventually make it so.

In the wake of the London bombings of 7 July Ayman al-Zawahiri, the al-Qaeda ideologue, made clear—and not for the first time—that al-Qaeda's focus was not the West but the West's role in the regions of the world the jihadists define as the Muslim heartland. In a statement broadcast by al-Jazeera television, al-Zawahiri said:

Nations of the crusader alliance, we proposed that you at least stop your aggression against the Muslims. The lion of Islam, mujahid Sheikh Osama bin Laden, may God preserve him, offered you a truce until you leave the lands of Islam. Has Sheikh Osama bin Laden not informed you that you will not dream of security until we live it in reality in Palestine and before all infidel armies leave the land of [the Prophet] Muhammad, may peace be upon him? You, however, shed rivers of blood in our land so we exploded volcanoes of anger in your land. Our message to you is crystal clear: Your salvation will only come in your withdrawal from our land, in stopping the robbing of our oil and resources, and in stopping your support for the corrupt and corrupting leaders.[2]

Being prepared to believe such statements is essential if those in the West who are engaged in defining and countering the terrorist threat are to be successful. But their task has been greatly complicated by the determination of the Bush administration to exploit the threat and use it as a mechanism for expanding western influence. The invasion of Iraq under the pretext that the war was a response to 9/11 and a necessary way to fight al-Qaeda, amounted to the most flagrant example of playing politics with terrorism.

---

2   Ayman al-Zawahiri. Statement issued on al-Jazeera TV, Doha, in Arabic 12:02 GMT, 4 August 2005. Source: BBC Monitoring.

## Know your enemy

Far from being a plot to overthrow western civilisation, the September 11, 2001 attacks were a result of the anger that had accumulated among generations of Arabs over several decades. Those who carried out the attacks saw them as a *reaction* rather than an *action*. It was on this basis that the attacks are justified by the jihadists as being part of a jihad, as the concept is justified in the Koran as a *defensive* act and not as an act of aggression. For Americans, whose ignorance of the world around them has become legendary, the 9/11 attacks came out of the blue; to much of the rest of the world the attacks were seen as the appalling price a country can pay for numerous cack-handed policies and—specifically—successive US administrations' unquestioning support for Israel's policies towards the Palestinians. But as Stefan Halper and Jonathan Clarke wrote in regard to the climate that was created in the aftermath of 9/11 and which permitted the Bush administration's policy responses:

The administration seemed intent, from the early stages of the war [in Afghanistan], to sell a policy that relied as much on the media as on the official statements of government officials. In waging a war of words to provide the basis for a war of weapons, the media was of paramount significance, and the extent to which the media outlets underpinned the successful formulation of neo-conservative foreign policy was of great importance. They amplified the administration's discursive rationale, broadly advancing the public neo-conservative policy agenda. Beyond the presentation of policy objectives, this process had the effect of diminishing and marginalising dissenting voices arising from other sections of the policy community. It created in effect an echo chamber, in which the administration's rationale was repeated and sustained in primary and secondary circumstances, such that opinion was formed and then reinforced through endless repetition of neo-conservative themes…Thus, by the time that speechwriters and neo-conservative officials within the administration began to construct the notional discourse, half the task had already been completed by the overwhelming and sensational coverage from much of the American media.[3]

---

3   Stefan Halper and Jonathan Clarke, *America Alone: the Neo-Conservatives and the Global Order* (Cambridge, 2004), pp. 194–5.

It is without doubt that the failure of the US media to break free of political loyalties, proprietorial influence and personal prejudice, together contributed to the intensity of the shock Americans felt when their country came under attack on September 11, 2001. Americans did not know what had hit them because they had been kept in the dark for so long about how their country's activities abroad were being regarded by those on the receiving end. The failure of the media *prior* to 9/11 to inform Americans generally of the sentiments that were later to be manifested in the terrorist attacks was followed by a failure *after* the attacks to encourage a response that was designed to address the issues that had encouraged the terrorist onslaught. The media generally voiced the view that because America had been bloodied, the perpetrators—wherever they may be found—should be bloodied in response, as a matter of pride and national interest. By doing so, the US media greatly contributed to the sense of confusion that continues to prevail among Americans.

A survey[4] by the Program on International Policy Attitudes (PIPA) issued on 21 October 2004, revealed the vast gulf between illusion and reality that prevailed in public attitudes in the run up to the presidential election and Bush's second term. On key issues, a reality fostered by media coverage determined the direction in which individual respondents were planning to vote in the election: among Bush supporters a large majority believed that Saddam Hussein's regime in Iraq had possessed weapons of mass destruction, despite a succession of official reports conclusively revealing it had not; among supporters of the Democratic contender John Kerry, the opposite view was held. Both Bush and Kerry supporters told the PIPA that Saddam Hussein had provided 'substantial support to al-Qaeda', even though this assertion has been widely acknowledged as wrong. According to the poll, Bush supporters were under the impression that global opinion supported Bush's re-election, when numerous polls worldwide revealed the opposite. Most startling perhaps, was PIPA's conclusion that 'majorities of Bush supporters misperceive

---

4   http://www.pipa.org/OnlineReports/Pres_Election_04/Report10_21_04.pdf.

his positions on a range of foreign policy issues. In particular, they assume he supports multilateral approaches.'

The misunderstanding of al-Qaeda's central aim as clarified for more than a decade by Ayman al-Zawahiri and Osama bin Laden, coupled with the quiescence or worse of the media and a tendency to ally one's view of the truth with one's political allegiance, together make it hardly surprising that Americans remain deeply confused about why the threats they face are multiplying rather than diminishing. A comparison with the UK is informative.

## Please forget I said that

In the wake of the 7 July bombings in London, the confusion of the British media in its attempts to explain what lay behind what had taken place, had multiple roots. The main political battleground has clearly focused on the question of whether Britain's role in Iraq explains its vulnerability to terrorism. Britain's historically close ties with the US, its links to Arab regimes that have been targeted by al-Qaeda, its oil interests in the Middle East, its colonial past: all these issues are contributory factors. But other issues have made for a more complex picture. Britons of most political hues cannot generally be said to have particularly high regard for President George W. Bush. In 2003 a million people of many political and other persuasions marched through the streets of London to protest against the impending invasion of Iraq. The nationalism of the 'neo-cons' who surround President Bush has isolated Britons from the US as much as it has isolated Americans from Germans or French. In addition, Britons do not particularly cherish playing second fiddle: the image of the UK as an American sycophant is one that makes Britons feel uncomfortable.

The July 2005 bombings provided an opportunity for the UK media to detach the threat to Britain from the experience of the US. Londoners showed their mettle; the British public, the emergency services, the government: all of them reacted in a cool and measured way, which contrasted sharply with the hysteria which prevailed throughout American society in the wake of 9/11. For the UK media the 7 July bombings—and the foiled attacks of 21 July—were moments to be savoured. The watershed had finally arrived, and Britain could once again assert its national character.

But the media's ability to rise to the occasion first necessitated that the public rapidly forget much if not all of what they had read in newspapers during the months that preceded those terrifying moments in London. As recently as 17 June 2005 the *Financial Times* had made great and uncritical play of a statement by the opposition Conservative Party's legal affairs spokesman in a story headlined: 'Threat of terrorism has been overstated, says MP'. The story then quoted the MP, Dominic Grieve, as saying that the introduction of control orders intended to place known radicals under intense surveillance 'appears to confirm our suspicion that the anti-terror bill before the general election was a cynical election ploy rather than a genuine attempt to protect British people.'[5] Similar politicisation of the issues was undertaken by other media seeking to force the terrorism threat through the political prism.

In a detailed analysis of the uses and abuses of the issue—as a stick to beat foreigners, as well as a ploy to curtail civil liberties—David Miller of Stirling University identified as long ago as 2003 how Britain's right wing media appeared intent on using the terrorist threat as a lever to strengthen its arguments in favour of tough laws to prevent foreigners being granted political asylum in Britain.[6] Miller wrote:

The ongoing spasms about asylum seekers and immigration flowed into the same ideological pool as the campaign on the war on terror. At the same time the government propaganda campaign aimed at winning public opinion to support the war in Iraq attempted to present Iraq as linked to al-Qaeda and Islamist 'terrorism'. In the event the government campaign

---

5   'Threat of terrorism overstated, says MP,' *Financial Times* (London) 17 June 2005.

6   '"They were all asylum seekers": The propaganda campaign to link Iraq to terrorism at the expense of refugees.' David Miller, 27 March, 2003. See: http://www.scoop.co.nz/stories/HL0303/S00262.htm.

failed to convince the public of the need for war, but the main effect of the campaign was to increase hostility towards asylum seekers.

But of perhaps greater concern than the extreme views of the anti-asylum tabloids has been the calm authoritativeness among the 'quality' newspapers that have sought as an alternative to project an image of well-informed 'expertise' in reporting and analysing the terrorist threat. On 7 November 2002, the *Sunday Times* published a now infamous story on its front page in which it stated that Algerian terrorists had been thwarted in their plans to carry out a 'gas attack' on the London underground.[7] The claims in the article were a concoction by the newspaper, comprising elements that had been brought together disingenuously: there had been concern among security officials about Algerian Islamists; the London underground was widely regarded as a potential target; some forms of gas—like the sarin used in a terrorist attack in Tokyo—were thought to exist within the al-Qaeda arsenal. But no security officials had brought these elements together: the newspaper's staff had done this for themselves. Even so, the truth behind the issues barely mattered: the article set the news agenda for the following couple of days and the *Sunday Times* never published a correction.

But if the media is not concocting stories of its own, it is accusing governments of doing so. On 13 March 2005, the *Observer* published a long analysis by its chief reporter. The theme of government exaggeration of the terrorist threat was given substantial space, though in the form of the views of its reporter himself rather than as a report of the views of an opinionated politician or informed security official. 'The threat to Britain from Islamic militancy is far less serious than the government is telling us' the strapline in the story informed readers. This particular assessment of the terrorist threat to the UK as seen through the eyes of a journalist is informative in several ways. The reporter wrote:

---

7   'MI5 foils poison-gas attack on the Tube.' *Sunday Times* (London), 17 November 2002.

As you read this, there are no 200 'Osama bin Laden-trained volunteers' stalking our streets, as is claimed by the government. Nor are there al-Qaeda networks 'spawning and festering' across the country. Nor are Islamic militants cooking up biological or chemical weapons. Nor indeed are there any 'terrorist organisations', as Charles Clarke, the Home Secretary, calls them, nor are there 'hundreds of terrorists', as the Prime Minister told Woman's Hour. Nor are there legions of young British Muslims, enraged by perceived injustices in the Islamic world and by the supposed iniquities of Western policy towards their co-religionists, preparing to mount violent attacks.[8]

Several important issues arise from these assertions. The key one is that the bombings of 7 July and the attempted bombings of 21 July 2005 disproved all the claims made in the article regarding terrorist organisation and motivation. A second issue regards the number of 'volunteers'. The article infers that the reporter himself knew how many such 'volunteers' there were in the UK at that time, which of course he did not and cannot know. In the months prior to the July bombings there were far more than 200 investigations underway in the UK relating to the terrorist threat. The bombings showed that there was meanwhile a clear process of 'spawning and festering' underway, and that without any doubt there were—and probably still are—'terrorist organisations'. The article then went on to say:

So what is the threat now? The Afghan training camps are gone, al-Qaeda is scattered and MI5 is pretty confident it has wrapped up anyone active in 2001. At a counter-terrorism conference at London's Royal United Services Institute last month, experts agreed that the term 'al-Qaeda' was defunct. [Charles] Clarke might like to take notice. After all, one of the speakers was Sir David Veness, Scotland Yard's former head of counter-terrorism. Instead, the threat comes from 'cleanskins', individuals with no training and no previous involvement in militancy. The police and the security services believe there are a 'dozen or so' such people in the UK who might be able to draw on a few core sympathisers.

Again, the lessons from the July plots must inform us. The 'scattering' of al-Qaeda did not imply a weakening of al-Qaeda. The

---

8 'Be afraid, perhaps. But very afraid? No: the threat to Britain from Islamic militancy is far less serious than the government is telling us, says Jason Burke', *The Observer* (London), 13 March 2005.

'wrapping up' of those who were previously active means nothing against the background of new recruitment and a global climate in which new radicalisation is so clearly evident and has been for several years. The bombings also proved that being a 'cleanskin' simply does not imply that a person has 'no training'. In addition, the figure of 'a dozen or so' is simply wrong.[9]

But the reason above all why the article is such a travesty of what reporting ought to be about is that it is an article that pretends to know what it cannot know. It then uses unproven assertions to attack the government for daring to think in a manner that does not correspond to the half-baked views of a reporter seeking to promote himself as a better-informed 'expert'. Bashing politicians for thinking the wrong thoughts is very easy. To retain credibility the reporter must prove with indisputable facts that these thoughts are wrong, that policies are ill-conceived, that counter-terrorism measures are draconian and inappropriate. Of course reporters rarely provide this proof. Nor do many feel the need to do so. And when London *was* suddenly crippled by a new reality, when a group *did* turn the worst fears into real-life carnage, the media rounded on those officials they had accused of exaggeration—and told them they had not done enough to protect the population.

## *The public's right to know... what exactly?*

The London bombings offered the British public an opportunity to see just how little the numerous *experts* within the media actually know about *the* major global issue currently facing the world. 'Al-Qaeda fanatics living in Ireland may have channelled critical dosh and data to the London bombers. Secret agents are now sifting mountains of intelligence at their Dublin HQ in search of any link'[10] the *News*

---

9   It is also worth noting that it was the reporter himself who was the sole 'expert' attending the conference at the Royal United Services Institute who referred to the term 'al-Qaeda' as being 'defunct', as I recall, having attended the conference myself.

10  'Agents search for Irish link to London blasts.' *News of the World* (London),

*of the World*—the UK's biggest-selling Sunday newspaper—stated confidently on 10 July. On the same day, the *Sunday Telegraph* told its readers: "'Foreign terrorist cell' was behind London bombings. Police believe 'tiny number' of fanatics entered Britain from mainland Europe on false passports."[11] It went on to tell its readers:

Police were last night searching for a foreign-based Islamic terrorist cell after it was disclosed that three of the four bombs that hit London last Thursday exploded 'almost simultaneously'. Ministers now believe that the bombings—which left at least 49 people dead in Britain's worst terrorist attack—were the work of a 'very, very small number' of individuals who arrived from mainland Europe or North Africa on false passports within the past six months.[12]

A month later, the media were still spewing forth their theories. The *Daily Mail* produced a new explanation on 5 August, telling its readers: The bombs used in the July 7 terror attacks in London were probably detonated by mobile phones, it emerged yesterday. Investigators believe alarm clocks on the handsets were used to trigger the blasts which killed 52 innocent people. The revelation increased speculation that the 7/7 atrocities were linked to the Madrid bombings last year which killed 191. The Spanish attacks, also on the city's public transport system, involved bombs detonated by mobile phones. Witnesses who saw the London bombers detonate the devices with wires must have been bemused by this and many other stories.

As we know, there has been no Irish angle to the 7 July bombings. Nor were police looking abroad for the key culprits, until it transpired that one had fled to Italy. Moreover, mobile phones were not used, and the suggestion of a link to the Madrid bombings—which would have had serious implications for the investigation—was wrong. Meanwhile, the hunt for an Egyptian chemist who left Leeds for

---

10 July 2005.

11 'Foreign Terrorist Cell was Behind London Bombings,' *Sunday Telegraph* (London), 10 July 2005.

12 Ibid.

Cairo just before the bombings, as well as the detention in Zambia of a man associated with al-Qaeda, gave many in the media the opportunity to pretend that the scenarios which had been invented for the purposes of telling a dramatic story—that it was foreign-based terrorists, and moreover that it was 'foreigners' rather than British people who were responsible for the carnage—were a gift to editors. The newspapers had no proof that those being tracked in Egypt and Zambia had anything to do with the deaths. But that did not matter, as long as they could be portrayed as the latest scene in the national drama. When both 'suspects' were declared to have had nothing to do with the attacks, the certainties about their guilt were simply dropped from the newspapers.

Just as it took the British media to invent all sorts of scenarios to keep their readers convinced that it was in *their* newspaper that the exclusive stories and privileged insights would be published, so it took some within the media to highlight the ill-informed nature of much of what was being printed. The internal mechanism of self-justification that exists within the media became clear, as the more cerebral commentators began to point out how spurious much of the reporting had been, either as fact or interpretation.

Matthew Parris, columnist with *The Times*, was early in his identification of the trend. In a critique published on 23 July 2005, he vilified the media in general and specific terms to a point where the reader could only be left wondering whether there was any real point in relying on journalists to ever report anything resembling the truth. Parris wrote:

At times of national emergency, the habit of the news media to drop a story or a lead in mid-air when it seems to be going nowhere unsettles the public. The media betray a sort of sheepish wish to 'move on' from an erroneous report, hoping that their audience will not notice. Rather than acknowledge this, they publish a new report, leaving us to compare it with what had previously been said—and draw our own conclusions. Or they start barking up a different tree, the inference being that the last tree may have been the wrong tree.[13]

---

13 'I Name the Four Powers Who Are Behind the Al-Qaeda Conspiracy,'

It is worth looking closely at Parris' commentary, though not because it contained any new details about the terrorist attacks. Its value lay in the fact that the kinds of criticisms he makes of the media are both strongly argued *and* almost completely ignored by the targets of his ire. The publication in a mainstream newspaper of a strong argument based on facts about media errors should be a matter of genuine concern. Instead it is brushed aside, if it is read at all. The immunity of the media from criticism is what emerges.

Parris continued:

Immediately after the first bombing, a report was splashed that two people had been arrested trying to leave Heathrow. The later report that they had been released without charge appeared as little more than a footnote. A few days after that, much was made of the arrest in Egypt of a British Muslim whom the less-scrupulous news reports called a 'chemist' (he is a biochemist). There was talk of British agents attending (or joining) his interrogation in Cairo. A statement from the Egyptian authorities denying that they had linked him to the bombing or that he was on their list of al-Qaeda suspects, did receive momentary attention—and then the story seemed to die. I do not know what has happened to it, or him. Then there were some big headlines about an alleged 'al-Qaeda operative' who had 'slipped' into Britain, and slipped out—just before the bombings. But it transpired that he was low on our counter-terrorist services' lists of security threats—and that story, too, has disappeared. Then there was an arrest in Pakistan of an alleged 'al-Qaeda mastermind', about which reports have become increasingly confused, dropping from their early position as leading news items. I do not know where we are now on these reports...This is only a small sample of the deadends (or possible deadends) in the July 7 and July 21 stories. You will have noticed many others. You will notice, too, that every one tends in the same direction. Each report, when first we read it, accentuated the impression that we face a formidable, capable, extensive and well-organized terrorist movement, with important links abroad, and that is almost certainly being masterminded from abroad.

And indeed we may. Nothing—I repeat, nothing—I write here is meant to exclude that possibility.... My purpose is more limited. To alert you to the enormous, insidious and mostly unconscious pressure that exists to talk up, rather than talk down, the efficacy of al-Qaeda. When all the pressures

---

Matthew Parris, *The Times* (London), 23 July 2005.

are to talk up a lethal characterisation of the forces at work, we need to be supercool in the way we look at these reports.

But as well as exposing the readiness of the media to publish baseless rubbish, Parris is serving the purposes of the media empire for which he works—Rupert Murdoch's News International—by writing such an article. His point seems to be that if the media are going to get things wrong, then at least they should get things wrong by downplaying rather than exaggerating the threat. By doing so, the media would at least then be publishing rubbish which would serve the national interest rather than rubbish that would serve the aims of the terrorists by making the threat seem worse than it might actually be. Either way, Parris does not seek to reprimand those guilty of publishing information that turns out to be wrong: he merely chides them, very gently.

If this is the best that the more thoughtful and intelligent of the UK's commentators can come up with, it is no surprise that when the truth of the bombings emerged the nation was taken by surprise. The truth was that Britain had produced its own suicide bombers, though with some help from operatives abroad. The question was: how and why? A media that had generally decided to believe that 'we' could not have done this to 'ourselves', had by then led the public so far in one direction that it was unlikely that it would have the capacity to turn the spotlight on Britain itself and ask awkward questions about the fragile state of British society. So, it turned the issue into a manhunt, a criminal investigation, a race against time, and a flag-waving exercise that warned al-Qaeda that Britain would not be cowed, as the *Express* made clear on August 5 after Ayman al-Zawahiri had issued a fresh threat. 'Threats won't defeat us' a headline said above the newspaper's leader column. It went on indignantly:

Just who do these people think they are? Ayman al-Zawahri, Al Qaeda's second in command, appeared on the Arabic TV channel Al Jazeera yesterday, warning Britain of another terror attack. It is a measure of these people's self-importance that they think they can frighten us. Al Jazeera is guilty of airing a lot of views from fanatics but it doesn't mean anyone in the wider world feels alarm. Our attitude is much better summed up by Gary Holness, who lost a leg in the July 7 bombing. 'I'm not down at all,' he said. 'If I have a bad day, they win.' Britain may be on high alert but it was business as usual yesterday. It is time people like al-Zawahri realise that the more threats they make, the more resilient the British people become.[14]

Far from being the source of factual material that could contribute to the national debate on how best to deal with the threat, the British media thereby reduced its role to one of forcing all facts through a political prism as it sought officials to blame, or 'dumbed down' the issues in an effort to raise national spirits during a time of difficulty. Every issue—the wisdom or not of introducing national identity cards, the extent to which the police, MI5, the Home Office, the Secret Intelligence Service and other institutions had failed in their duty, or the government's policy on asylum seekers, in addition to fresh new definitions of what it is to be British—all of these have been incorporated into the reporting of the terrorist threat since July 7, 2005. Britons cannot even come to a consensus over whether the British role in the invasion of Iraq is a cause of the terrorist threat to the UK: all views on the issue are political, with little impartial truth having emerged from any of the debate.

## Meanwhile, the threat is real

Two important lessons will nevertheless have been learned from the appalling events in London. First, that the terrorists' capacity existed within the UK despite all the efforts to thwart it. Second, that the *jihadist-salafist* ideology propagated by al-Qaeda had become entrenched in the UK in its purest form—in the creation of the suicide bomber—implying that efforts to dilute it by countering its message with the propagation of 'moderate' alternatives have only had limited success.

In such circumstances, the media has a vital role to play: not in identifying 'our values' and explaining how they must and should be protected, but in informing people about the reality of the society in

14 'Threats Won't Defeat Us,' *Daily Express* (London), 5 August 2005.

which they live and why it is that the way we live has spawned such antipathy within a tiny minority. It would be wrong to assume that 'society' was to blame for producing the 7 July bombers: they made their own decisions to kill. But the sentiments that have developed into extremism and the readiness to kill and die are now a part of what Britain has become. These people are evidently a part of what we now are, whether we like it or not.

It is the role of the media to explain what we are, not what we would like to be. But how good is the media at confronting the public with reality, after so many years of exploiting the freedoms democracies enjoy in order to turn truth into a political weapon?

'Attack is the best defence against terror,'[15] the *Sunday Telegraph* announced in an editorial on 10 July 2005. The editorial revealed very clearly the ambiguities that prevail within the media, seeking as it does to ally a perception of what is the factual reality with the preferred political perspective of the newspaper. The *Telegraph* argued:

It is difficult for most people who live in tolerant, liberal, secular societies to realise how utterly devoted al-Qaeda's adherents are to their alien vision of the world. Those fanatics believe—as Osama bin Laden himself has stressed—that they have a God-given duty to 'kill unbelievers'. They are not interested in compromise and negotiation. As one Islamic terrorist has said: 'We are not trying to exact concessions from you. We are trying to destroy you.'

It then went on to state:

...There is in fact no foreign policy initiative that will make the slightest difference to the murderous intentions of the people responsible for last week's bombs. Indeed, there is no policy of any kind that will make any difference at all—short of adopting the extreme, Wahaabi version of Islam advocated by Osama bin Laden and his supporters. That is why it is also a mistake to believe that fundamentalist-inspired terrorism can be stopped if only we address its 'causes'. Those causes are, it is frequently asserted, poverty and political disenfranchisement. It simply is not true, however, that poverty is an

15 'Attack is the Best Defence Against Terror', *Sunday Telegraph* (London), 10 July 2005.

incubator of terrorism, or that terrorists come from backgrounds that mean the only opportunities open to them are the ones which involve violence.

Then the newspaper concluded:

The reality is that we cannot address the 'causes' of terrorism, for the simple reason that no one knows what they are: no one knows why people decide to become mass murderers, or how to prevent them from doing so. The only defence we have is to penetrate and destroy the terrorist organisations them-selves: to identify, arrest and imprison the terrorists and their leaders.

It is evident that the successes the US in particular has had in identifying and arresting al-Qaeda's leaders have in fact done little to diminish the terrorist threat. The main perpetrators and planners of the 9/11 attacks are either dead or in jail. Their legacy now lives on in the recruitment of new radicals—recruitment to an ideology that is extreme, real and strong as a mobilising force. The *Telegraph*'s assertion that measures 'to identify, arrest and imprison the terror-ists and their leaders' will address the problem is therefore spurious. Equally, its reference to the claim that poverty is given as an excuse for extremism is a red herring. Today's Muslim extremists rarely ut-ter a word about poverty; they are on a religious mission. Discontent borne of social conditions may have made some more prone to look for ways to escape their circumstances, and fostered the climate of discontent in Egypt and Algeria in the early 1990s which undoubt-edly fed into the emergent Muslim radicalism. But a phenomenon far more powerful than one inspired by unemployment in Upper Egypt or a leaking roof in a grimy town in north-west England, lies behind the readiness to become a *shaheed*, a martyr.

## Not such blissful ignorance

On both sides of the Atlantic Ocean, the confusion of the West in trying to discern what that phenomenon is has been made far more difficult by a media that does not know whether it should be run-ning towards the gunfire to find out more about those who are doing the shooting, or running away from it as part of a 'patriotic duty' to condemn. It is very difficult for western media commentators and pundits to address the profound issues arising from the challenge presented by al-Qaeda and its affiliates. This is primarily because of the lack of understanding of where or why anti-western sentiment actually fits into the ideology of the jihadis. The simplistic explanation for *jihadist* violence in the West itself—as opposed to in Iraq or elsewhere—is that the perpetrators are seeking to subvert 'our' way of life. It is a simple way of deriding the jihadist terrorists' ideological position. The purpose of taking this line—and all media have done it, either by condemning the jihadists for being 'anti-democratic', or by stirring feelings of nationalism—is to avoid seeking real answers to the question with which this essay began: why do they hate us?

In his powerful account of the likely future of Muslim-Christian relations, the Indian journalist M.J.Akbar wrote of the terrorist campaign launched by al-Qaeda: 'This is a war being fought in the mind as much as anywhere else.'[16] He continued: 'In an age of despair the need for a hero who can inspire pan-Islamic victories becomes acute...There is no such hero on the horizon now. Despair can become a breeding ground for mavericks who believe in themselves and their version of the faith.'

The psychological war that is going on—the threatening videos, the courtroom defiance, the violent language of extremist statements—suggest that much is going on in 'the mind'. But where Akbar is probably wrong is in failing to see that there *is* indeed a new 'hero'. It is bin Laden who is both the 'maverick' and the 'hero who can inspire pan-Islamic victories' and who can thereby try to secure victory in the minds of those he seeks to have follow him, inspiring them to commit acts which will chip away at western influence in the Islamic world.

Bin Laden has gripped the minds of many Muslims because his emergence as the man with the will to confront the West is consistent with a long historical tradition. It is a tradition with its roots in the anti-imperialist campaigns that emerged in the Middle East

---

16  M. J. Akbar, *The Shade of Swords: Jihad and the Conflict Between Islam and Christianity* (London, 2002), p. 195.

in the late-nineteenth and early twentieth centuries, of which most people in the West are entirely ignorant. The emergence of the Muslim Brotherhood in Egypt in the 1930s, and the coalescence of academic writings and popular activism that produced the extremist violence of the 1990s, combined religious doctrine with political ambition.[17] The subsequent emergence of al-Qaeda as a powerful mobilising force is explicable largely because it identified a far clearer target than the groups which it brought together. But by identifying the West as its target, was al-Qaeda pulling an opportunistic target out of a hat? No. It was drawing together strands of religious belief, historical experience and cultural identity which are deep-rooted in the Muslim world.

These strands have been shaped by a history from which the West had hoped to move on, after playing a vital role in creating it for more than a century. The challenge from al-Qaeda is fundamentally rooted in its determination to prevent the West from being permitted to extricate itself. The Islamists are determined to use the 'anti-imperialist' fight as the means by which they can redefine the Muslim world, and use their confrontation with the West as a platform from which to launch their bigger struggle—that within the Muslim world itself. Al-Qaeda wants to fight the West because jihad is its means of defining what the Muslim world actually is. For a century, Arab Islamists have *defined* themselves by way of their response to foreign influence, though not always by using the concept of jihad. That has been their guide, and the reason 'they hate us' is because they *need* the western presence with all its violence, arrogance and stupidity. Without it there could be no jihad, and the war in Iraq has allowed them to lure the West into a protracted battle during which their ranks are swelling and their fighters being trained for future conflicts.

But just as the jihadis must one day look to themselves rather than their enemies in order to establish what it is they are trying to achieve, so those in the West now fighting against them must be

---

17 For a comprehensive study of this historical process, see Mark Huband, *Warriors of the Prophet: The Struggle for Islam* (Boulder, 1998).

prepared to examine the contributory role they and their forefathers had in creating the extremism in the first place. *Jihadist-salafism* did not come out of nowhere. It emerged out of a conflict rooted in imperialism. It is simply not true that western influence has *per se* been a force for good in the world. Al-Qaeda's horrifying behaviour is one appalling consequence, and it will certainly not be the last.

For democracy to prevail over extremism in this appalling climate, and for those who opt for terrorism to be convinced that their behaviour is aberrant, knowledge is the most powerful weapon. Osama bin Laden has chosen his knowledge very carefully, which is why his exhortations are not being countered in any meaningful way by either the co-religionists or the non-Muslims who oppose him. To counter his message, the media has a crucial role to play in broadening knowledge, in carefully reporting what is taking place, and in aspiring to tell the truth rather than foisting polemics on the public under the guise of 'reportage'. The truth is never political, but most media prefer to *report* the *truth* of the terrorist threat by way of telling who it is that is *winning* the arguments for and against the measures that together amount to the 'war on terror'. This approach diminishes rather than increases knowledge, as the public think they are learning facts when they are only hearing opinions.

To redress this dangerous trend, the media 'experts' on terrorism or religion or the Middle East must ask themselves whether they really are what they say they are, before they peddle their views on unsuspecting readers who are ill-equipped to know whether their insights are genuinely borne of knowledge and sound judgment. The 'security experts'—many of them former civil servants, whose knowledge often becomes redundant as soon as their access to official secrets is cut off—must ask themselves whether the 'authoritative' views which the media pays them well to express, really do have 'authority' beyond that endowed by their status as *former* civil servants. Most importantly the media itself—the newspapers, the television, the radio—must be a conduit for information rather than a prism through which they tell the story in a manner befitting the prejudices of editors. The challenge from al-Qaeda is not just a story of violence. It is a sprawling struggle within and between societies. It will not end until it is understood. To achieve that understanding requires that we examine it from all sides. This means that we look at ourselves as much as we look at the enemy we are seeking to thwart. To achieve such understanding the media must begin to tell the story as it is rather than as it would like it to be.

# 13

# THE TERRORISM INDUSTRY: THE PROFITS OF DOOM

## John Mueller

Thus far at least, terrorism is a rather rare and, in appropriate context, not a very destructive phenomenon: in fact, international terrorism generally kills only a few hundred people a year worldwide—about the number who drown yearly in bathtubs in the United States. Americans worry intensely about 'another 9/11', but if one of these occurs every three months for the next five years, the chance of being killed in one of them is two one-hundredths of one per cent. Astronomer Alan Harris has calculated that at present rates, the lifetime chances that a resident of the globe will die at the hands of terrorists is one in 80,000, about the same likelihood that one would die over the same interval from the impact on the earth of an especially ill-directed asteroid or comet.[1]

But such numbers are almost never discussed. Instead, most Americans seem to have developed what Leif Wenar of the University of Sheffield has characterised as a false sense of insecurity

---

[1] About 320 Americans per year drown in bathtubs: John Stossel, *Give Me a Break* (New York, 2004), p. 77. The posited 9/11s would kill 60,000 which is about .02 per cent of 300,000,000, Harris: personal communication. See also Bruce Schneier, *Beyond Fear: Thinking Sensibly about Security in an Uncertain World* (New York, 2003). International terrorism figures derive from State Department tallies as presented, for example, in the United States Department of State, *Patterns of Global Terrorism, 1997* (April 1998). In recent years, the definitions have shifted to include a considerable amount of domestic terrorism and insurgency activity in the count.

about terrorism. Thus, since 9/11, over a period in which there have been no international terror attacks whatever in the United States and in which an individual's chances of being killed by a terrorist have remained microscopic even if one did occur, nearly half of the population has continually expressed worry that they or a member of their family will become a victim of terrorism. Moreover, when asked if they consider another terrorist attack likely in the United States within the next several weeks, less than 10 per cent have usually responded with what has proven to be the correct answer: 'not at all likely'. Yet, this group has not notably increased in size despite continual confirmation of its prescience.[2]

A major reason for this remarkable, if somewhat bizarre, phenomenon may be that the fear of terrorism is constantly being stoked by members of what might be called the 'terrorism industry', an entity that includes not only various risk entrepreneurs and bureaucrats, but also most of the media and nearly all politicians. However, in most cases, the terrorism industry did not create the fear, but rather is reacting to, and profiting from, anxieties that are already out there. And even if the stoking stops, the fears may still continue to linger for decades.

## The terrorism industry

Responding to the apparent needs of their constituencies, reporters, bureaucrats, politicians, terrorism experts mostly find extreme and alarmist possibilities much more appealing than discussions of broader context, much less of statistical reality.

## Politicians

There is no reason to suspect that George W. Bush's concern about terrorism is anything but genuine. However, his approval rating did receive the greatest boost for any president in history after September 11, 2001, and it would, of course, be politically unnatural for him not

2  Data are available at www.pollingreport.com.

to notice. Indeed, his chief political adviser, Karl Rove, was already declaring in 2003 that the 'war' against terrorism would be central to Bush's re-election campaign the following year.[3] It was, and it worked. And as fears about terrorism continued at a constant level in the next years, Rove announced in January 2006 that he was already gearing up to make it a major theme in the congressional campaigns later that year.[4]

In all this, the White House may have been able to enhance things just a bit from time to time by aggressively urging the Department of Homeland Security into putting the country on higher alert levels than it might have been inclined to embrace on its own. Indeed, one study has found a consistent positive relationship between government-issued terror warnings and presidential approval.[5] In 2005, outgoing homeland security czar Tom Ridge attempting to 'debunk the myth' that he had been responsible for repeated alerts, particularly in the 2004 election year, observed that 'more often than not we were the least inclined' to do so. But, he continued, 'there were times when some people were really aggressive about raising it, and we said, 'For that?'[6]

The administration also has a terrific political incentive to stoke fear by portentously pointing to bad people who are out there and citing evidence of terrorist intrigues. Thus in 2005 President Bush touted a list of ten terrorist plots that he claimed had been uncovered even though some of these seem to have been nearly trivial and most did not even take place in the country.[7] Then, shortly after Vice

---

3 Francis X. Clines, 'Karl Rove's Campaign Strategy Seems Evident: It's the Terror, Stupid,' *New York Times,* 10 May 2003.

4 Dan Balz, 'Rove Offers Republicans A Battle Plan For Elections,' *Washington Post,* 21 January 2006.

5 Robb Willer, 'The Effects of Government-Issued Terror Warnings on Presidential Approval,' *Current Research in Social Psychology,* 10, 30 September 2004.

6 Mimi Hall, 'Ridge Reveals Clashes on Alerts,' USA Today, 11 May 2005.

7 Sara Kehaulani Goo, 'List of Foiled Plots Puzzling to Some,' Washington Post, 23 October 2005.

JOHN MUELLER

President Dick Cheney had publicly lamented that 'as we get farther away from September 11, some in Washington are yielding to the temptation to downplay the ongoing threat to our country and to back away from the business at hand', the president brought up one of these plots again as if it were new news: a 2002 conspiracy in Asia to hijack a commercial airliner using a shoe bomb to get into the cockpit, and then to fly it into a tall building in Los Angeles.[8] No one has apparently been charged, still less convicted, of any crime connected to this episode, and the 'plot' appears to have been idle aspiration rather than anything remotely operational.[9] Moreover, the notions that passengers and crew would allow the takeover of a plane in the wake of 9/11 and that a shoe bomb could blow off a cockpit door without downing the plane itself (and thereby ending the possibility of using it as a weapon) went unexamined. But the president was successful in floating a bit of fear into the atmosphere, something likely to be politically beneficial.

The Democrats are at a decided political disadvantage on the terrorism issue. They do not want to seem to underplay the terrorist threat, and so, like the Republicans, they find it—or believe it—politically expedient to be as hysterical as possible, to exaggerate, and to inflate. For the most part, they have scurried to keep up, desperate not to be thought soft on terrorism. Those with long memories probably remember with some pain how the Republicans once tried to label them 'soft on communism', perhaps with some effect in some elections. In consequence, they have stumbled all over each other to appear tough and strong while spewing out plans to expend even more of the federal budget on the terrorist threat, such as it is, than President Bush. Thus, in the 2004 presidential campaign, Democratic candidate John Kerry repeatedly urged that 'I do not fault George Bush for doing too much in the war on terror, I believe he's done too little'. In contrast to Bush who 'has no comprehensive strategy

8   Peter Beinart, 'Elevated Threat,' *New Republic,* 6 February 2006.
9   David Cole, 'Are We Safer? An Epilogue,' *New York Review of Books,* 23 March 2006.

for victory in the war on terror—only an ad hoc strategy to keep our enemies at bay', proclaimed Kerry, 'if I am Commander-in-Chief, I would wage that war by putting in place a strategy to win it'.[10]

The political jockeying and outbidding process on this issue could be seen in two episodes during that campaign. In September, Bush as columnist Gwynne Dyer sardonically noted, had 'a brush with the truth' by opining that the war on terror could not be won, but that conditions could be changed to make terrorism less acceptable in some parts of the world. 'This heroic attempt to grapple with reality', notes Dyer, 'was a welcome departure from Bush's usual style'; but his Democratic opponents quickly pounced, declaring irrelevantly, 'What if President Reagan had said that it may be difficult to win the war against Communism?' Bush promptly fled to safer ground, sanctimoniously intoning in a later speech, 'We meet today in a time of war for our country, a war we did not start, yet one that we will win'.[11]

In October, it was Kerry's turn. In an interview in the *New York Times* he suggested, presumably by accident, that Americans would be able 'to feel safe again' when we 'get back to the place we were, where terrorists are not the focus of our lives, but they're a nuisance'. Like prostitution, illegal gambling, and organised crime, the idea would be to 'reduce it to a level where it isn't on the rise', where 'it isn't threatening people's lives every day', and where 'it's not threatening the fabric of your life'. Bush and Cheney quickly jumped on that one, declaring it to be proof that Kerry was 'unfit to lead'. Kerry, chastened, was soon back to his more usual macho mantra.[12]

Other opportunities for American politicians of all stripes are opened up by the popular, if sudden, massive increases in expendi-

---

10 Quoted, Ian S. Lustick, *Trapped in the War on Terror* (Philadelphia, PA, 2006), ch. 6.

11 Gwynne Dyer, 'Politicking skews needed perspective on terror war,' *Columbus Dispatch*, 6 September 2004.

12 Lustick, *Trapped in the War on Terror*, ch. 6; Benjamin Friedman, 'Leap Before You Look: The Failure of Homeland Security,' *Breakthroughs*, 13, Spring 2004.

tures designed to enhance security against terrorism. Not surprisingly, much of this hasty spending has been rendered inefficient by any standards as porkbarrel and politics-as-usual formulas have been liberally applied. Local politicians are quick to get in on the action as well, leading to such excesses as the $63,000 decontamination unit that gathers dust in a warehouse because the locals do not have a team that knows how to use it.[13]

## Bureaucrats

Meanwhile, Bush's hastily-assembled and massively-funded Office of Homeland Security seeks to stoke fear by officially intoning on the first page of its defining manifesto that 'Today's terrorists can strike at any place, at any time, and with virtually any weapon.'[14] The interactive, if somewhat paradoxical, process between government and public is crisply described by Ian Lustick: the government 'can never make enough progress towards 'protecting America' to reassure Americans against the fears it is helping to stoke.'[15]

Threat exaggeration is additionally encouraged, even impelled, because politicians and terrorism bureaucrats also have, as Jeffrey Rosen points out, an 'incentive to pass along vague and unconfirmed threats of future violence, in order to protect themselves from criticism' in the event of another attack.[16] 'Far better', notes Peter Beinart, 'to warn of an attack that never comes than to remain silent and appear to be taken by surprise.'[17]

As always in the United States, the Federal Bureau of Investigation is on the job, in this case intoning 'I think, therefore they are' spookiness when the purported terrorist menace is assessed.

13  Veronique de Rugy, 'Bad News for Homeland Security,' *Tech Central Station*, 8 June 2005.

14  Office of Homeland Security, 'The National Strategy for Homeland Security,' July 2002.

15  Lustick, *Trapped in the War on Terror*, ch. 5.

16  Jeffrey Rosen, *The Naked Crowd* (New York, 2004), p. 79.

17  Beinart, 'Elevated Threat.'

Thus, in testimony before the Senate Committee on Intelligence on 11 February 2003, FBI head Robert Mueller proclaimed that 'the greatest threat is from al-Qaeda cells in the US that we have not yet identified'.[18] He rather opaquely judged that the threat from those unidentified entities was 'increasing in part because of the heightened publicity' surrounding such episodes as some sniper shootings in the Washington DC, area in 2002 and the anthrax letter attacks of 2001, and that 'al-Qaeda maintains the ability and the intent to inflict significant casualties in the US with little warning.' The terrorists he opined, would 'probably continue to favor spectacular attacks', and he judged its 'highest priority targets' to be 'high profile government or private facilities, commercial airliners, famous landmarks, and crucial infrastructure such as energy-production facilities and transportation nodes'.

However, if the bad guys had *both* the ability *and* the intent in 2003 and if the threat they presented was somehow increasing, they had remained remarkably quiet by the time Mueller testified before the same committee two years later on 16 February 2005. Despite that posited ability, intent, and increasing threat, despite (God knows) continued publicity about terrorism, and despite presumably severe provocation attending the subsequent US invasion of Iraq, no casualties (significant or otherwise) were suffered in spectacular (or non-spectacular) attacks in the US (with or without warning), and all high (and low) profile facilities, airliners, landmarks, and crucial (and non-crucial) infrastructure nodes (and non-nodes) remained unmolested by terrorists. Nonetheless, Mueller remained unflappable, calmly retreating to his comfortable neo-Cartesian mantra: 'I remain very concerned about what we are not seeing', a profundity this time dutifully rendered in bold type in his published script. As it happens, he failed to mention a secret FBI report that had in the meantime wistfully noted that after more than three years of intense hunting,

---

18  Testimony can be found through www.fbi.gov/congress/congress.htm.

the agency had been unable to identify a single true al-Qaeda sleeper cell anywhere in the country.[19]

Not to be left behind in the fear-mongering sweepstakes, analysts in the CIA who have convinced themselves that al-Qaeda already has a nuclear weapon, respond to the observation that no abandoned nuclear material was found when the terrorist organisation was routed in Afghanistan with the artful riposte, 'We haven't found most of the al-Qaeda leadership either, and we know that they exist.'[20] We also know that Mount Rushmore exists which must be taken to mean, I suppose, that the tooth fairy does as well.

## The media

Since 9/11 the American public has been treated to endless yammering about terrorism in the media. Politicians and bureaucrats may feel that, given the public concern on the issue, they will lose support if they appear insensitively to be downplaying the dangers of terrorism. But the media like to tout that they are devoted to presenting fair and balanced coverage of important public issues. As has often been noted, however, the media appear to have a congenital incapacity for dealing with issues of risk and comparative probabilities—except, of course, in the sports and financial sections.[21] I may have missed it, but I have never heard anyone in the media stress that in every year except 2001 only a few hundred people in the entire world have died as a result of international terrorism, a simple fact that ought really to be embraced as conventional wisdom, but one instead that is little known or appreciated.

---

19 Brian Ross, "Secret FBI Report Questions Al-Qaeda Capabilities: No 'True' Al Qaeda Sleeper Agents Have Been Found in US," ABC News, 9 March 2005, http://abcnews.go.com/WNT/Investigation/story?id=566425&page=1.

20 Graham Allison, *Nuclear Terrorism: the Ultimate Preventable Catastrophe* (New York, 2004), p. 27.

21 On the issue more generally, see Eleanor Singer and Phyllis M. Endreny, *Reporting on Risk: How the Mass Media Portray Accidents, Diseases, Disasters, and Other Hazards* (New York, 1993).

Even in their amazingly rare efforts to try to put terrorism in context—something that would seem to be absolutely central to any sensible discussion of terrorism and terrorism policy—the process never goes very far. For example, in 2001 the *Washington Post* published an article by a University of Wisconsin economist that attempted quantitatively to point out how much safer it was to travel by air than by automobile even under the heightened atmosphere of concern inspired by the September attacks. He reports that the article generated a couple of media inquiries, but nothing more. A cover story by Gregg Easterbrook in the *New Republic* in 2002 forcefully and effectively argued that biological and especially chemical weapons were hardly capable of creating 'mass destruction', a perspective relevant not only to concerns about terrorism, but also to the drive for war against Iraq that was going on at the time.[22] *The New York Times* asked him to fashion the article into an op-ed piece, but that was the only interest the article generated in the media.

A cynical aphorism in the newspaper business holds that 'if it bleeds, it leads'. And there is a obvious, if less pungent, corollary: if it doesn't bleed, it certainly shouldn't lead and, indeed, may well not be fit to print at all.

Another problem concerns follow-up. It was widely reported that a band of supposed terrorists arrested in London in 2003 had been producing a poison, ricin. Contrary to initial reports, no ricin was ever actually found in their possession, but by the time that was cleared up, the press had mostly gone on to other things.[23] When a major political figure makes some sort of fear-inducing pronouncement or prediction about terrorism, it tends to get top play in the media, as, generally, it should. Although many of these dire assertions have been

---

22 Gregg Easterbrook, 'Term Limits: the meaninglessness of "WMD",' *New Republic*, 7 October 2002, pp. 22–5.

23 Milton Leitenberg, *Assessing the Biological Weapons and Bioterrorism Threat* (Carlisle, PA, 2005), pp. 27-8. Leitenberg notes that those arrested did have in their possession a readily-available book that contained a recipe for making ricin. If followed out, the recipe would have yielded enough poison to kill one person if the substance were *injected*.

subjected to later analysis in the media (and very often have proved to be based on skimpy evidence and intelligence), the follow-up reports receive much less play than the initial assertions.[24] In addition, there have been almost no efforts, systematic or otherwise, to go back to people who have prominently made dire predictions about terrorism that proved to have been faulty (and, indeed, thus far almost *all* of them have been), to query the predicters about how they managed to be so wrong.

Finally, a large number of what seem to be rather ordinary propositions about terrorism and about the threat it may—or may not—present should at least be part of the public policy debate, yet few are. Isn't it true that an American's chance of being killed by a terrorist is very, very small? Shouldn't that proposition at least be *discussed* in the media? How about the proposition that another hijacking attack like the one on 9/11 is impossible because passengers and crew would forcefully interfere? Or that chemical weapons can't wreak mass destruction? Or that the number of people killed annually in the world by international terrorists is only a few hundred?

## Risk entrepreneurs

The monied response to 9/11 has also created a vast and often well-funded coterie of risk entrepreneurs. Its members would be out of business if terrorism were to be back-burnered, and accordingly they have every competitive incentive (and they are nothing if not competitive) to conclude it to be their civic duty to keep the pot boiling. As 'a rising tide lifts all boats,' suggests Lustick, 'an intractable fear nourishes all schemes.'[25] Moreover, notes Rosen, since they are

---

24 On problems of lack of follow-up in the Vietnam War, see Peter Braestrup, *Big Story: How the American Press and Television Reported and Interpreted the Crisis of Tet 1968 in Vietnam and Washington* (New Haven, CT, 1983). On the problem in the Gulf War of 1991, see John Mueller, *Policy and Opinion in the Gulf War* (Chicago, 1994), pp. 136–7.

25 Lustick, *Trapped in the War on Terror*, ch. 5.

'dependent on the public for status and recognition, 'terrorism experts have an 'incentive to exaggerate risks and pander to public fears.'[26]

For example, Allison, intent on hyping the threat of nuclear terrorism in a book that ended up selling rather well, soberly relays—without the slightest effort at critical evaluation much less skepticism—a report by an Arabic-language magazine that bin Laden's boys by 1998 had purchased no less than twenty nuclear warheads 'from Chechen mobsters in exchange for $30 million in cash and two tons of opium.'[27] Meanwhile, some of those intent on spreading alarm about bioterrorism have soberly included *hoaxes* in their tabulations of 'biological events'.[28]

There have also been creative efforts by people with political agendas to fold them into the all-consuming war on terror. The gun control lobby has proclaimed that 'We have a responsibility to deny weapons to terrorists and to actively prevent private citizens from providing them,' while the National Rifle Association has espied an 'increased momentum since September 11 for laws permitting concealed guns' and its executive director patiently explains that people would rather face the terrorist threat 'with a firearm than without one'. Meanwhile, notes Lustick, 'organizations fighting AIDS in Africa have been torn between arguments that compare casualty rates to show that AIDS is a bigger threat than terrorism, to arguments that the devastation AIDS causes in African countries creates breeding grounds and safe havens for terrorists'. In her campaign against breast cancer, one senator probed 'the rhetorical limits of the War on Terror', suggests Lustick, by urging people to 'think of the terror a breast cancer patient feels when she needs tamoxifen and

---

26  Rosen, *Naked Crowd*, p. 222.

27  Allison, *Nuclear Terrorism*, p.27. For news fit enough to print in the *Times of London* suggesting that bin Laden had already collected tactical nuclear weapons by 1998, see Michael Binyon, 'Bin Laden "now has nuclear arsenal",' Times (London), 7 October 1998.

28  Leitenberg, *Assessing the Biological Weapons and Bioterrorism Threat*, p. 21.

cannot afford the $135 a month'.[29] And, upon discovering that his roadside water park in Florida had been included on the Department of Homeland Security's list of over 80,000 potential terrorist targets, Weeki Wachee Springs' marketing and promotion manager quickly and creatively began to work to get a chunk of the counterterrorism funds allocated to the region by that well-endowed, anxiety-provoking, and ever-watchful agency.[30]

## Envisioning doom

Members of the terrorism industry are truly virtuosic at pouring out, and poring over, worst case scenarios—or 'worst case fantasies', as Bernard Brodie once labelled them in a different context.[31] But there are, of course, all sorts of things that are 'not impossible'. Thus, a colliding meteor or comet could destroy the earth, Tony Blair or Vladimir Putin and their underlings could decide one morning to launch a few nuclear weapons at Massachusetts, George Bush could decide to bomb Hollywood, an underwater volcano could erupt to cause a civilisation-ending tidal wave, Osama bin Laden could convert to Judaism, declare himself to be the Messiah, and fly in a gaggle of mafioso hit men from Rome to have himself publicly crucified.

Brodie's cautionary comment in the 1970s about the creative alarmists in the defence community holds as well for those in today's terrorism industry:

[It] is inhabited by peoples of a wide range of skills and sometimes of considerable imagination. All sorts of notions and propositions are churned out, and often presented for consideration with the prefatory works: 'It is conceivable that...' Such words establish their own truth, for the fact that someone has conceived of whatever proposition follows is enough to establish that it is conceivable. Whether it is worth a second thought, however, is

---

29  Lustick, *Trapped in the War on Terror*, ch. 5.

30  Mary Spicuzza, 'Weeki Wachee mermaids in terrorists' cross hairs?,' *St. Petersburg Times*, 22 April 2005.

31  Bernard Brodie, 'The Development of Nuclear Strategy,' *International Security*, 2, Spring 1978, p.68.

another matter. It should undergo a good deal of thought before one begins to spend much money on it.[32]

That is, what we mostly get from the terrorism industry is fear-mongering and doom-saying, and much of it borders on hysteria. Some prominent commentators, like David Gergen, have argued that the United States has become 'vulnerable', even 'fragile'. Others, like Indiana senator Richard Lugar are given to proclaiming that terrorists armed with weapons of mass destruction present an 'existential' threat to the United States, or even, in columnist Charles Krauthammer's view, to 'civilization itself'.[33]

Allison, too, thinks that nuclear terrorists could 'destroy civilization as we know it' while Joshua Goldstein is convinced they could 'destroy our society' and that a single small nuclear detonation in Manhattan would 'overwhelm the nation'. Not to be outdone, Michael Ignatieff warns that 'a group of only a few individuals equipped with lethal technologies' threaten 'the ascendancy of the modern state'.[34]

Two counterterrorism officials from the Clinton administration contend that a small nuclear detonation 'would necessitate the suspension of civil liberties,' halt or even reverse 'the process of globalization', and 'could be the defeat that precipitates America's

---

32  Brodie, 'Development of Nuclear Strategy,' p. 83.

33  David Gergen, 'A fragile time for globalism,' *US News and World Report*, 11 February 2002, p. 41. Lugar: Fox News Sunday, June 15, 2003. Charles Krauthammer, 'Blixful Amnesia,' *Washington Post*, 9 July 2004. The threat to Israel from terrorism and from its reaction (or overreaction) to the internal terrorist challenge, however, could conceivably be existential, and this is perhaps what Krauthammer means by 'civilization'. For a suggestion along this line, see Francis Fukuyama, 'The Neoconservative Moment,' *National Interest*, Summer 2004, p. 65. Krauthammer replies, however, by parsing 'existential', arguing that what Israel faces is more nearly 'Carthaginian extinction': 'In Defense of Democratic Realism,' *National Interest*, Fall 2004, p. 18.

34  Allison, *Nuclear Terrorism*, p.191. Joshua S. Goldstein, *The Real Price of War: How You Pay for the War on Terror* (New York, 2004), pp.145, 179. Michael Ignatieff, *The Lesser Evil: Political Ethics in an Age of Terror* (Princeton, 2004), p. 147.

decline', while a single explosion of any sort of weapon of mass destruction would 'trigger an existential crisis for the United States and its allies.'[35] A best-selling book by a once-anonymous CIA official repeatedly assures us that our 'survival' is at stake and that we are engaged in a 'war to the death'.[36] It has become fashionable in some alarmist circles extravagantly to denote the contest against Osama bin Laden and his sympathisers as (depending on how the Cold War is classified) World War III or World War IV. And, General Richard Myers, chairman of the Joint Chiefs of Staff, has meticulously calculated that if terrorists were able to kill 10,000 Americans in an attack, they would 'do away with our way of life'.[37]

---

35  Daniel Benjamin and Steven Simon, *The Age of Sacred Terror* (New York, 2002), pp. 398-9, 418.

36  Michael Scheuer, *Imperial Hubris: Why the West is Losing the War on Terror*, (Dulles, 2004), pp. 160, 177, 226, 241, 242, 250, 252, 263. One of the book's many hysterical passages runs: 'To secure as much of our way of life as possible, we will have to use military force in the way Americans used it on the fields of Virginia and Georgia, in France and on the Pacific islands, and from skies over Tokyo and Dresden. Progress will be measured by the pace of killing and, yes, by body counts. Not the fatuous body counts of Vietnam, but precise counts that will run to extremely large numbers. The piles of dead will include as many or more civilians as combatants because our enemies wear no uniforms. Killing in large number is not enough to defeat our Muslim foes. With killing must come a Sherman-like razing of infrastructure. Roads and irrigation systems; bridges, power plants, and crops in the field; fertilizer plants and grain mills–all these and more will need to be destroyed to deny the enemy its support base. Land mines, moreover, will be massively reintroduced to seal borders and mountain passes too long, high, or numerous to close with US soldiers. As noted, such actions will yield large civilian casualties, displaced populations, and refugee flows'. In the acknowledgements, the author thanks Ms. Christina Davidson, his editor, 'who labored mightily to delete from the text excess vitriol' (xiii, 241-42). Perhaps Ms. Davidson should have laboured just a bit more mightily.

37  Jennifer C. Kerr, 'Terror Threat Level Raised to Orange,' Associated Press, 21 December 2003. For a contrast with such views, see Daniel L. Byman, 'Al-Qaeda as an Adversary: Do We Understand Our Enemy?' *World Politics*, 56, October 2003, pp. 160, 163; Russell Seitz, 'Weaker Than We Think,' *American Conservative*, 6 December 2004.

But as the subtext (or sometimes the text) of these hysterical warnings makes clear, the 'existential' threat comes not from what the terrorist would do to us, but what we would do to ourselves in response. It seems, then, that it is not only the most-feared terrorists who are suicidal.

However, the United States is hardly 'vulnerable' in the sense that it can be toppled by dramatic acts of terrorist destruction, even extreme ones. In fact, the country can readily, if grimly, absorb that kind of damage—as it 'absorbs' some 40,000 deaths each year from automobile accidents. As military analyst William Arkin points out forcefully, 'Terrorists can not destroy America.' However, 'every time we pretend we are fighting for our survival we not only confer greater power and importance to terrorists than they deserve but we also at the same time act as their main recruiting agent by suggesting that they have the slightest potential for success.'[38]

## The public as prime motivator

It is easy, even comforting, to blame the terrorism industry for the distorted and context-free condition under which terrorism is so often discussed, and to want to agree wholeheartedly with H. L. Mencken's crack, 'The whole aim of practical politics is to keep the populace alarmed (and hence clamorous to be led to safety) by menacing it with an endless series of hobgoblins.'[39]

In many respects, however, the alarm is not so much aroused by the politicians and other 'opinion leaders' as by their auditors. Rosen quotes Tocqueville on the phenomenon: 'the author and the public corrupt one another at the same time', and he updates the lesson with a pointed observation about exaggerated fears of mad cow disease in Britain: 'Unwilling to defer to any expert who refused to confirm its unsupported prejudices, the crowd rewarded the scientists who were willing to flatter its obsessions by cheering

38 William M. Arkin, 'Goodbye War on Terrorism, Hello Long War,' 26 January 2006, http://blogs.washingtonpost.com/earlywarning.

39 H. L. Mencken, *A Mencken Chrestomathy* (New York, 1949).

it on to self-justifying waves of alarm.'[40] As it happens, then, hysteria and alarmism often sell. That is, although there is great truth in the cynical newspaper adage, 'If it bleeds, it leads', this comes about not so much (or at any rate not entirely) because journalists are fascinated by blood, but because they suspect, probably correctly, that their readers are.

Fears are stoked, then, because the stokers are responding to the apparent needs of the stoked. And dealing with the resulting problem of exaggerated fear is no easy task. In summarising some of the literature on this issue, risk analyst Paul Slovic points out that people tend greatly to overestimate the chances of dramatic or sensational causes of death, that realistically informing people about risks sometimes only makes them more frightened, that strong beliefs in this area are very difficult to modify, that a new sort of calamity tends to be taken as a harbinger of future mishaps, that a disaster tends to increase fears not only about that kind of danger but of all kinds, and that people, even professionals, are susceptible to the way risks are expressed—far less likely, for example, to choose radiation therapy if told the chances of death are 32 per cent rather than that the chances of survival are 68 per cent.[41] Studies have also shown that when presented with two estimations of risk from reasonably authoritative sources, people choose to embrace the high risk opinion regardless of its source; that is, there is a 'predilection toward alarmist responses and excessive weighting of the worst case scenario'.[42]

In some respects, fear of terror may be something like playing the lottery except in reverse. The chances of winning the lottery or of dying from terrorism may be microscopic, but for monumental events which are, or seem, random, one can irrelevantly conclude

40  Rosen, *Naked Crowd*, pp. 77, 87.

41  Paul Slovic, 'Informing and Educating the Public about Risk,' *Risk Analysis*, 6, 1986, pp. 403-15.

42  W. Kip Viscusi, 'Alarmist Decisions with Divergent Risk Information,' *Economic Journal*, 107, November 1997, p. 1669.

that one's chances are just as good, or bad, as those of anyone else. As Cass Sunstein notes,

Those who operate gambling casinos and lotteries...play on people's emotions in the particular sense that they conjure up palpable pictures of victory and easy living, thus encouraging people to neglect the question of probability. With respect to risks, insurance companies, extreme environmental groups, and terrorists do exactly the same.[43]

Sunstein focuses on what he calls 'probability neglect' and relates it directly to the experience with terrorism. 'When their emotions are intensely engaged,' he finds, 'people's attention is focused on the bad outcome itself, and they are inattentive to the fact that it is unlikely to occur.' Under such conditions, he argues, 'attempts to reduce fear by emphasizing the low likelihood of another terrorist attack' are 'unlikely to be successful'.[44]

For example, although they could responsibly point to all sorts of studies that prove the point, airline companies do not routinely stress how safe flying is, especially when compared to driving. The reason for this, I strongly suspect, is that the airlines have come to conclude that telling people how safe it is to fly will increase their fear of flying. And indeed, concern about safety has been found to rise when people discuss a low-probability risk even when what they mostly hear are apparently trustworthy assurances that the danger is infinitesimal.[45]

Risk, then, tends to be more nearly socially constructed than objectively calculated. And sometimes it gets constructed differently in societies that otherwise are quite similar.[46]

---

43 Cass R. Sunstein, 'Terrorism and Probability Neglect,' *Journal of Risk and Uncertainty*, 26, March–May 2003, p. 128.

44 'Terrorism and Probability Neglect,' p.122. See also George F. Lowenstein et al., 'Risk as Feelings,' *Psychology Bulletin*, 127, 2001, pp. 267-86.

45 Sunstein, 'Terrorism and Probability Neglect,' p. 128.

46 For a discussion, see Bernd Rohrmann and Ortwin Renn eds., *Cross-Cultural Risk Perception: a Survey of Empirical Studies* (Dordrecht, 2000). See also Mary Douglas and Aaron Wildavsky, *Risk and Culture* (Berkeley, CA, 1982).

Also puzzling in this regard are the dogs that don't bark. Despite a huge number of books and movies depicting the danger of asteroids, comets, and other space objects colliding with the earth, no one seems to have gotten terribly hysterical over this distinct, dramatic, and vivid possibility. Moreover, despite the efforts and machinations of legions of agitators, Americans seem to be substantially unmoved by threats supposedly presented by global warming and genetically modified food.

For all these gloomy difficulties, however, risk assessment and communication should at least be part of the policy discussion over terrorism, something that may well prove to be a far smaller danger than is popularly portrayed. By contrast, the constant unnuanced stoking of fear by politicians, bureaucrats, experts, and the media, however well received by the public, is on balance costly, enervating, potentially counterproductive, and unjustified by the facts.

## *The decline of fear*

The reduction of fear in emotion-laden situations like terrorism, then, is a very difficult one. In fact, suggests Sunstein, 'if officials want to reduce fear' in such cases, the best response may be to 'alter the public's focus'. That is, 'perhaps the most effective way of reducing fear of a low-probability risk is simply to discuss something else and to let time do the rest.'[47]

Evidence from the past suggests this could be an extended process. The closest historical parallel to fear about terrorism in the United States is probably with fears about domestic Communism. This issue attracted a great deal of press in the early and middle 1950s—the high point of the McCarthy era—but interest declined thereafter, and press attention to the internal enemy had pretty much vanished entirely by the 1970s.[48]

---

47 'Terrorism and Probability Neglect,' pp. 122, 131.
48 John Mueller, 'Trends in Political Tolerance,' *Public Opinion Quarterly*, 52, Spring 1988, p. 16.

Interestingly, however, even though attention to the threat (if any) posed by domestic Communists greatly diminished, even though the party itself essentially ceased to exist, and even though there were no more dramatic, attention-arresting revelations like those of the Hiss and Rosenberg cases of the late 1940s, public concern about the danger posed by domestic communism declined only gradually in the United States. In 1954, at the zenith of the McCarthy era, some 42 per cent of the public held American Communists to be a great or very great danger. Ten years later, this had changed, but not all that much: 38 per cent still saw danger. And when the relevant question was last asked, in the mid-1970s, around 30 per cent continued to envision danger.[49] Of course, the Cold War continued during the period surveyed, but credible (or even non-credible) suggestions that domestic communism was much of anything to worry about became almost non-existent as did press attention to the issue. Yet concern about this 'danger' diminished only gradually.

The phenomenon suggests there is a great deal in dramatic first impressions: once a perceived threat is thoroughly implanted in the public consciousness, it can become internalised and an accepted fact of life and existence. Eventually, it may become a mellowed irrelevance, but, unless there is a decisive eradication of the threat itself (as presumably happened in 1945 for the 'threat' posed by domestic Japanese) the process, it seems, can take decades. An internalised fear can continue even when evidence of, and attention to, its existence fades.

Americans, then, are hardly likely to relax any time soon, and the terrorism industry will continue to find profit in envisioning doom and in stoking fears about this particular hobgoblin. People, even those who proudly sing about how they reside in the 'home of the brave,' will always jump at some spooks (but it is not always predictable which ones) and imagine them to be far more potent than they are, and they will always evaluate some risks perversely and fancy them to be becoming increasingly threatening. Politicians will always

49 Data from Roper Public Opinion Research Center.

sanctimoniously play to those fears, become convinced themselves, and expend funds and deploy armed force unwisely, even counter-productively. Bureaucrats will always stoke the same fears since they need, after all, to protect their anatomies, particularly the posterior portion thereof, against any conceivable uncertainty, and, needless to say, they have no incentive to work themselves out of a job. The entrepreneurs of the terrorism industry may eventually move on to the next governmental cash cow, but they will always first work very hard to sustain and milk their current one. And the press, ever true to its central precept, will continue to make sure that if it bleeds, it will always, always, always lead.

EPILOGUE
# THE DANGERS OF PLAYING
# POLITICS WITH TERRORISM

*Paul Wilkinson*

This volume is one of the best advertisements for the independent academic study of terrorism and responses to terrorism. None of the essayists is trying to sell the reader an official 'party line' on terrorism, and none has hesitated to offer a candid critique of the ways in which the terrorism issue has been exploited for partisan purposes. With the exception of Mark Huband, who has provided a devastating critique of the sloppy journalism that sometimes purports to be 'expertise' on terrorism, and Peter Oborne, all the essayists are leading academic specialists in the study of terrorism, and all provide valuable insights on the extremely broad topic of 'playing politics with terrorism'.

The author found himself using the expression frequently in the course of discussions about the statements made by the UK government and opposition parties about proposals for new anti-terrorism legislation after the 7 July London bombings. However it is clear that the phrase is clearly open to numerous alternative interpretations and can be applied in a host of different contexts. The present volume's editor has wisely left it to the authors of the essays he has commissioned to choose their own interpretation of what it means to 'play politics'. For example, Martin A. Miller makes clear that he sees terrorism as: 'the result of an interactive dynamic between agencies of states and sectors of society who seek to resolve political problems by resorting to tactics of violence. Miller later observes: 'The overlooked aspect of the history of terrorism over the last century is that there are always two kinds of players, and as often as not the state has been the provoking agent.

It is noteworthy that all the scholars contributing to this volume share the view that the threat from the al-Qaeda network of cells and affiliates is serious: it was not invented by politicians. Mark Huband in his chapter in this book provides an incisive critique of the kind of journalism which professes to be 'expert' but which confidently announces that the al-Qaeda problem is over. Al-Qaeda terrorism is by no means the worst threat to human security but it certainly exists. What are the reasons for viewing it as the most dangerous international terrorist threat we face? Many Europeans are still under the illusion that al-Qaeda is just the same as any other terrorist group. This assumption is not only misinformed, it is positively dangerous because it grossly underestimates the nature of the threat the al-Qaeda movement poses to international peace and security.

Al-Qaeda means 'the base'. It evolved in the 1990s under the leadership of Osama bin Laden and his deputy, Ayman al-Zawahiri, and from an early stage in its development it was clear that it was not going to resemble traditional terrorist groups with their monolithic structures and centralised control: instead it was developed into a world-wide network of networks.[1] This 'horizontal' network structure means that although bin Laden and al-Zawahiri provide ideological leadership and inspiration it is left to the affiliated networks and cells to carry out attacks against the types of targets designated in al-Qaeda ideology and combat doctrine. The al-Qaeda movement is able to maintain its 'global reach' through its widely dispersed network of cells and affiliates in over sixty countries, making it the most widely dispersed non-state terrorist network in history. Thousands

---

1   See Mariam Abou Zahab and Olivier Roy, *Islamist Networks: the Afghan-Pakistan Connection* (London, 2004); Olivier Roy, *Globalised Islam: Fundamentalism, De-territorialisation and the Search for the New Ummah* (London, 2004) and Mark Sageman, *Understanding Terror Networks*, (Philadelphia, 2004).

of militants from many countries have been through the al-Qaeda training camps in Afghanistan prior to the overthrow of the Taliban regime which gave al-Qaeda safe haven up to the autumn of 2001.

Another key feature of al-Qaeda is that although it uses the language of extreme fundamentalist Islam its core ideology is a grandiose plan to wage a global jihad against America and its allies and against all existing Muslim governments in order to bring about nothing less than a revolutionary transformation of international politics. Al-Qaeda aims to expel the US presence and influence from every part of the Muslim world, to topple all existing Muslim governments on the grounds that they are all 'apostate' regimes because they maintain friendly relations and co-operation with what al-Qaeda terms the 'crusaders and Zionists', i.e. America and its allies including, of course, Israel. Ultimately al-Qaeda wants to create a pan-Islamist caliphate to rule all Muslims on lines dictated by bin Laden and al-Zawahiri. Their ideology is absolutist and hence 'incorrigible', i.e. there is no basis for diplomatic or political compromise.

However impracticable this ideological project may seem to most in the West, al-Qaeda certainly believe that their revolutionary global transformation will happen because they believe that Allah is on their side and that they will ultimately be victorious, however long it takes. A key feature of the al-Qaeda movement is its explicit commitment to mass-killing terrorist attacks. In a notorious 'fatwa' announced to the world in February 1998, bin Laden and a group of leading fellow extremists declared that it was the duty of all Muslims to kill Americans, including civilians and their allies, whenever the opportunity arises. The 9/11 attacks which killed almost 3,000 and a whole series of other al-Qaeda attacks, including those in Nairobi, Bali, Iraq, Madrid and London, demonstrate that the movement has no hesitation or compunction about killing hundreds of innocent civilians including fellow Muslims.

Closely connected with al-Qaeda's congenital tendency to engage in mass killing is its modus operandi in tactics, targets and areas of operations. Its typical tactic is to mount co-ordinated no-warning suicide attacks using car or truck bombs designed to maximise carnage and economic destruction. Its choice of targets shows that it has no compunction about attacking soft targets where crowds of civilians are likely to be gathered, such as public transport systems, tourist hotels and restaurants, etc. These suicide no-warning co-ordinated attacks on the general public are particularly difficult for the police to prevent in open, democratic societies.

Bearing these key features of the al-Qaeda network of networks in mind, we can clearly differentiate this form of terrorist threat from the typical patterns of terrorism committed by more traditional groups. A leading example of a traditional group is the Irish Republican Army (IRA).[2] The IRA can justifiably be regarded as the best armed, richest and most experienced terrorist group active in Western Europe between 1970 and 1996. It was responsible for killing more civilians than any other terrorist group in Europe.

However it is clear that there are many striking differences between the terrorism posed by the IRA prior to the Good Friday Agreement of 1998 and the threat posed by al-Qaeda. In contrast to al-Qaeda the IRA's aims were focused specifically on their ethno-separatist objectives in Ireland. They aimed to rid Ireland of the British presence in the North and to unite the whole of Ireland under a single Republican government. Their leaders and their political wing, Sinn Fein, have shown a degree of realism and pragmatism in recognising that they were not going to achieve their aims by terrorism, but that they have a better chance of pursuing their political agenda by political means. They signed up to the Good Friday Agreement and have maintained their ceasefire and, although the peace process is still fragile, it is still holding and has saved hundreds of lives that would have undoubtedly been lost if the Northern Ireland conflict had continued. Contrast al-Qaeda's stance.

2   On the history of the IRA and its terrorist campaign from the 1970s to 1998 see Richard English, *Armed Struggle: the History of the IRA* (Basingstoke, 2003); Martin Dillon, *25 Years of Terror: the IRA's War Against the British* (London, 1996); and Ed Maloney, *A Secret History of the IRA* (London, 2002).

Another key difference between traditional terrorist groups and the al-Qaeda movement is that the former have not been conducting a global war, they have concentrated most of their violence on the country or region where they claim to have the right to a separate state. It is true that the IRA and other traditional groups went to great trouble to establish diaspora support networks to raise money and weapons and political support for their campaigns but they did not aim to alter the whole international system. Another crucial difference is that traditional groups used terror, as Brian Jenkins once expressed it, to have 'a lot of people watching, not a lot of people dead'.[3] Al-Qaeda, on the other hand specifically aims to have a lot of people dead as well as a lot of people watching.

For all the above reasons the al-Qaeda network is far and away more dangerous than traditional terrorist groups. We are fooling ourselves if we pretend otherwise. Moreover it is a serious threat to all the countries of the European Union and the security and economic well-being of the EU as a whole. It is a dangerous illusion to think Europe is immune from attack. If the al-Qaeda plot to attack the Strasbourg Christmas market had not been thwarted by police action the first mass killing of civilians in a western state would have been in France, not in the United States. Hundreds of suspected members of al-Qaeda have been arrested in Europe and many cells have been uncovered. Between September 2001 and December 2004 over 700 people suspected of involvement in the al-Qaeda network were arrested in Europe. According to the US Congressional Research Services August 2005 report on al-Qaeda, about 3,000 suspected al-Qaeda members have been detained or arrested worldwide. The cells that did the major planning for the 9/11 attacks were based in Hamburg and Spain. EU countries have been repeatedly specifically threatened in al-Qaeda videotape messages. Finally the deadly attacks of Madrid and London show that the danger is real and we

---

3   Brian Jenkins, 'International Terrorism: A Balance Sheet', *Survival*, vol. 17, no. 4, p. 158.

need to respond effectively, avoiding overreaction, but also avoiding under-reaction.

In my experience, a very large number of scholars specialising in the study of terrorism would agree with this and would thus share the view of the contributors to this volume that we need to investigate and analyse the ways in which terrorist groups themselves, as well as governments and political parties, play politics with terrorism. Jonathan Stevenson, in his contribution, provides an extremely perceptive and objective analysis of both the republicans' and the British government's political tactics in the period leading up to the Good Friday Agreement and since. Stevenson brings out the positive aspect of the politics involved, on both sides. He argues that the main reason that the Northern Ireland troubles have been 'provisionally consigned to history' has been 'both the British and the republicans' political savvy—and the mutual recognition of each of the others political limits. Both sides played politics with terrorism, but predominantly with an eye towards its termination.

However, as Stevenson concedes, international events also played a key role. Few can doubt that the enormous US hostility to terrorism in the wake of 9/11 and the huge damage to the IRA's image in the US as a result of its involvement with FARC in Colombia played a key role in pushing the IRA into its belated and grudging decommissioning of weapons. International and domestic developments can exert a considerable influence not only on governments but also on non-state players in potentially corrigible conflict situations which spawn terrorism.

Richard Drake's outstanding discussion of the kidnapping and murder of Aldo Moro reminds the reader of the complex nature of the modern state. Readers may recall that the Red Brigades spoke of attacking the 'heart' of the Italian Republic, only to find that it had no 'heart'. It is essential to be aware of the many institutions and agencies which together compromise components of the state, and to be aware that organisations such as the police and the intelligence services are not all working in splendid harmony. They all have their different cultures, aims and motivations and methods of operating and are in constant competition for power, influence, status and resources with rival organisations in the same sector. Often playing politics with terrorism is a by-product of the inter-agency struggles to acquire power and to serve their own interests.

Richard Drake's case study of Italy is particularly valuable because somehow and *in spite of* the traditionally rather fragmented and weak central structure of the state, the authorities managed to take the initiative and took the powers necessary to defeat the Red Brigades. It was the judiciary who took the most effective and extreme measure of all: the *pentiti* law, the law of repentant terrorists. By providing huge reductions in sentences to terrorists who turned state's evidence and gave valuable testimony leading to the capture of other terrorists, the authorities were able to crack open the cells and columns of the Red Brigades. Moreover, unlike the Fujimori government in Peru, so well described in Jo-Marie Burt's chapter, the Italian government did not use the anti-terrorist emergency as a means of establishing a permanent authoritarian regime. When the Red Brigades were on the ropes they rescinded the special anti-terrorist measures, including the *pentiti* law.

The Spanish case provides a stark warning of the consequences of the cynical manipulation of terrorist events and threats for the integrity of liberal democratic political systems. Jordan and Horsburgh conclude that the attempt by the ruling PP to manipulate information by trying to insist that ETA had been responsible for the Madrid bombings was not the sole reason for the PP's defeat. Their detailed examination of the political impact of the attacks leads them to conclude that both major political parties tried to play politics with terrorism, and that the major consequences have been that the reputations of both parties have been 'seriously tarnished' by this behaviour, and that this has led indirectly to prejudicing the legitimacy of the political system.

From my point of view, as one who has specialised in the study of responses to terrorism by democratic governments and societies,

Leonard Weinberg and William Eubank provide one of the most penetrating analyses of the way the government of the world's most powerful democracy was able to exploit the issue of terrorism to win the 2004 Presidential election. As they observe Karl Rove and other presidential advisers and Republican Party strategists quickly recognised the advantages to stressing Bush's vigorous response to the 9/11 attacks. In fact, as Rove pointed out to a meeting of the Republican Party National Committee in 2002, Republican congressional candidates would be helped by depicting their party as better able to protect the country against the terrorist threat than the rival Democrats. The tactic appears to have worked. Before 9/11 the Democrats held a slim majority in the US Senate; following the 2004 elections, the Republicans held a ten-seat majority in mainly the same body. But Weinberg and Eubank rightly conclude that although playing politics with terror undoubtedly played a decisive role in Bush's election victory in 2004, in the longer term, the realities of the 'war on terror' are likely to do great harm to their support base. The Iraq war is increasingly unpopular with a growing number of Americans.

It would be foolish to imagine that we could stop people playing politics with terrorism. However, there may be ways in which we can reduce it and, by exposing it, forewarn governments and publics about its dangers. I make no apology for providing a reprise of the major dangers involved. These distinguished essays have covered many but by no means all of them.

## *Major dangers of playing politics with terrorism*

- Manipulating intelligence and threat assessments for political advantage almost inevitably involves exaggerating or deliberately understating threats with the concomitant risks of creating a climate of fear, panic or complacency. Either way it is likely to lead to the wrong counter-measures being taken. People's lives may be put at greater risk.

- Political manipulation of the terrorism threat is likely to leak and, once generally known, it is likely to undermine morale and public confidence not only among the public as a whole but particularly in groups with a key role in preventing and combatting terrorism, such as the police, the military, the emergency services, the judiciary etc.

- In the event of a genuine terrorism emergency, when it is vital for the public to be given clear and authoritative advice on what they should do to help protect their families and themselves, the public may no longer believe anything said by the authorities.

- If new anti-terrorist legislation is seen to be needed it is far preferable to enlist the support of all the main political parties in the legislature, thus maximising its legitimacy and popular mandate.

- All-party support helps to bring about mass public support and this is essential if such measures are to work effectively on the ground.

- The mass media are more likely to help explain the measures and to back them if they are seen to be based on an all-party consensus and the support of the overwhelming majority of the public.

The authoritative case studies in this collection all throw light on the complexity of the relationship between democracy and terrorism. And as Richard Jackson argues in his perceptive assessment of the 'war on terror': 'responding effectively to the actual terrorist threat requires an alternative politics based on realistic assessment, proportionality and genuine social involvement in democratic debate.' The attentive reader will find this collection a compelling argument for such a debate.

# INDEX